MW01233127

Lord, He Hit Me Again

An Insider's Look at Intimate Partner Violence

Smiley Grace

© Bringing your words to life

Acknowledgement

The Heavenly Father knows how to keep us hidden until it is time to present us center stage. He knows when we are ready and waiting for that perfect moment to shine. In Exodus 40:1-38, we are reminded to enter God's holy presence (The Tabernacle). I must go beyond the veil, leaving my comfort zone. Although I prefer backstage, the curtain has risen, and I cannot hide forever.

Special thanks to Pastor Veronica "Vee" Nicholson for her prophetic words that encouraged me to start working on my book.

I also want to acknowledge Bishop Frank A. White for his inspiring message on *The Power of Possibilities*, which has motivated me to continue drafting my book, *Lord, He Hit Me Again: An Insider's Look at Intimate Partner Violence*.

I express gratitude to the incredible Gina McGowan-Cade with Trinity Writing and Publishing, LLC., and her team, who made this book a reality. This project would not have been possible without their unwavering support and guidance throughout the publishing process.

To the men who abused me, thank you for providing the essence of this book to empower others to go from victim to victor.

I am humbled, overwhelmed, and grateful to acknowledge the depth of encouragement from my family, friends, college peers, academic advisor, sisters-in-Christ, and extended family for their support and individual heartwarming feedback to book excerpts.

A special mention goes out to my cousin, Jamila Davenport, for providing insight into a suggested area to incorporate into the book: trauma bonding.

To Valerie Collins (who wrote the foreword), the Rogers family, and the Perez family, thank you for being there during my post-intimate partner violence ordeal!

Most importantly, I thank the God of Glory (Jesus), who brought me into a wealthy place out of despair and abuse.

Contents

List of Figures

List of Tables

Disclaimer

Section 107 of the Copyright Act provides the statutory framework for determining whether something is fair use and identifies certain types of uses—such as criticism, comment, news reporting, teaching, scholarship, and research—as examples of activities that may qualify as fair use.

The views, information, or opinions of numerous resources are solely those of the individuals involved and do not necessarily represent mine or those of Trinity Writing and Publishing, LLC. I made great strides to ensure the book's content was palatable, considering the delicate topic. If you disagree with the assessment that your material does not constitute fair use, please notify me immediately in writing to remove the data. The book's content is provided for informational purposes only and does not substitute medical and mental health clinical consultations. Please seek professional treatment or counseling.

Content Warning: Due to the graphic nature and sensitive topic of intimate partner violence, the information shared may be emotionally or psychologically disturbing and unbearable to some readers.

Foreword

I am delighted to count Smiley Grace as a daughter since our introduction more than 40 years ago when she was a teenager entirely devoted to God as a faithful member of the same Pentecostal congregation. I saw firsthand her first domestic violence relationship with her spouse (an inspiring minister). Consequently, my immediate family and her members performed an intervention for Smiley Grace to enable her to escape from an abusive boyfriend after a physical assault upon such a beautiful soul. Although experience is a good teacher, being battered is not. I watched her go from a victim (being abused and then homeless after the attack) to a victor. It's been a joy to have known her all these years, and what a blessing she has been in my life. I am so proud of how God has used her through the trials and tests of life to help others along the way.

Lord, He Hit Me Again: An Insider's Look at Intimate Partner Violence is a beautiful book and an open door to freedom: heart, mind, and soul. Everything in this book, from the beginning to the end, reveals so much truth that even a blind person can see the snares and traps of an abuser. The book is worth every penny invested as it's an investment in your life. If you seek to be delivered, this book is the answer.

I want to emphasize the vast content of complex dynamics of intimate partner violence relationships, the intricacies of entanglement, and how to heal after escaping is priceless. This informative book contains graphics and extensive research on intimate partner violence. For your life to change, you must admit that you are involved in an abusive relationship, and sometimes you must walk away. If you read this book, you can change and reclaim your life. With your eyes shut, the truth is known; the person can run away when they know it. This book does an excellent job of explaining how to start again.

Finally, I pray that men, women, boys, and girls receive insight into what I reviewed, the author researched, and invested hours in for all to be delivered. This book, I pray, will be so successful that men will benefit once they pick it up because they also experience relationships. As a former victim of intimate partner violence, I endorse this book, and may God add a blessing to its readership that people say, "Wow, let me check it out."

Pastor Valerie Collins,
Co-Pastor-House of David Deliverance & Transforming Ministries, Brooklyn, NY, USA

Introduction

> *"Has he ever trapped you in a room and not let you out? Has he ever raised a fist as if he were going to hit you? Has he ever thrown an object that hit you or nearly did? Has he ever held you down or grabbed you to restrain you? Has he ever shoved, poke, or grabbed you? Has he ever threatened to hurt you? If the answer to any of these questions is yes, then we can stop wondering whether he'll ever be violent; he already has been."*
> — *Lundy Bancroft*

*L*ORD, HE *Hit Me Again: An Insider's Look at Intimate Partner Violence* provides extensive research on intimate partner violence (IPV), incorporating personal accounts of traumatic occurrences wherein my abuser was imprisoned and pleaded guilty to third-degree assault. A cycle of intimate partner violence existed within my family dynamic. This memoir's events are factual. Pseudonyms have been used to protect the identities of the individuals mentioned in this book. The World Health Organization's (WHO's) website asserts intimate partner violence as "one of the most common forms of violence against women." Intimate partner violence permeates all socioeconomic levels, genders, ethnicities,

1

and racial backgrounds. Likewise, different races, classes, and backgrounds respond to intimate partner violence differently (Antiracism & Interpersonal Violence).

Figure 1. Check out this compelling graphic display that portrays the harrowing reality of domestic violence victims. It's truly eye-opening and a must-see for anyone who wants to understand the gravity of this issue. Source: Freepik.com

Domestic and family violence occurs in all races, ages, and genders with no cultural, socioeconomic, educational, religious, or geographic limitations (Huecker and Smock). In the book *Forensic Psychology*, Matthew T. Huss defined the nature of domestic violence as any act of violence perpetrated within the context of significant interpersonal relationships (Rakovec-Felser, 2014). The effects on the individual who has experienced narcissistic abuse can be fatal or highly debilitating and long-lasting, and individual recovery can be a complex process (Howard, 2019).

Intimate partner violence has various forms: threats of physical or sexual violence, psychological violence/aggression (including coercive tactics), emotional violence/abuse, and stalking by a current or former intimate partner. Many researchers have found a link between childhood experiences of aggression behind domestic walls and violence and abuse in adulthood (Rakovec-Felser, 2014). Abusers may be manipulative and use humiliation, intimidation, threats, and coercion on their victims, but "dominating you is their main interest (Lambert, 2016)." Utilizing these tools, the intimate partner in this toxic relationship keeps victims from reaching out to others for help and causes them to become dependent on their abusers.

✶ ✶ ✶ ✶

My story encapsulates and embodies the intimate partner violence experience, highlighting that staying with Maverick was also detrimental to my emotional and psychological well-being. Judge Faith Jenkins, author of *Sis, Don't Settle: How to Stay Smart in Matters of the Heart,* expressed in an interview, "How people treat you is a reflection of their character." While I was a member of a church in Texas, a Woman of God said to me, "What's in you will come out of you."

My intimate partner violence experience included the following:

- A cycle of abuse/toxic relationship
- Psychological abuse. One day in Maverick's Bronx single-room occupancy housing, he told me, "I know you do not have anywhere to go." I assume this is the reason he treated me wrongly. I was hopeless and downtrodden.
- Isolation from my support network. I was isolated from family, friends, and neighbors and prohibited from communicating with males (e.g., family members, co-workers, neighbors, friends, Microsoft Office Specialist instructor).
- Barriers to leaving my abuser
- Revictimization

- Emotional attachment to the abuser
- Mental health issues. I experienced Post Traumatic Stress Disorder (PTSD), moderate recurrent major depression, psychological care, and medication.
- Law enforcement and court system involvement. Third-degree assault charges were brought against my abuser. Police officers arrested him, a final order of protection was granted, and my abuser pled guilty to the crime.
- I re-established a relationship with my abuser. A criminal court's seven-year order of protection was a deterrent to my abuser's violent physical attacks, and he was frightened at the thought of imprisonment.
- Chronic homelessness: I lived in a domestic violence shelter for a short period. For over two years, I resided in the New York City Department of Homeless Services' in-take shelter, transitional housing until final placement in a permanent housing program. I couch-surfed and lodged at an extended-stay hotel. I slept in New York's 34th Street Penn Station, New York's Grand Central Terminal Station, and New York City's Port Authority. I freshened up at a drop-in center and utilized hotels or restaurants. I relocated to a safe haven in another state to escape my abuser's friend's retaliation at my sibling's advice.

Throughout our on-and-off reconciliation, my abuser's jealous behavior remained. Thankfully, I am no longer in an abusive, intimate partner violence relationship. As Dr. Larry D. Reid asserted in his YouTube video on June 27, 2023, "I am the gift that everyone doesn't deserve."

★ ★ ★ ★

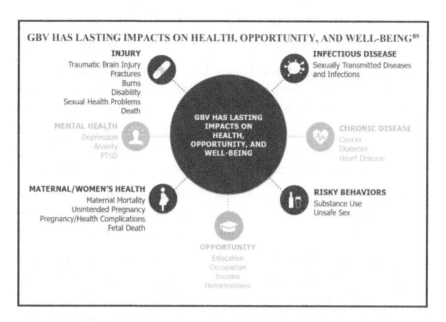

Figure 2. Gender-based Violence has a lasting impact on health, opportunity, and well-being. Source: https://www.whitehouse.gov/wp-content/uploads/2023/05/National-Plan-to-End-GBV.pdf

A Yorkshire Evening Post article dated February 17, 2021, vividly depicts an intimate partner violence incident wherein "[t]he woman had been in a relationship for ten weeks at the time of the incident (Gardner, 2021)."

- **Physical abuse:** The IPV abuser, Thomas Dalby, gouged the victim's eye with his thumb, kicked her in the face, and bit her arm during the prolonged attack at the property in Armley (England). The attack happened October 24-25, 2021, at Dalby's home on Armley Grove Place, where he lived with his grandparents. The victim was unable to leave the property and was attacked again the next day when Dalby kicked her in the chin.

- **Jealousy:** Dalby accused her of being unfaithful and shouted, "Why don't you tell me the truth." The violently jealous boyfriend kept his partner prisoner in his home.

- **Alcohol and drug abuse:** The defendant appeared drunk and under the influence of drugs when the victim arrived.

- **Emotional abuse/isolation:** Dalby took her phone, snapped the device in two, and said, "You won't be able to contact anyone now." The woman went to pack her belongings, but the defendant said, "You are not going anywhere. You are staying here tonight. I am ruining your plans tonight." Dalby locked the front door and took the victim's keys from her.

- **Medical treatment:** The IPV victim had an operation to remove part of a dislodged jawbone after the attack and needed dental work costing $5,603.78 US dollars.

- **Law enforcement:** Judge Penelope Belcher said, "This was a thoroughly horrible incident. You took the alcohol, and you took the drugs. They may have affected your behaviour, but you took them, and you have to live with the consequences, which are appalling. This will live with (the victim) for the rest of her life." Thomas Dalby pleaded guilty to false imprisonment and inflicting grievous bodily harm. He was jailed for three years (Gardner, 2021).

The National Intimate Partner and Sexual Violence Survey (NISVS) is an ongoing, nationally representative random-digit-dial (RDD) telephone survey of adults in the United States using a dual frame approach that includes both landline and cell phones (What You Need to Know: The National Intimate Partner and Sexual Violence Survey (NISVS) 2016/2017 Report on Sexual Violence, 2022). NISVS' disturbing report findings on sexual offenses are as follows:

Sexual coercion

- Nearly one in four women (23.6% or 29.4 million) in the United States reported sexual coercion victimization at some point in her lifetime. Almost four percent (3.7% or about

4.6 million) reported sexual coercion in the 12 months before taking the survey. About one in nine men (10.9% or 12.8 million) in the United States reported sexual coercion victimization during his lifetime. About 1.9% (or 2.3 million) reported sexual coercion in the 12 months prior to taking the survey.

- During their lifetimes, more than half (58.3%) of female victims of sexual coercion reported that their perpetrator was an intimate partner, followed by two in five (41.8%) by an acquaintance, one in 10 (10.1%) by a person of authority, one in 11 (9.1%) by a family member, one in 21 (4.7%) by a stranger, and one in 22 (4.6%) by a brief encounter. In the previous 12 months, about two-thirds (66.7%) of female victims of sexual coercion reported that their perpetrator was an intimate partner, and about one in three (31.8%) reported an acquaintance. Previous 12-month estimates for the remaining categories of perpetrators were based on numbers too small to produce statistically stable estimates and were not reported.

- In their lifetimes, nearly half (49.1%) of male victims of sexual coercion reported that their perpetrator was an acquaintance or an intimate partner (45.8%), followed by one in 10 (10.0%) who reported a person of authority, one in 15 (6.8%) a brief encounter, one in 19 (5.3%) a family member, and one in 25 (4.2%) a stranger. In the previous 12 months, more than half (55.0%) of male sexual coercion victims reported an intimate partner perpetrator, and 41.2% reported an acquaintance. Twelve (12)-month estimates for the remaining categories of perpetrators were based upon numbers too small to produce statistically stable estimates and were not reported.

Sexual assault (rape)

- In their lifetimes, more than half (56.1%) of female victims were raped by an acquaintance, more than one in three (39.3%) by an intimate partner, about one in six (16.0%) by a family member, about one in eight (12.1%) by a stranger, one in 10 (9.6%) by a brief encounter, and one in 25 (4.0%) by a person of authority. In the 12 months before the survey, almost half of female rape victims were raped by an intimate partner (45.4%) or an acquaintance (48.1%). Previous 12-month estimates for the remaining categories of perpetrators were based on numbers too small to produce statistically stable estimates and were not reported.

- During their lifetimes, more than half of male victims were raped by an acquaintance (57.3%), about one in six (16.0%) by a family member, nearly one in seven (13.7%) by a stranger, one in eight (12.8%) by a brief encounter, one in eight (12.5%) by an intimate partner, and one in 11 (9.2%) by a person of authority. Twelve (12)-month estimates for the type of perpetrator of male rape victims were based upon numbers too small to produce statistically stable estimates and were not reported.

Being made to penetrate (men)

In their lifetimes, more than three in five male victims were made to penetrate by an acquaintance (62.2%) followed by more than one in four (26.3%) by an intimate partner, one in seven (14.3%) by a brief encounter, one in 10 (10.4%) by a stranger, and one in 17 (5.9%) by a person of authority and a family member (5.9%). In the 12 months before the survey, about one in three male victims of being made to penetrate reported an intimate partner perpetrator (29.7%), and more than half of male victims reported an acquaintance perpetrator (55.5%). Twelve (12)-month estimates for the remaining categories of perpetrators were based upon numbers too small to produce statistically stable estimates and were therefore not reported.

Unwanted sexual contact

- During their lifetimes, more than half (59.9%) of female victims of unwanted sexual contact reported that their perpetrator was an acquaintance, followed by one in five (22.9%) who reported a family member, one in five (22.4%) a stranger, nearly one in six (16.8%) an intimate partner, nearly one in nine (11.7%) a brief encounter, and one in 11 (9.4%) a person of authority. In the 12 months before the survey, more than half (55.1%) of female victims of unwanted sexual contact reported an acquaintance perpetrator, 18.0% an intimate partner, 16.1% a stranger, and 8.4% a brief encounter perpetrator. Twelve (12)-month estimates for the remaining categories of perpetrators were based upon numbers too small to produce statistically stable estimates and were therefore not reported.

- In their lifetimes, more than one in two (62.4%) male victims of unwanted sexual contact reported that their perpetrator was an acquaintance, followed by one in five (21.9%) reporting a stranger, one in nine (11.1%) a brief encounter, one in 11 (9.2%) an intimate partner, one in 12 (8.3%) a family member, and one in 14 (7.2%) a person of authority. In the 12 months before the survey, almost two-thirds (62.9%) of male victims of unwanted sexual contact reported an acquaintance perpetrator, 18.0% an intimate partner, and 11.8% a stranger perpetrator. Twelve (12)-month estimates for the remaining categories of perpetrators were based upon numbers too small to produce statistically stable estimates and were not reported.

✶ ✶ ✶ ✶

Family and domestic violence is a common problem in the United States, affecting an estimated 10 million people yearly; as many as one in four women and one in nine men are victims of domestic violence (Huecker and Smock). Some 47,000 women and girls worldwide were killed by their intimate partners or other family members in 2020 (United Nations Office on Drugs and Crime). About 41% of women and 26% of men experienced contact with sexual violence, physical violence, or stalking by an intimate partner and reported an intimate partner violence-related impact during their lifetime (National Center for Injury Prevention and Control, Division of Violence Prevention). The link between mental health and intimate partner violence perpetration is well established (Maldonado et al., 2020). A meta-analysis found that men's physical assault perpetration was associated with depression, anxiety, and PTSD (Maldonado et al., 2020).

"IPV perpetration in the past year was assessed via 6 items that are a combination of multiple items from the Conflict Tactics Scale (CTS), Form R with modified response options [39]. This approach is consistent with other research on IPV that has been published using the NESARC [9,18,26]. Participants who endorsed being in a relationship were asked how frequently in the past year (0 = never to 5 = more than once a month) they: (1) pushed, grabbed, or shoved; (2) slapped, kicked, bit, or hit; (3) threatened with a weapon; (4) cut or bruised; (5) forced sex; and (6) injured their spouse/partner. Participants were categorized as perpetrators (1) or non-perpetrators (0). Twelve participants did not have valid responses to any of the CTS items and were coded as missing. (Maldonado et al., 2020)

The intergenerational cycle of violence and trauma can cause a legacy of suffering (Knaul et al.). To that end, multi-country studies show that boys who witnessed their mother being beaten have more than two to five times the odds of ever perpetrating violence against their partner. The article further asserts that gender-based violence and maltreatment of young people violates fundamental human rights to equality and non-discrimination, life, health, security of the person, privacy, and freedom from torture and cruel, inhumane, or degrading treatment. In multivariate analyses examining risk factors for men ever perpetrating physical violence against a partner, witnessing parental violence was the strongest risk factor, reinforcing previous research suggesting the intergenerational transmission of violence (Fleming et al.).

Coupled with the humanitarian side, gender-based violence reduces global gross domestic product by 2% per year, equivalent to an annual loss of more than $1.6 trillion when considering only direct medical costs and immediate productivity losses per The Lancet Commission (Knaul et al.). Violence against women is a transparent barrier to sustainable development, which has been acknowledged and adopted in the United Nations' Agenda 2030 for Sustainable Development (Puri). United Nations Transforming Our World: The 2030 Agenda for Sustainable Development new Agenda number 20 reveals, "All forms of discrimination and violence against women and girls will be eliminated, including through the engagement of men and boys" (United Nations). Strand and Storey (2019) reported that victims living in rural and remote areas had more vulnerability factors present than victims residing in urban areas, and the severity of violence was higher in rural and remote areas (Petersson & Thunberg, 2021).

Native American women experience higher rates of intimate partner violence than other U.S. racial/ethnic groups (Jock et al., n.d). Nevertheless, previous research has not sufficiently examined the complex determinants shaping their intimate partner violence experiences. The article's authors emphasized that research participants described how intergenerational exposure contributed to normalizing violence. More than four in five American Indian and

Alaska Native men and women (83%) have experienced a form of violence in their lifetime — whether it be physical violence or psychological aggression from an intimate partner, sexual violence, or stalking — according to the National Institute of Justice (NIJ). In addition, more than 1.5 million American Indian and Alaska Native women have experienced violence in their lifetime per a NIJ-funded study (PSAs Highlight Domestic Violence Awareness among Native Americans, 2022). This Specialty Institute will introduce the newly created Indigenous Safe Housing Center—STTARS (Safety, Training and Technical Assistance, Resources and Support), offering important and timely presentations designed to address the spectrum of housing issues for Indigenous victims/survivors, showcase promising or best practices related to domestic violence and housing, and provide valuable resources, support, and recommendations (Specialty Institute June 2022: Addressing the Spectrum of Housing for Victim/Survivors for DV, Sexual Violence and Trafficking in Tribal Communities | NIWRC, 2023).

Regression analyses using a nationally representative sample indicated that interracial couples demonstrated a higher level of mutual intimate partner violence than monoracial white couples but a level similar to monoracial Black couples (Martin et al., 2013). Evidence suggests that domestic violence incidents against South Asian women in high-income countries are often unreported and unrecorded, and this demographic represents an intersection of diverse identities and challenges (religion, socio-cultural norms, race, ethnicity, language, migration), which can affect help-seeking amongst those who experience domestic violence (Sultana et al., 2022).

* * * *

"Non-intimate partner violence" is violence between individuals who are not intimate partners but have a familial relationship, such as mother/adult son or brother/sister (Domestic Violence Dynamics – What Domestic Abuse What It Does to Family, 2011).

Elderly domestic violence may be financial or physical (Huecker & Smock, 2023). The abuse of older people, also known as elder abuse, is a single or repeated act, or lack of appropriate action, occurring within any relationship where there is an expectation of trust, which causes harm or distress to an older person (World Health Organization, 2022). Elder abuse, a heartbreaking crime, is thought to occur in three to 10% of the population of elders (Huecker & Smock, 2023), including physical abuse, emotional abuse, sexual abuse, exploitation, neglect, and abandonment (National Council on Aging, 2021). I mention this because perpetrators include children, other family members, spouses (associated with an elevated risk of abuse), and staff at nursing homes, assisted living, and other facilities (National Council on Aging, 2021).

According to the National Institute of Justice website, teen dating violence — also called intimate relationship violence or intimate partner violence among adolescents or adolescent relationship abuse — includes:

- Physical, psychological, or sexual abuse.
- Harassment.
- Stalking of any person ages 12 to 18 in the context of a past or present romantic or consensual relationship.

Being a victim, perpetrator, or bystander to such violent behavior can significantly impact teenagers' developmental processes.

The American Psychological Association published a journal article on intimate partner violence victimization in Lesbian, Bisexual, Gay, Transgender, and Queer + (LBGTQ+) young adults. The study included an ethnically diverse sample of 172 LGBTQ+ young adults who completed self-report measures of intimate partner violence, sexual behavior, mental health, and substance abuse at two-time points (four and five-year follow-ups) of an ongoing longitudinal study of LGBTQ+ youth. The study showed that participants experienced intimate partner violence nonuniformly across demographic groups. Specifically, female, male-to-female trans-gender, and Black/African American young adults were at higher risk than those who identified as male, female-to-male transgender, and other races (APA PsycNet, n.d.). Interventions targeting intimate partner violence in LGBTQ+ young people may benefit from programs tailored to address this community's specific needs, such that individuals with multiple gender, racial, or sexual minority identities may be at even greater risk for intimate partner violence.

Forty-three and eight-tenths percent (43.8%) of lesbian and 61.1% of bisexual women have experienced rape, physical violence, or stalking by an intimate partner at some point in their lifetime. Twenty-six percent (26%) of gay men and 37.3% of bisexual men have experienced rape, physical violence, or stalking by an intimate partner in their lifetime (LGBTQ: Sexual Assault, Partner Violence, and Stalking, n.d.).

****

Trauma bonding occurs when an abuser uses manipulation tactics and cycles of abuse to make the victim feel dependent on them for care and validation, causing a solid attachment or bond. Trauma bonding often occurs in romantic narcissistic relationships and families, friendships, or work relationships (The 7 Stages of Trauma Bonding, 2022).

The Cycle of Violence (Abuse) is a tool developed by Dr. Lenore Walker, an educator and forensic psychologist, who explains the complexity and co-existence of abuse with loving behaviors and describes intimate partner violence's cyclical nature and effect on victims. The cycle of violence model helps those who have never experienced domestic violence understand that breaking the violence cycle is much more complicated than just leaving (Blue Cloud Studio).

There are direct and indirect entanglements or risk factors that occur with intimate partner violence relationships: separation violence, homicides, murder-suicide, filicide-suicide, child abuse, Adverse Childhood Experiences (ACEs), barriers to safety, homelessness, and criminalization of survivors who murder their abusers.

✶ ✶ ✶ ✶

Maverick, my handsome, golden-complected, wavy-haired, African-American boyfriend with a great deal of swag, was upset that his numerous unwarranted phone calls went unanswered in late 2009. This well-built, muscular, burly man's fist punched my face and head for more than five minutes in the presence of a male neighbor who did not come to my aid. After frequent physical beatings, this domestic violence incident was my final straw. Maverick's conviction granted me a seven-year order of protection from the Kings County District Attorney's Office.

✶ ✶ ✶ ✶

A powerful tool to elaborate on intimate partner violence is an individual who has survived it. In the Holy Bible, Jesus visited where His disciples assembled after He arose from the dead following His crucifixion on the Cross. One of the disciples, Thomas, was not in attendance during the other disciples' glorious encounter with Jesus. John 20:25-27 (AMPC) proclaims, "So the other disciples kept telling him, We have seen the Lord! But he said to them, Unless I see in His hands the marks made by the nails and put my finger into the nail prints, and put my hand into His side, I will never believe [it]. Eight days later, His disciples were again in the house, and Thomas was with them. Jesus came, though they were behind closed doors, and stood among them and said, Peace to you! Then He said to Thomas, Reach out your finger here, and see My hands; and put out your hand and place [it] in My side. Do not be faithless and incredulous, but [stop your unbelief and] believe!"

This memoir is an authentic, transparent account where you will visualize the scars on my heart and the physical, psychological, and emotional abuse inflicted by my abusers. I experienced the cycle of violence and trauma bonding, which affected my self-esteem, sense of identity, and health (mental, physical, and emotional). My abuser repeatedly belittled me and did not adulate me often. A Gospel group, The Williams Brothers, had a song called *Misery* years ago. The lyrics declared, "Lord, you took my misery, all of the things that had me down and feeling so low, and you turned it into my ministry and gave me a word that I can share with others." I hope this book can give strength to people who are going through intimate partner violence in various populations across the globe. The Power and Control Wheel addresses dating violence dilemmas. At the start of a new relationship, it is not always easy to see the signs or red flags that the relationship will later become abusive. Many people who are abusive appear like ideal partners in the early stages of a relationship. Possessive and controlling behaviors do not always appear overnight and may intensify as the relationship grows. I strongly advise you not to ignore dating overt or covert red flags signaling that you are in a toxic relationship and your partner is a potential abuser.

The Cycle of Abuse

THE POWER and Control Wheel assumes she/her pronouns are for the victim and he/him pronouns are for the perpetrator. However, the abusive behavior that it details can happen to people of any gender or sexuality (National Domestic Violence Hotline, n.d.). The wheel is a diagram of tactics an abusive partner uses to keep their victims in a relationship. The inside of the wheel is made up of subtle, continual behaviors over time, while the outer ring represents physical and sexual violence. Abusive actions like those depicted in the outer ring often reinforce the regular use of other, more subtle methods found in the inner ring.

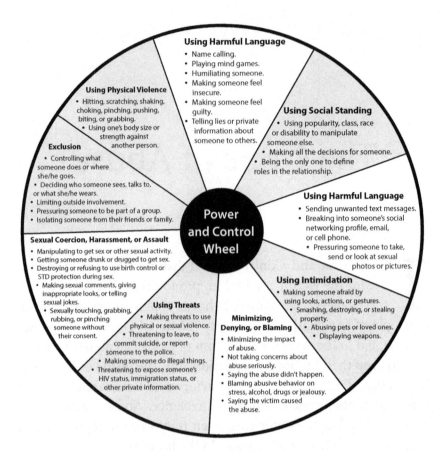

Figure 3. The Power and Control Wheel is an informative illustration of abusive partners' subtle, continual behaviors over time and represents physical and sexual violence. Source: (Power and Control Wheel | Michigan State University, n.d.)

There are many reasons abusers need to control their partners, including:

- Anger management issues;
- Jealousy;
- Low self-esteem;
- Feeling inferior;

Figure 4. Domestic violence infographic defining specific areas of IPV.
Source: Freepik.com

- Cultural beliefs that they have the right to control their partner;
- Personality disorder or psychological disorder;

- Learned behavior from growing up in a family where domestic violence was accepted; or
- Alcohol and drug use, as an impaired individual may be less likely to control violent impulses (Huecker & Smock, 2023)

✳ ✳ ✳ ✳

Amy Brunell, a psychology professor at The Ohio State University whose research focuses on narcissism in social and romantic relationships, affirms that while there is not much research on intimate partner abuse and narcissism, there is a connection. Controlling a person's social life from the beginning may leave the person with nowhere to turn when a relationship sours. "It does plant the seeds for intimate partner violence because typically a person will finally have enough and want to get out of it, and then it's really hard," Dr. Brunell said in a phone interview (Cherelus, 2010).

Authors argue that the Model Systemic Relational Violence presentation model provides a potential extension for the two existing theoretical models, the Cycle of Violence and the Duluth Power and Control Wheel (McLeod et al., 2021.).

"The Model of Systemic Relational Violence, with visual depiction in Figure 1, highlights the non-physical elements of control which exist within intimate partner abuse. The model was developed in response to an abundance of field data and qualitative responses, which described a continual state of control. Those experiencing relational violence describe a constant state of control that is not depicted in the current models of domestic violence—survivors and helping professionals describe these relationships as a perpetual system of domination. The Model of Systemic Relational Violence illustrates the constant expression of behavioral control that may fluctuate and then later be enforced through physical and non-physical sentinel acts. The model demonstrates how

the abuser constantly maintains dominance and behavioral control and acts in unique and/or discreet ways to enforce their dominance and maintain that control. For example, hitting a partner is not the focus of domestic violence, it is merely a symptom of a more extensive disease of systematic daily interpersonal control and domination (McLeod et al.)."

According to the National Domestic Violence website, below are common signs of abusive behavior in a partner:

1. Telling you that you never do anything right.
2. Showing extreme jealousy of your friends or time spent away from them.
3. Preventing or discouraging you from spending time with friends, family, or peers.
4. Insulting, demeaning, or shaming you, especially in front of others.
5. Preventing you from making your own decisions, including working or attending school.
6. Controlling finances in the household without discussion, including taking your money or refusing to provide money for necessary expenses.
7. Pressuring you to have sex or perform sexual acts with which you are uncomfortable.
8. Pressuring you to use drugs or alcohol.
9. Intimidating you through threatening looks or actions.
10. Insulting your parents or threatening to harm or take away your children or pets.
11. Intimidating you with weapons like guns, knives, bats, or mace.
12. Destroying your belongings or your home.

✶ ✶ ✶ ✶

The four phases in the Cycle of Violence are Phase 1: Tension-Building; Phase 2: Incident/Acute or Crisis-Explosion; Phase 3: Reconciliation; and Phase 4: Calm or Honeymoon.

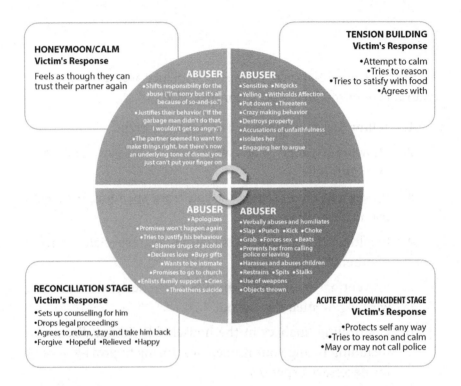

HONEYMOON/CALM
Victim's Response

Feels as though they can trust their partner again

ABUSER
•Shifts responsibility for the abuse ("I'm sorry but it's all because of so-and-so.")
•Justifies their behavior ("If the garbage man didn't do that, I wouldn't get so angry.")
•The partner seemed to want to make things right, but there's now an underlying tone of dismal you just can't put your finger on

TENSION BUILDING
Victim's Response
•Attempt to calm
•Tries to reason
•Tries to satisfy with food
•Agrees with

ABUSER
•Sensitive •Nitpicks
•Yelling •Withholds Affection
•Put downs •Threatens
•Crazy making behavior
•Destroys property
•Accusations of unfaithfulness
•Isolates her
•Engaging her to argue

ABUSER
•Apologizes
•Promises won't happen again
•Tries to justify his behaviour
•Blames drugs or alcohol
•Declares love •Buys gifts
•Wants to be intimate
•Promises to go to church
•Enlists family support •Cries
•Threathens suicide

ABUSER
•Verbally abuses and humiliates
•Slap •Punch •Kick •Choke
•Grab •Forces sex •Beats
•Prevents her from calling police or leaving
•Harasses and abuses children
•Restrains •Spits •Stalks
•Use of weapons
•Objects thrown

RECONCILIATION STAGE
Victim's Response
•Sets up counselling for him
•Drops legal proceedings
•Agrees to return, stay and take him back
•Forgive •Hopeful •Relieved •Happy

ACUTE EXPLOSION/INCIDENT STAGE
Victim's Response
•Protects self any way
•Tries to reason and calm
•May or may not call police

Figure 5. Four Phases in the Cycle of Violence. Sources: (Bottaro, 2022) (The 4 Stages of the Cycle of Abuse: From Tension to Calm and Back, 2022)

Phase 1: Tension-Building

The San Bernardino County District Attorney's Office's website describes this phase perfectly. During the tension-building phase, a victim and abuser's relationship becomes increasingly unhealthy (Domestic Abuse: A Cycle of Violence, n.d.). Victims may frequently feel like they are walking on eggshells, never knowing what will set the abuser off. The tension-building phase culminates in an inevitable blow-up (i.e., the abusive incident.)

Psychological aggression is verbal and non-verbal communication intending to harm another person mentally or emotionally or exert control over another person (Health, n.d.). A study based on data from the U.S. National Epidemiologic Survey of Alcohol and Related Conditions (NESARC) found that perpetrators of intimate partner violence were more likely to report any mental health disorder than non-perpetrators, including generalized anxiety, depression, PTSD, alcohol dependence, and drug dependence (Maldonado et al., 2020). Among U.S.-born Latinos, racial/ethnic discrimination had positive, significant correlations with all mental health measures (i.e., anxiety symptoms, depression symptoms, PTSD, alcohol dependence symptoms, and drug dependence symptoms) and intimate partner violence perpetration (Maldonado et al., 2020).

INJURY
Sprains, contusions, lacerations, fractures, strangulation, head, neck, and facial, traumatic brain injury, thoracic and abdominal injuries, sexual assault, and homicide.

CHRONIC CONDITIONS
Asthma, diabetes, joint disease, chronic pain, cardiovascular disease (hypertension, lipid disorders, and stroke).

MENTAL HEALTH CONDITIONS AND SUBSTANCE MISUSE
Depression, anxiety disorders including PTSD, suicidal behavior, tobacco addiction, misuse of alcohol and other drugs, prescription and opioid misuse.

Figure 6. Common Medical and Psychiatric Sequelae of Exposure to Intimate Partner Violence. Source: (Miller & McCaw, 2019); Pictures: Freepik.com

A batterer may establish uncanny rules for the victim to follow and consequences if not adhered to, isolate the individual from their support network, or say demeaning, degrading, and derogatory phrases toward the victim to objectify the victim (Domestic Violence: Understanding the Cycle of Violence, n.d.).

Listed below are potential terminologies or behaviors a batterer may display during the tension-building phase during the cycle of violence:

TERMINOLOGIES	VICTIM FEELS/BEHAVIOR	BATTERERS' BEHAVIOR
"Don't push it" "If you love me..."	**Feels:** angry, unfairly treated, hopeless, tense, afraid, embarrassed, humiliated, disgusted, depressed. **Behavior:** nurturing, submissive, "walking on eggshells," afraid to express feelings, may use alcohol or drugs to avoid the situation.	**Verbal abuse/Argumentative:** display anger or angry gestures; shortness of temper; yells or shouts profanity at the victim. **Manipulation and mind games:** silent treatment, ridiculing or making fun of you, coercion, criticism (critique you), blaming, questioning and jealousy, withdrawing, and sulking as well as emotional outbursts of irritability **Behavior:** Tense, frustrated, disgusted, self-righteous **Feels:** controlling, arrogant, possessive, may use alcohol or drugs, treats, minor fights or altercations, broken promises.

Figure 7. What vocabularies or behaviors may a batterer show during the Cycle of Violence as a tension-building step to manipulate or control their victim?

Below are examples of lifetime and 12-month psychological aggressions upon both men and women as illustrated in *The National Intimate Partner and Sexual Violence Survey 2016/2017 Report on Intimate Partner Violence* chart (NISVS) (2016/2017 Report on Sexual Violence, 2022):

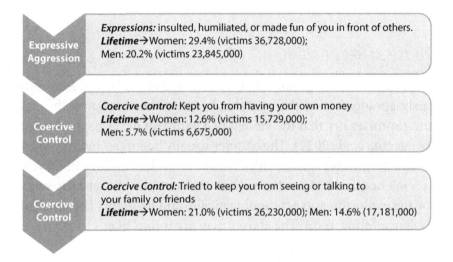

Expressive Aggression
Expressions: insulted, humiliated, or made fun of you in front of others. *Lifetime*→Women: 29.4% (victims 36,728,000); Men: 20.2% (victims 23,845,000)

Coercive Control
Coercive Control: Kept you from having your own money *Lifetime*→Women: 12.6% (victims 15,729,000); Men: 5.7% (victims 6,675,000)

Coercive Control
Coercive Control: Tried to keep you from seeing or talking to your family or friends *Lifetime*→Women: 21.0% (victims 26,230,000); Men: 14.6% (17,181,000)

Figure 8. Examples of Lifetime and 12-month psychological aggressions upon both men and women. Source: (2016/2017 Report on Sexual Violence, 2022)

Phase 2: Incident/Acute Explosion

In the incident stage, the batterer will release tensions accumulated during Phase 1, in which they become extremely aggressive, endangering and injuring the women (Sangeetha et al., 2022). During this phase, the batterer exhibits uncontrolled violent outbursts, which may start as minor, such as a slap, a pinch, or hair pulling, becoming increasingly brutal and escalating into a significant bodily injury or death (Domestic Violence: Understanding the Cycle of Violence, n.d.). This phase is when the woman wishes to leave the abusive relationship. Intervention occurs during this phase as the woman is utterly helpless in the hands of an abuser's impending danger, notwithstanding that her basic feelings are focused on survival (Sangeetha et al., 2022). An article in the National Library of Medicine notably unmasks, "In addition to physical and emotional abuse, she is subjected to brutal sexual abuse in which her husband uses sex, in fact, rape, as a weapon to subdue her (Anderson et al., 2014)."

Phase 3: Reconciliation

During this stage that follows severe abuse, the batterer copiously apologizes for the mistake, bestows the woman with gifts, and promises her that the violent behavior will never happen again (Sangeetha et al., 2022). The batterer usually begins an intense effort to win forgiveness (Domestic Violence: Understanding the Cycle of Violence, n.d.). After the violent incident, the abuser feels sorry for the explosion and acts apologetically and lovingly (The Cycle of Violence|Mpdc, n.d.). The abuser may say things like:

1. I will never do it again.
2. I am sorry, and I never meant to hurt you.
3. I promise I will change.
4. I promise I will get help.
5. I only did it because I was drunk, high, lost my temper, etc.

Phase 4: The Calm or Honeymoon Phase

According to Envision Counselling & Support Centre Inc.'s website, this phase is how the relationship starts. The individual who is abusive creates a safe space filled with love and a sense of security in the relationship (Cycle of Abuse – Envision, n.d.). A calm or honeymoon phase holds a significant draw for the person experiencing the abuse, as feelings of love are persuasive. The abusive person acts in ways they know their partner will desire and appreciate. The abuser may compliment the victim on their good looks, venture on usual outings, and provide extra affection, alluring the victim to stay with him/her. Unfortunately, as the idiom says, "sweet words can hide dark intentions." In this remorseful phase, the batterer demonstrates loving behavior and convinces victims to believe that prior abuse will not occur again. The cycle of violence commences due to a victim's willingness to believe a batterer because the tension has dissipated.

✶ ✶ ✶ ✶

Breaking the Cycle of Abuse

A majority of those in prison for violent crimes were either emotionally, physically, or sexually abused as children; consequently [t]hose who are mistreated perpetuate a culture of violence that affects us all (Engel, 2020). Violence refers to the concept of power and usage of superiority over others (Both et al., 2019), underscoring why including this section on empowering victims dealing with fear and trepidation to break the cycle of abuse and move forward.

Constant violence causes changes in the structural functioning and psychological conflict of the victims: difficulties in mentalization, instability in relationships, emotional dependence, abandonment of her own life for her partners, difficulty in having a sense of identity. Victims presented difficulties in making significant changes in daily life to break the cycle of violence. (Both et al., 2019)

The dynamics of domestic violence imply repetitive behavioral patterns in relationships, maintaining the cycle of violence (Both et al., 2019). Methods to breaking the cycle of abuse include:

- Become aware – recognize the problem

- Create an exit or safety plan
- Prioritize yourself
- Establish your boundaries
- Do not blame yourself
- Establish a support network
- Share truth – reclaim your power from the abuser's control over you.

Engels states that offering courses or therapeutic programs will help individuals from abusive or neglectful backgrounds clear up the debris of their childhood before embarking on a new life with a spouse (Engel, 2020).

CATEGORIES	SUBCATEGORIES
Previous history	Parental relationship and previous relationships.
Behavioral aspects	Female submission, escalated discussions in the relationship, difficulties breaking with the cycle of violence (independence), and recurring assaults.
Emotional aspects	Fear, sadness, devaluation, and guilt.
Reason for being in the relationship	Feeling of being taken care of, receiving affection, and love for the partner.
Type of violence and explanation of the reason for the violence	Psychological violence, physical violence, and sexual violence. Causes: alcoholic beverage and jealousy.
Support network and daily activities	Family support, job, and study.
Referrals	Protective measures, assets, child custody, and treatment.

Table 1. Psychodynamics of women in the cycle of violence considering the aspects of psychological trauma illustrated in categories and subcategories. The sample was composed of ten women victims of domestic violence. Data collection was based on the OPD-2 Clinical Interview. Content analysis was performed from categories created by a posteriori: (a) Previous history; (b) Behavioral aspects; (c) Emotional aspects; (d) Reason for being in the relationship; (e) Type of violence and explanation for the reason of violence; (f) Support network and daily activities; and (g) Clinical and legal referral. Source: (Both et al., 2019)

Factors identified as being related to breaking the cycle of abuse among children who grew up in abusive homes and did not become abusive as adults include:

- Good self-esteem
- School achievement
- A caring and supportive relationship with a caregiver or other adult in childhood
- Social supports

- Having participated in therapy (Choosing Therapy, 2023)

✶✶✶✶

Shame is a significant factor in the continuation of the cycle of abuse (Engel, 2020). Society should refrain from making "monsters out of those who continue the cycle of violence by abusing their children or their partner" (Engel, 2020) and proactively provide mental health services to heal their souls.

"If you were emotionally, physically, or sexually abused as a child or adolescent, or if you experienced neglect or abandonment, it isn't a question of whether you will continue the cycle of abuse or neglect, it is a question of how you will do so—whether you will become an abuser or continue to be a victim. Individuals with a history of childhood abuse are four times more likely to assault family members or sexual partners than are individuals without such a history (Engel, 2020)."

Previous research suggests that survivors of intimate partner violence experience stigma, which may affect their willingness to seek help and their recovery process following the end of the abusive relationship (Murray et al., 2015). Effective treatments for survivors of domestic abuse typically include:

- Connection with an advocate or mentor to assist the survivor by providing information, access to support (e.g., legal, financial, housing, other community support), and developing a safety plan.
- Cognitive-behavioral therapy interventions offered individually and/or in groups help the survivor develop skills in emotion management, communication, and assertiveness.
- PTSD therapies for those experiencing PTSD and complex trauma because of domestic abuse (Choosing Therapy, 2023).

Toxic Relationships

"The most painful thing is losing yourself in the process of loving someone too much and forgetting that you are special too." — Ernest Hemingway, Men Without Women

D R. LILLIAN Glass, a California-based communication and psychology expert, coined the term toxic relationship in her 1995 book *Toxic People*. Dr. Glass defines a toxic relationship as "any relationship [between people who] do not support each other, where there is conflict, and one seeks to undermine the other, where there is competition, where there is disrespect and a lack of cohesiveness (Ducharme, 2018)." In the search for acceptance, people look for love in the wrong places or from the wrong people and go from one dissatisfying relationship to the next (Rafferty, n.d.). This article argues that even the most maladaptive and self-defeating of compulsive, repetitive behaviors seek love and validation that an individual was denied through early life experiences. In preparing this book, recurring victimization of toxic relationships was apparent in my life (Rafferty, n.d.). Webster-Merriam Dictionary describes toxic as "containing or being poisonous material especially when capable of causing death or serious debilitation."

When we form secure attachments with a parent or parents based on unconditional love and acceptance, we learn that we are acceptable and deserve respect and polite treatment from others (Why Do I Keep Attracting Toxic Partners? | Psychology Today, n.d.). In contrast, with toxic partners, Dr. Jack affirms that a person will "find it hard to feel content and safe within a relationship, no matter how loving and supportive you are." Defining what a toxic person is can be a moving target precisely because of how a toxic person acts:

- A toxic person is deft at deflecting blame or responsibility.
- A toxic person can prey on both the goodwill and fear of others.
- A toxic person is adept at gaslighting-making someone else feel dysfunctional (Break Free from the Trap of Toxic People | Psychology Today, n.d.).

Toxic relationships start with jealous rage or controlling behavior and can include, but are not limited to, unrealistic expectations, isolation, blame, hypersensitivity, dual personality, criticism, and contempt (King, 2018). In enduring profound love, which involves the personal growth of each partner, self-fulfillment is not egoistic, and the tension drives mutual thriving (Ben-Ze'ev, 2019). Isolation alienates a victim and amputates a sense of community and belonging. Abuse is an extreme form of toxicity (10 Signs You're in a Toxic Relationship, n.d.). A *New York Times* article, *Stop Treating Domestic Violence Differently From Other Crimes, The Criminal Justice System Isn't Preventing Intimate Partner Violence. It Might Be Making It Worse,* gives a heartbreaking story of a victim who was in a toxic, romantic relationship who cried for him to law enforcement and did not receive help (Goodmark, 2019):

"Second, a woman from Connecticut named Tracey Thurman won a multimillion-dollar judgment against the city of Torrington. Ms. Thurman sued after the police failed on numerous occasions to arrest her husband, despite her reports of violence; he eventually left her partly paralyzed. Jurisdictions around the country took notice, concerned that they too could be held liable for police inaction (Goodmark, 2019)."

✶ ✶ ✶ ✶

The Digital Age presents another hidden danger we cannot undermine, recoil, or downplay-digital domestic abuse. Technological intimate partner violence or cyber abuse, an emerging trend in intimate partner violence (Woodlock, 2016), was explored in an increasing number of studies that emphasized its adverse psychological consequences (Maftei & Dănilă, 2021). Despite the prevalence and impact of domestic violence enacted through technology, there has been a scant academic review of what we have also termed digital coercive control (Harris & Woodlock, 2018). A quote from the University of California Berkeley research article *A Domestic Violence Dystopia: Abuse Via the Internet of Things and Remedies Under Current Law* highlights the impact of technology, "The increasing prevalence of Internet of Things (IoT) devices has given abusers a powerful new tool to expand and magnify the traditional harms of domestic violence, threatening the progress advocates have made in the past thirty years and creating novel dangers for survivors (HeinOnline, 2021)." Digital coercive control is introduced to highlight the nature and impacts of technology-facilitated abuse in the context of domestic violence (Woodlock et al., 2019). The authors of *Technology as a Weapon in Domestic Violence: Responding to Digital Coercive Control* article shared, "A major dilemma faced by practitioners is how to promote and facilitate client safety from [digital coercive control] DCC while still enabling safe use of technology so clients can remain connected to family, friends, and community (Woodlock et al., 2019)."

"Mcfarlane et al. (2002) suggested, for example, that among the most frequent stalking behaviors before homicide were spying and victim surveillance. Technology provides abusers a quick and easy method to harass their partners, even when they are not physically close, using social media, GPS tracking, constant texting or sexting, and other related forms of intimidation, embarrassment, and control (Maftei & Dănilă, 2021)."

Technology plays a significant role in today's intimate partnerships, wherein we might meet our future husband or wife online, and we can communicate fast and efficiently, share pictures, and stay connected to our loved ones (Maftei & Dănilă, 2021). "[T]he dark side of digital technologies within relationships might include stalking and the surveillance of victims by abusive partners using digital location services, monitoring the partners' social networking activity and their e-mails through stolen passwords, remote cameras and microphones, spyware, or simply by forcing them to reveal their passwords and share their accounts (Maftei & Dănilă, 2021)."

Toxic relationships have been augmented into another dimension by countless modes of communication across digital age platforms. Embedded is a list of various forms of technology in existence today:

Internet (World Wide Web)	Dark web (ability to secretly share provocative photos)	Social media	YouTube
Apple watch	Smart phone mobile devices	Laptops	Desktop computers
Chromebook	iPad	Multimedia	AI or ChatGPT – OpenAI
File sharing (upload documents or imagery)	Satellite	Drones	Smart TVs
Alexa	Ring Security and Door Cameras	The Cloud	Webcam
Dashcam (car digital video recorder device)	Zoom video conferencing	Spyware	Stalkerware
Tracking devices	Live streaming broadcast	Podcasts	Online banking
Mobile banking	Cryptocurrency	eBooks (e.g, Kindle and Amazon Fire)	3D printers (make untraceable deadly weapons like a gun)
Apps (Ride-share provides an abuser the ability to stalk a victim in an unfamiliar vehicle)	Streaming services	Self-driving vehicles	Dating apps (Check to see if an individual is seeking another relationship if no longer together.)

Table 2. Modes of communication across digital age platforms.

According to an article from *Forbes, Eleven Ways Tech Is Preventing and Reducing Domestic Violence,* "On a somewhat uplifting note, technology and AI enable us to help domestic abuse victims in many effective and creative ways:

- Crowdsourcing data
- Using AI to predict trends, prevent domestic abuse, and alert police
- Safety through apps and SMS-based services
- Helplines and hotlines with AI-powered chatbots and virtual agents
- E-governments and safety tools
- Wearable tech
- Social media campaigns
- Responsible design
- Education through gaming
- Pro bono CSR programs
- NGOs, social impact VCs, and grants (Ates, 2021)"

"Crowdsourcing is a powerful way to understand domestic violence and sexual harassment, as well as for triggering policy-making and institutional change. Crowdsourcing sites such as #StopFemicides, HarassMap and Hollaback! Are not only raising awareness of the scale and seriousness of this issue, but they are also bringing the much-needed transparency required to accelerate change by calling on governments and policymakers to take action. On an equally exciting level, various AI and NLP tools have been developed to spot domestic violence and online harassment trends during COVID-19. Tools such as artificial intelligence can help protect victims of domestic violence, identifying patterns during lockdown to enable subject matter experts, local authorities,

＊ ＊ ＊ ＊

The COVID-19 pandemic caused devastation for people world-wide — psychologically, financially, and socially; most importantly, intimate partner violence substantially increased while everyone in respective countries was under governmental mandates "order-ing quarantines and lockdowns to keep people indoors and curb the spread of the coronavirus (Gajanan, 2020)." Social isolation is considered one of the main risk factors leading to intimate partner violence episodes; this evidence also emerged during the applica-tion of stay-at-home policies to contain the COVID-19 pandemic (Lausi et al., 2021). The COVID-19 pandemic has forced a rapid shift to virtual delivery of treatment and care to individuals affected by domestic violence and sexual violence (Ghidei et al., 2022).

According to a *New York Times* article dated March 18, 2021, President Joseph Biden's $1.9 trillion pandemic relief package had tens of millions of dollars for organizations dedicated to curtail-ing domestic abuse (Ryzik & Benner, 2021). The relief package had vouchers for people fleeing violence at home to help them find safe shelter and rebuild their lives. President Biden signed a version of the American Rescue Plan that funnels $49 million in aid and hundreds of millions of dollars in housing assistance to victims trapped during the pandemic with their abusers. Experts also warned that COVID-19 would increase rates of teen dating violence as adolescents and young adults also spent more time at home (COVID-19 and Its Impact on Intimate Partner Violence | SSRI COVID-19 Resources, 2020).

*Domestic violence consists primarily of aggravated and
so-called simple assaults committed against domestic*

partners or family members. The monthly domestic violence rate, displayed in Figure 8, exhibited a cyclical pattern and a [slight] downward trend that persisted through the end of 2022. Across the sample of 11 cities, domestic violence decreased by 3.9% from 2021 to 2022. Domestic violence offenses were 5% lower in 2022 compared to 2019. The number of domestic violence offenses during the first half of 2023 was 0.3% higher, on average, than during the same period in 2022, representing 148 more domestic violence incidents in the cities that reported data. The domestic violence rate from January to June 2023 remained 4.8% lower than in the first half of 2019 (Crime Trends in U.S. Cities: Mid-Year 2023 Update - Council on Criminal Justice, 2023)

Figure 9. Monthly domestic violence rates are now in a slight downward trend that persisted through the end of CY 2022. Source: (Crime Trends in U.S. Cities: Mid-Year 2023 Update - Council on Criminal Justice, 2023)

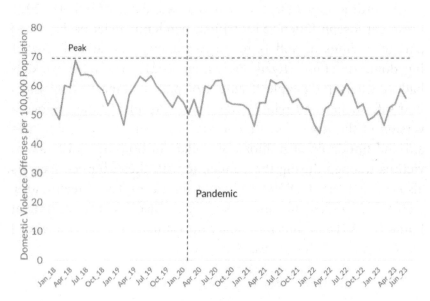

The economic and social stressors brought on by the pandemic have also contributed to a greater risk of violence and conflict in the home (Ghidei et al., 2022). People who lost their jobs due to the pandemic were three to four times more likely to perpetrate intimate partner violence than those who remained employed (Davis et al. (2021). By October 2021, 52 countries had integrated violence against women and girls' prevention and response into COVID-19 plans, and 150 countries had adopted measures to strengthen services for women survivors of violence during the global crisis (Facts and Figures: Ending Violence Against Women, n.d.). The United Nations Women's article, *Facts and Figures: Ending Violence Against Women*, asserts, "Less than 40 percent of the women who experience violence seek help of any sort" (Facts and Figures: Ending Violence Against Women, n.d.).

Evidence of the adverse effects of the pandemic on domestic violence is still emerging, even as violence prevention strategies are iteratively being refined by service providers, advocacy agencies, and survivors to meet stay-at-home mandates (Emezue, 2020). Furthermore, the author remarked, "Emotional and material support for survivors is a critical resource increasingly delivered using digital and technology-based modalities, which offer several advantages and challenges (Emezue, 2020)."

"Technology use during COVID-19 has also raised some ethical challenges related to protecting clients' safety and the coercive control tactics used by perpetrators. For instance, it has been reported that the risks to a woman's safety increases when she uses app-based interventions that can easily be accessed by her perpetrator (El Morr & Layal, 2020). Moreover, some individuals may be struggling with unstable or unavailable internet connections, or they may not be able to afford the required devices, such as a smart phone or tablet, to receive treatment or support virtually (Fiolet et al., 2020; Rossi et al.,

According to the *American Journal of Emergency Medicine* and the United Nations group, *U.N. Women*, when the pandemic began, domestic violence incidents increased by 300% in Hubei, China; 25% in Argentina; 30% in Cyprus; 33% in Singapore; and 50% in Brazil. The U.K., where calls to domestic violence hotlines have soared since the pandemic hit, was particularly shaken that June by the death of Amy-Leanne Stringfellow, 26, a mother of one and a veteran of the war in Afghanistan, allegedly at the hands of her 45-year-old boyfriend (Kluger, 2021).

The *National Library of Medicine* article, *Intimate Partner Violence in the COVID-19 Era: A Health, Psychological, Forensic and Legal Perspective* Section *Supporting IPV Survivors in Health Services during the COVID-19 Pandemic*, underscores dynamics individuals should reassess enduring a toxic relationship:

"About 30% of women worldwide have experienced some form of gender violence in their lifetime, with long-lasting adverse health consequences. Several different diseases, particularly musculo-skeletal, respiratory, cardiovascular, and gastrointestinal disorders, and chronic pain diseases are more likely to be encountered in women who survived IPV. Moreover, gynecological disorders, including sexually transmitted infections, sexual dysfunctions, chronic pelvic pain, and adverse pregnancy outcomes, are prevalent in women suffering from domestic violence. A possible explanation of this high frequency of chronic diseases could be attributed to high-stress levels and/or reduced healthy practice (Barbara et al., 2022)."

* * * *

The line between healthy and unhealthy relationships can be quickly crossed and potentially challenging to define, even with signs that might seem obvious to others (Torrisi, 2022). Social support is a key factor in mediating, buffering, and improving the outcomes of survivors of violence and improving mental health outcomes (Ogbe et al., 2020). Conversely, social isolation and lack of social support are linked with poor health outcomes for survivors of violence (Ogbe et al., 2020).

"If you know the enemy and know yourself, you need not fear the result of a hundred battles. If you know yourself but not the enemy, for every victory gained you will also suffer defeat. If you know neither the enemy nor yourself, you will succumb in every battle." – Sun Tzu, The Art of War

---

The article, *7 Signs of A Toxic Relationship and What to Do to Fix It*, from *Insiders Global News Publication*'s website, points out seven signs of a toxic or abusive relationship (Fielding et al., 2022):

1. *Lack of trust.* A partner is someone you can rely on, be vulnerable with, and have in your corner. In the absence of trust, none of these things are possible.

2. *Hostile communication* can cause tension and create further distrust between partners. Instead, healthy relationships rely on open communication, cooling down before things get too heated, and respect. According to Kamil Lewis, AMFT, a sex and relationship therapist in Southern California, overt forms of hostile communication include:

   - Yelling
   - Name-calling or other hurtful phrases
   - Throwing and breaking things

- Using your body for physical intimidation or force

According to Woodfin, subtler signs of hostile communication include (Fielding et al., 2022):

- The silent treatment
- Using 'you-statements' or blaming statements
- Constantly interrupting
- Listening to respond instead of listening to hear and understand your partner.

3. *Controlling behaviors.* Your partner has no right to control your actions or beliefs (Fielding et al., 2022). According to Woodfin, one controlling behavior to look out for is threatening the loss of something, such as financial stability, time with your children, or companionship. Other signs of controlling behavior include:

- Telling you what is right.
- Threatening to out you.
- Needing to know everything you do and who you are with.
- Trying to manage your money.
- Secluding you from loved ones or always being present when you are with others.
- Acting like you do not know what you are talking about.
- Requiring access to your personal devices, such as phone or email accounts.

4. *Frequent lying.* When a partner lies to you, it signals they do not respect you as a mutual partner who deserves honesty and care (Fielding et al., 2022).

5. *All take, no give.* If your relationship consistently revolves around what makes your partner happy and ignores your needs, it can be a sign of toxicity. "If they dismiss, belittle, or

bulldoze your boundaries, which could also signify a toxic relationship (Fielding et al., 2022)."

6. *You feel drained.* Think about the last time you did something for yourself, spent time — even virtually — with a loved one, or slept soundly. Try shifting some of your energy to care for yourself and see how your partner reacts. If their response is negative, that signals toxic traits in the relationship. (Fielding et al., 2022)

7. *You are making excuses for their behavior.* Do you often find yourself forced into a position to defend your partner? While it's easy to fall back on the mentality of 'you don't know them like I do,' an outside perspective from someone you know loves you— such as a friend or family member you trust — may be able to see your partner's negative characteristics that are hard to acknowledge yourself. (Fielding et al., 2022)

My analogy for a toxic relationship is how cigarette use harms humans; nevertheless, consumers disregard the Surgeon General's warning labels or commercial ads to deter user consumption. The writing is always on the wall of whether their partner's love is genuine and sincere. People who smoke are exposed to a toxic mix of over 7,000 chemicals, including more than 70 that can cause cancer, when they inhale cigarette smoke (Products, 2023). The Food and Drug Administration (FDA)'s website cautions that cigarettes are "also responsible for the vast majority of all tobacco-related disease and death in the U.S.; basic components are tobacco, chemical additives, a filter, and paper wrapping (Products, 2023)."

As stated earlier, non-intimate partner violence is violence between individuals who are not intimate partners; hence, we are talking about secondary-level abuse (e.g., family members, neighbors, friends, and support networks that decide to get involved) and others who may be killed at the hand of a victim of intimate partner violence's abuser. "Inhaling secondhand smoke is called involuntary or passive smoking" of nonsmokers (Cigarette Smoking: Health Risks and How to Quit, 2023). The cause-and-effect scenarios in toxic relationships may result in a non-intimate partner's death or bodily harm. Likewise, nonsmokers exposed to secondhand smoke have a higher risk of lung cancer and coronary heart disease (Cigarette Smoking: Health Risks and How to Quit, 2023).

Healthy Relationships

"A healthy relationship is a feast of affection/giving for both people; not one receiving crumbs and trying to convince themselves it's enough." — Shannon Thomas

Healthy Relationship

RESEARCH SHOWS that women are specifically damaged in their ability to have healthy love relationships due to the absence of their fathers at some point in their lives (Romero, 2014). A father is typically a daughter's first introduction to males: her first hero, role model, and usually her primary measuring stick for all other men involved in her life (Team, 2022). Women are likely to have unhealthy love relationships due to insecurity caused by the emotional absence of a father throughout childhood (Romero, 2014). Fathers play a significant role in a child's development and can affect a child's social competence, performance in school, and emotional regulation (Lansford, 2021). Other studies revealed that daughters with absentee fathers experienced psychological effects such as insecurities, difficulty establishing intimate relationships with the opposite sex, development of attention-seeking behavior, and negative perceptions of men and relationships (Brown, 2018).

The term 'father absence' in this study refers to biological fathers who are absent in the lives of their children due to disappearance in the early stages of the child's life or those who are known to be alive or perceived to be alive but since the early stages of the child's life, have been emotionally and economically absent leading to children feeling neglected or abandoned (Sikweyiya et al., 2016). Notwithstanding this, evidence from a few studies conducted in South Africa suggests that young people who grew up with absent fathers tend to be treated differently (compared to other children who have involved fathers) in their maternal homes or often suffer physical, sexual, and emotional abuse perpetrated by significant people in their lives (e.g., maternal uncles, aunts, and/or maternal grandparents) (Sikweyiya et al., 2016).

Ways God designed the importance of a father

Here are a few ways that God designed dads to have a unique influence on their families (Cuppy, 2022):

- A father's *strength* can be *powerful.*
- A dad's *words* can be *fueling* and *inspirational.*
- *Hugs* from a dad can be deeply *comforting.*
- A dad's *smile* can instill *joy* and *confidence.*
- *Time* with a dad can be *fun* and *productive.*
- A dad's *physicality* can be *challenging.*
- A dad's *guidance* can be *life-changing* and *foundational.*
- A father's *correction* can be *life-saving* and *life-giving.*
- *Adventures* with a dad can be *exciting* and *memorable.*

✶ ✶ ✶ ✶

My childhood home's family dynamic, which consisted of married parents with young children, changed. My parents separated, and Dad no longer resided there. I do not recall my biological father, who passed during my child-rearing years (I was 10). I missed these important impartations of my biological father's presence, albeit there were other male role models in our tight-knit family (maternal grandfather, uncles, cousins) and at church (pastors, elders, deacons, brothers-in-Christ).

Although my biological father was absent, I had a great relationship with my Heavenly Father, whom I affectionately call Daddy. One day, I went into the restroom and cried out to Daddy about a situation at work. With all the great male role exemplars, especially the late Apostle H.L. McGowan (who was like a dad to me), where did I go wrong in partner selection?

Life and business strategist Tony Robbins declares, "A healthy relationship is one in which you feel valued, trusted, and respected – period, certain core traits as well as these qualities: Communication, Honesty, Vulnerability, Growth, and Intimacy (13 Proven Ways to Maintain a Healthy Relationship with Tony, n.d.). Furthermore, Robbins stated we should recognize signs of an unhealthy relationship:

1. *Criticism:* There is a difference between honesty and criticism. When your partner is honest, you will still feel respected and valued because their feedback is constructive.

2. *Controlling behavior:* If your partner pressures you to change your appearance, quit activities you love, or stop seeing friends or family, those are big red flags.

3. *Distance:* Healthy relationships are both emotionally and physically close.

4. *Lack of conflict resolution:* Sometimes, it is best to *defuse arguments* over minor things. However, your communication skills may be lacking if you are always burying conflict – or constantly arguing without seeing any improvement.

Establishing Healthy Boundaries

Tony Gaskins' quote, "You teach people how to treat you by what you allow, what you stop, and what you reinforce," explains healthy boundaries quite well. We must be clear about our expectations of ourselves and others and what we are uncomfortable with in specific situations (Selva, 2018). The author shares that setting healthy boundaries requires effective communication skills that convey assertiveness and clarity. Notwithstanding, we should recognize the difference between healthy relationships, unhealthy relationships, and behavioral patterns of intimate partner violence. We can abstain from falling prey to intimate partner violence by knowing what a healthy relationship is, establishing boundaries, and educating ourselves about abuse.

I found the statement "Men want women for two reasons: that is for keeps or the ride" quite intriguing in a Nollywood drama. If I recall correctly, the male actors gathered and openly discussed their relationship perspectives. Evaluate the person's intention in pursuing you for a romantic relationship. Dating is about collecting data on an individual. What are your core values, and does your love partner have a differentiation or opposition to it? It is best to determine clear expectations of your official title (position) or the type of relationship dynamic you have (e.g., platonic friends, casually dating non-committal, friends with benefits, asexual, someone to be with on the rebound, someone on reserve, "a girl for the streets" aka promiscuous women who are not relationship material, a placeholder, side chick, or someone they are stringing along) eliminating confusion or gray areas.

Brand Awareness is a business term individuals should consider when assessing a mate while dating because it plays a vital role in most aspects of marketing. Consumers are inundated with coercive marketing or advertising agencies' tactics that effectively become embedded into their psyches. Brand awareness consists of brand familiarity, brand recognizability, and consistency in brand reputation (Foroudi, 2019). Practical marketing tools build an organization's credibility and brand identity, luring customers with products or services that influence consumer loyalty and purchasing behavior (Foroudi, 2019).

According to the *Forbes* article *The Power of Symbols to Transform Your Business*, "When harnessed effectively by companies, symbols can have a strong impact on corporate culture, recruiting, morale, and brand longevity (Council, 2023)." At the start of a relationship, people present an image of themselves, which can be considered a representation of their identity or mascot. Another symbolic advertising ploy or secret weapon in marketing is using embodied brand mascots (symbolic characters) to sell their products or services.

A resident in a homeless shelter where I lived years ago accidentally drank Clorox bleach, thinking water was inside the bottle. The homeless shelter resident was inattentive, and she placed bleach inside the empty water bottle for her laundry. Surface appearance may bamboozle you, which is this scenario's dangerous lesson, as the individual required medical attention. In business, a true glimpse into their character is acquired through the lens of employees and whistleblowers. In personal relationships, whistleblowers are family members, friends, co-workers, acquaintances, partners, etc.

Consumers recognize a company's brand, whether product or service, without visually seeing their name because the symbolic imagery, though intangible, has allocated space in their brains. This is impressive, considering a standard television commercial advertisement lasts 15 seconds. The aspect of a lifetime partner requires research into who they are. Dating is acquiring data (an interview), being eagle-eyed, and viewing past the surface (their brand image). I strongly recommend being vigilant for a potential mate's fictitious display or portrait of their actual self.

The Five Love Languages

Miscommunication, misreading, and misinterpretation of verbal and non-verbal cues can cause friction in a relationship because we do not understand love languages. John Gray's book, *Men Are from Mars, Women Are from Venus: A Practical Guide for Improving Communication and Getting What You Want in Your Relationships*, garnered attention years ago. Gary Chapman, Ph.D., a well-known marriage counselor and director of marriage seminars, published *The 5 Love Languages: The Secret to Love That Lasts, Things I Wish I'd Known Before We Got Married*, and it "has helped thousands of people to understand the miscommunication that happens in their intimate relationships (https://www.facebook. com/TheLadiesCoach, 2016)."

"The premise of The 5 Love Languages® book is quite simple: different people with different personalities give and receive love in different ways. By learning to recognize these preferences in yourself and in your loved ones, you can learn to identify the root of your conflicts, connect more profoundly, and truly begin to grow closer (Chapman, n.d.)."

The five love languages Mr. Chapman revealed were: 1) Words of affirmation, 2) Acts of service, 3) Receiving gifts, 4) Quality time, and 5) Physical touch. After deliberating over it, I declined a marriage proposal from an individual who had not vocalized the intimate words *I love you* to me. A spiritual mom heard a lack of excitement about marriage in our telephone discussion. If I recall correctly, my sister indicated Stephan did display love, albeit it was not expressed through words. Dr. Chapman explained on his website that (Chapman, n.d.):

- Acts of Service™: For these people, actions speak louder than words.

- Receiving Gifts™: For some people, receiving a heartfelt gift is what makes them feel most loved.
- Quality Time™: This language is all about giving the other person your undivided attention.
- Words of Affirmation™: This language uses words to affirm other people.

How to Speak Your Partner's Love Language

WHICH LOVE LANGUAGE	HOW TO COMMUNICATE	ACTIONS TO TAKE	THINGS TO AVOID
Words of Affirmation	Encourage, affirm, appreciate, and listen actively	Send an unexpected note, note, or card	Not recognizing or appreciating effort
Physical Touch	Non-verbal use of body language and touch to show love	Hugs, kisses, and cuddling.	Physical neglect or abuse
Receiving Gifts	Thoughtfulness, make your spouse a priority	Give thoughtful gifts and gestures. Express gratitude when receiving gifts	Unenthusiastic gift receiving and forgetting special occasions
Quality Time	Uninterrupted and focused conversations. One-on-one time is important	Create special moments, take walks, and do small things with your partner	Distractions when spending time together. Long time without one-on-one time
Acts of Service	Let them know you want to help and to lighten their load.	Make them breakfast or dinner. Go out of your way to help with chores	Lacking follow-through on small and large tasks

Table 3. The Ladies Coach ~ How to Speak Your Partner's Love Language. Source: (https://www.facebook.com/TheLadiesCoach, 2016)

Build Fundamental Relationship Skills

Tony Robbins' online article, *13 Proven Ways to Maintain a Healthy Relationship with Tony (n.d.),* proclaimed that "developing positive habits and patterns to create and maintain an extraordinary relationship requires a conscious application and repetition of good behavior and communication." Below are Tony Robbins' 13 proven ways to maintain a healthy relationship:

1. *Love yourself first* – "Like attracts like." – This is the law of attraction – the idea that we attract the things that we focus on and surround ourselves with – and it applies to relationships and life.

2. *Raise your standards* – You must hold yourself to high standards if you want a healthy relationship.

3. *Meet your partner's core needs* – What is a healthy relationship? It is two people making each other's needs their own.

4. *Communicate effectively* – Healthy relationships depend on effective communication.

5. *Grow together* – Lack of growth is better known as stagnation, which can lead to deterioration in a relationship.

6. *Appreciate your differences* – You do not need to ignore or play down the differences between you and your partner. On the contrary, appreciating your differences is essential to maintaining a sense of excitement in the relationship.

7. *Develop trust* – Trust is the foundation of all productive and healthy relationships. Trust springs respect; both are necessary for sharing, interaction, and growth.

8. *Be honest* – When thinking about a healthy relationship, honesty is vital – including being honest with yourself. Being honest and courageous when you face disappointment, pain, and surprise is essential.

9. *Redefine intimacy* – Intimacy is not just physical; it is not always about "big moments." Real intimacy is about the smaller, everyday moments.

10. *Discover the power of polarity* – Polarity is the attraction between opposite energies. This polarity attracted you to each other, and this powerful interplay can maintain passion between you.

11. *Align your values* – Healthy relationships can encounter disagreements about values and long-term goals. A successful relationship will use these problematic situations as a chance to re-align and grow instead of using them as an excuse to break down.

12. *Shift your focus* – Choose to focus on solutions, and you will be able to work through issues and celebrate how your differences enrich your life together.

13. *Keep it going* – You have worked on having a healthy relationship and reached a satisfactory place. Now, you move forward, leading by example and nurturing a healthy, loving connection.

Romantic Competence

Romantic competence is "the ability to function adaptively across all areas or all aspects of the relationship process [including] figuring out what you need, finding the right person, building a healthy relationship, [and] getting out of relationships that are unhealthy (The 3 Core Skills That Every Person Needs for Healthy Romantic Relationships, 2019)." The construct of romantic competence was introduced by Joanne Davila, a professor of psychology and the director of clinical training at Stony Brook University in Stony Brook, New York, and her colleagues (2009) in the context of understanding adolescent romantic functioning (Davila et al., 2017).

According to these researchers, romantic competence consists of three components:

1. *Insight* — the ability to reflect on romantic experiences and to anticipate the impact of one's behavior on the quality of the relationship.

2. *Mutuality* — the understanding that relationships are about meeting each other's needs and that each partner has diverse needs that are equally valid.

3. *Emotion regulation* — an awareness of the emotions you are feeling and the ability to channel them in ways that will benefit both members of the relationship (How Good Is Your Romantic Competence? | Psychology Today, n.d.).

Unrequited Love

A relationship should have reciprocity of emotions between two individuals. Unrequited love (one-sided love) transpires in platonic friendships or romantic relationships. Unrequited love may take a few different forms, including:

- The partners stay together but love to different degrees or for different outcomes (Unrequited Love, n.d.).
- People will reject offers of love if they come from people who do not live up to their standards for a romantic partner (Administrator, 2016).
- The individual you desire romantically is emotionally unavailable.
- Mutual attraction between people who are both in other relationships (Lpc/Mhsp, 2023).
- Desire for an ex after a relationship has ended (Lpc/Mhsp, 2023).

At its core, unrequited love is a love that is not reciprocated from one person to another, explains Leanna Stockard, LMFT, a marriage and family therapist with LifeStance Health (Varina, 2023). "One person either has stronger feelings for the other or there is no feeling at all from the other." To underscore this notion, the author of a *Cosmopolitan* article points out,

---

"When you think about it, the term "unrequited" is pretty spot on. Since "requited" means "returned," unrequited means all those ooey-gooey feels you have aren't being returned. Clinical psychologist Monica Vermani, PsyD, says this imbalance of affection can cause "tremendous emotional turmoil" and can make someone feel anxious, depressed, stressed, and unworthy—not ideal, to say the least. And even though unrequited love sounds a lot like an intense crush, it's typically much stronger because there are real feelings...on one end, at least."

Some signs can help you understand what is going on and if the love you are feeling for someone is being reciprocated (Lpc/Mhsp, 2023):

- *You Reach Out to Connect.* Are you the only person trying to communicate? When you are the only one taking the time to reach out and connect with the other person, follow up with them about things, or inquire about their life, it can be a sign that this love is unrequited.
- *You Long for Physical Touch.* Do you desire to touch the other person, hold hands, kiss, or hug? If you find that you are always the one initiating any physical touch or that when you attempt to connect physically, you are met with resistance or the other person pulling away, it can signal that this is a one-sided longing.

- *You Put the Person on a Pedestal.* Many times, in situations of unrequited love, one person has the other on a pedestal. Each party can see and hear each other and their areas of vulnerability. Only the emotionally invested person can see and hear the other party in an unrequited love dynamic. There is no mutual, healthy acknowledgment of each other in unrequited love.

- *They Never Take Time to Get to Know You.* Have you ever found yourself in a situation where someone exerted excessive control over your life, leaving you feeling undervalued and powerless? It is crucial to remember that your worth is significant, and you should not allow anyone, including an intimate partner, to possess too much power over you. I'd like to point out that exploring avenues to help you take charge of your life and showcase your true worth is prudent.

- Tactics to bounce back from unrequited love are gaining self-awareness, building self-compassion and self-restraint, and seeking professional help if needed (Grande). People who fail to return our love are not best described as harming us but as merely failing to benefit us by saving us from harm (Gheaus, 2021).

I admonish against giving an individual that much power over your life because they underestimate your value. As the proverb declares, "One man's trash is another man's treasure." Stephan Labossiere, Certified Life Coach & Relationship Expert, and YouTube's Stephan Speaks statement, "You'll never be good enough for the wrong person," was so profound to me.

"Romantic love is defined as a state of psychological euphoria, passion, and intimacy with another person (Gibson, 2015). Physiologically, romantic love is known to activate the ventral tegmental area, a region of the brain associated with feelings

> *of pleasure, ecstasy, and arousal (Aron, Fisher, & Strong, 2006). From a psychosocial perspective, according to Chung (2005), romantic love is one of the most powerful discourses that informs our understanding of femininity and masculinity, and it is imbued with expectations and notions of how one behaves when in love (Kirkman, Rosenthal, & Smith, 1998; Rose, 2000). It is distinct, for example, from the platonic love that we may feel for a close friend, or the paternal love of a child (Pocock et al., 2019)."*

Support networks or individuals observing an intimate partner violence relationship believe abusers' love for their victims is scarce. According to a *Health Care for Women International* peer-reviewed article, "The review provides a rare (but much needed) explanation and acknowledgment that love does sometimes exist in abusive relationships." Furthermore, "many women in abusive relationships view these experiences as evidence of a partner's love for her, and reason enough to endure the fear and the abuse (with the hope that the abuse will stop). Manipulation and control that the abuser exerted is so powerful that women's understanding of romantic love becomes distorted (Pocock et al.)."

Trauma Bonding

"How did you get here? Nobody's supposed to be here. I've tried that love thing for the last time. My heart says no, no. Nobody's supposed to be here, But you came along and changed my mind." — Lyrics from Deborah Cox's song "Nobody's Supposed To Be Here."

TRAUMATIC BONDING is a strong emotional attachment between an abused person and his or her abuser (Effiong et al., 2022). The term trauma bonding was introduced by Patrick Carnes, Ph.D., author of *The Betrayal Bond: Breaking Free of Exploitative Relationships* and founder of the International Institute for Trauma and Addiction Professionals (IITAP). According to a team of scientists led by Dr. Helen Fisher at Rutgers, romantic love can be broken into three categories: lust, attraction, and attachment. Each category is characterized by hormones stemming from the brain (Table 1) (SITNFlash, 2020).

LUST	ATTRACTION	ATTACHMENT
Testosterone	Dopamine	Oxytocin
Estrogen	Norepinephrine	Vasopressin
	Serotonin	

Table 4. What is Love? Love can be distilled into three categories: lust, attraction, and attachment. Though overlaps and subtleties exist, each type is characterized by its hormones. Testosterone and estrogen drive lust; dopamine, norepinephrine, and serotonin create attraction; and oxytocin and vasopressin mediate attachment. Source: (SITNFlash, 2020)

Testosterone and estrogen drive lust; dopamine, norepineph-rine, and serotonin create attraction; and oxytocin and vasopressin mediate attachment (SITNFlash, 2020).

According to the article, *Traumatic Bonding In Victims Of Intimate Partner Violence Is Intensified Via Empathy*, traumatic bonding is developed as the result of ongoing cycles of abuse in which the intermittent reinforcement of reward and punishment creates powerful emotional bonds that are resistant to change (Dutton & Painter, 1981). Dutton and Painter have theorized that solid emotional bonds are produced in relationships where the abuse is not constant. However, the abuse is often counterbalanced by positive behaviors, subjecting the victim to periods of both abuse and positive behaviors (Christman, 2009).

"Dutton and Painter, in the 1980s, developed a theory of "traumatic bond": the development of powerful emotional bonds starting from two specific characteristics of abusive relationships: the imbalance of power (in which the maltreated person perceives herself to be subjugated or dominated by the other) and intermittent good–bad treatment (i.e. periods characterized by participatory behaviors, affectionate from the dominant person, interspersed with episodes of intense abuse). The situation of alternating adverse and pleasant

conditions is a form of reinforcement which is very effective in producing persistent patterns of behavior that are difficult to extinguish or terminate and which develops strong emotional bonds. For this reason, the process of detachment from an abusive relationship is more difficult since the traumatic link is increased by relational dynamics (Tullio et al., 2019)."

Trauma bonding often occurs due to a specific type of abuse cycle that can look like the following, according to Dr. Moore:

- The abuser establishes a positive relationship with the victim.
- When the abuse occurs, the abuser follows the abuse with an act of kindness.
- The victim believes the kind and non-abusive version of the abuser was the authentic version of them.
- The cycle between abuse and kindness continues, leaving the victim feeling trapped in the relationship and eliciting complex and confusing emotions (Trauma Bonding: What You Need to Know—and How to Get Help, 2023).

Additional signs of trauma bonding, according to experts in the *Forbes Health* website article, include:

- Being unable to state your feelings, opinions, or desires without fear of upsetting the other person.
- Altering your behavior in a way that violates your moral code to keep the other person happy.
- Setting a boundary that is ignored or dismissed.
- Feeling like you would be lost without the other person.
- Being love-bombed at the beginning of a relationship (which can look over-the-top, extreme displays of attention, affection, and romantic gestures).

Some predisposing psychological factors lead to a woman's vulnerability to forming and maintaining an attachment to an abusive partner. According to trauma literature, victims of intimate partner violence may develop strong bonds with their perpetrators – a phenomenon known as identification with the aggressor – to survive the abuse (Lahav, 2021). As author Yael Lahav acknowledges, "this defensive reaction may endure after the abuse has ended and may adversely affect victims' mental health."

★★★★

There are seven stages to trauma bonding: Stage 1: Love Bombing; Stage 2: Trust & Dependency; Stage 3: Criticism; Stage 4: Manipulation & Gaslighting; Stage 5: Resignation & Giving Up; Stage 6: Loss of Self, and Stage 7: Addiction to the Cycle.

The psychological phenomenon labeled Stockholm syndrome, or trauma bonding, has been explained as a product of interpersonal trauma whereby the perpetrator elicits fear in the victim that is experienced as venerating gratitude for being allowed to survive (Reid et al., 2022). Researchers indicate that women succumb to relational abuse with maladaptive attachment, identity enmeshment, and implicit maltreatment (Women of Intimate Partner Abuse: Traumatic Bonding Phenomenon – ProQuest, n.d.).

Stage 1: Love Bombing

Love bombing is a manipulative dating tactic used by narcissistic and abusive individuals (L'Amie, 2019). "Love bombers seek to quickly obtain the affection and attention of someone they are romantically pursuing by presenting an idealized image of themselves," says Lori Nixon Bethea, Ph.D., owner of Intentional Hearts Counseling Services. Sometimes, in some harsh circumstances, the abuser may seem oblivious to their manipulation; however, that is typically not the case in a trauma bond (The 7 Stages of Trauma Bonding, 2022). "One partner, typically male but not exclusively, showers the other person with attention, affection, compliments, flattery, and essentially creates this context where she feels like she's met her soul mate, and it's effortless," Dr. Raghavan said in a phone interview. "The reality is the person who is doing the love bombing is creating or manipulating the environment to look like he's the perfect or she's the perfect mate (Cherelus, 2010)."

Lori Nixon Bethea, Ph.D., lists how a love bomber may act (L'Amie, 2019):

1. The love bomber will demand your attention and time and may isolate you from your family and friends (for example, they may become angry and make you feel guilty for making plans with others).

2. The love bomber will excessively compliment you and shower you with affection.

3. The love bomber will persuade you to commit to them early in the courtship.

Licensed therapist Sasha Jackson, LCSW, stated the following signs that you are being love-bombed (L'Amie, 2019):

1. "I want to spoil you." (Aka, if your partner buys you excessive gifts in a short amount of time).

2. "I just want to be with you all the time." If you feel guilty for wanting boundaries or space, it is not a good sign.

3. "I like to check on you because I get worried." If they check in occasionally, it is cute. Constantly checking in on your whereabouts, checking on social media pages, or asking for passwords? Love bombing.

4. "We are meant for each other." Be cautious if things feel intensely fast or they mention you are their soul mate or twin flame early on.

5. "It's you and me forever, right?"

Stage 2: Trust & Dependency

The person will work hard to gain your trust and loyalty and show signs of dependence (Shapper, 2022). In this stage, an abuser may purposefully assess the victim's trust and dependency, usually leading to the target feeling guilty for questioning their partner (The 7 Stages of Trauma Bonding, 2022). Another critical thing to remember is that "doubts are expected in a healthy relationship, and it takes time to get to know someone–not only for what they say but also for what they do." The following red flags indicate that emotional dependence is present (Beer-Becker, 2022):

- The dependent person has a constant fear of abandonment;
- Feels insecure and anxious;
- Has an always-present fear of rejection;
- Has the incessant need for reassurance;
- Sees true happiness as dependent on their romantic partner;
- Does not know how to meet their emotional needs by themselves; and
- Sometimes they even say their life is not worth living without their partner.

Stage 3: Criticism

Slowly but surely, the abuser will criticize the person, belittling and blaming them while also seeking validation (Shapper, 2022). Once they have your trust, emotional abusers may start to pick apart some of your qualities, identifying them as insignificant or problematic (The 7 Stages of Trauma Bonding, 2022). Moreover, the article states, "[T]his criticism can feel sudden, especially after experiencing the love bombing stage." However, it is common for abusers to test a victim's trust before they begin criticizing them.

Stage 4: Manipulation & Gaslighting

Merriam-Webster's Dictionary defines manipulation as "to control or play upon by artful, unfair, or insidious means, especially to one's advantage." To put it another way, the American Psychological Association (APA, n.d.) explains the psychology definition of manipulation as "behavior designed to exploit, control, or otherwise influence others to one's advantage." Gaslighting characterizes the manipulation of "another person into doubting his or her perceptions, experiences, or understanding of events (APA Dictionary of Psychology, n.d.)."

The sufferer will begin to constantly question themselves due to the abuser attempting to change the way they think and take the blame, even when not at fault (Shapper, 2022). Gaslighting and manipulation are two forms of psychological abuse often seen in trauma bonds that make victims question their reality and perception (The 7 Stages of Trauma Bonding, 2022). According to the Choose Therapy website, "gaslighters will never fully or honestly take responsibility for their behaviors and tend to shift blame onto the other person." It is common for gaslighters to suddenly seem calm, cool, and collected once they have pushed their target to its breaking point. Gaslighting is a textbook behavior among common abusers like narcissists, sociopaths, and psychopaths.

Stage 5: Resignation & Giving Up

The victim begins coping with uncertainty by doing what the abuser says, trying to feel the emotions, and triggering the person to act the way they did in stage one (Shapper, 2022). In *The 7 Stages of Trauma Bonding* article (2022), the author suggests that when dealing with a trauma bond, it is common for perpetrators of abuse to start giving in at some point to avoid more conflict.

The "fawn" trauma response, or bargaining and people-pleasing behaviors, may ensure the relationship can remain somewhat stable; however, targets may have some awareness that they are being manipulated (The 7 Stages of Trauma Bonding, 2022). Author Erica Laub, MS, LICSW, cautions that small awareness may not be enough to exit the relationship yet because the target may still be questioning whether they are to blame for the abuser's behavior.

Stage 6: Loss of Self

The sufferer will lack confidence and may feel mentally drained from fighting and decide not to fight back with the abuser since the behavior seems to worsen (Shapper, 2022). Throughout the stages of a trauma bond, there is a progressive loss of self, which brings tremendous pain and a disconnection from the world we once knew (The 7 Stages of Trauma Bonding, 2022). Erica Laub, MS, LICSW, states in her article, "People who leave abusive relationships may not seem like their usual selves due to losing their identity and personal boundaries."

Furthermore, "trauma bonds can be incredibly isolating, as you can lose many of your social connections due to the changes in self-identity that no longer match what people close to you are used to (The 7 Stages of Trauma Bonding, 2022)." The author provides additional insight, sharing, "This psychological destruction may lead to a complete loss of confidence and even suicidal ideation." Sadly, for many individuals, Ms. Laub proclaims, "this emotional torture, shame, and guilt have been built up for years, making it very difficult to face and move forward."

Stage 7: Addiction to the Cycle

The body feels cortisol spikes, which causes stress, and then an increase in dopamine, or the reward chemical in the brain. These highs and lows formulate a physical dependence on the person (Shapper, 2022). According to Ms. Laub's article, *Choose Therapy*, often in trauma bonds, the stages can be cyclical; after a significant conflict, there may be a cool down or honeymoon period. At this moment of peace, the abuser might apologize and start the love-bombing process again. This makes the target feel relieved and desired, thus positively reinforcing a dependency on this vicious cycle (The 7 Stages of Trauma Bonding, 2022). Vanessa Vaughter, with The Center for Integrative Counseling and Psychology in Dallas, stated in the *Forbes Health* article, *Trauma Bonding: What You Need To Know—And How To Get Help*, "Once someone has moved past their traumatic experiences, they may need further skills such as how to set, communicate, and hold healthy boundaries and healthy communication skills (McDermott, 2023)."

Why do Women Stay?

What is the correlation between women staying in intimate partner violence relationships and trauma bonding? What are the unrecognized hidden difficulties or obstacles (e.g., Stockholm syndrome, intimacy, financial, physiological, psychological, or emotional) these intimate partner violence victims or survivors challenging their ability to escape the cycle of abuse?

"In a biological sense there are two types of pair bonds: the social pair bond and the sexual pair bond. The social pair bond is a strong behavioral and psychological relationship between two individuals that is measurably different in physiological and emotional terms from general friendships or other acquaintance relationships. The sexual pair bond is a behavioral and physiological bond between two individuals with a strong sexual attraction component. In this bond the participants in the sexual pair bond prefer to have sex with each other over other options. In humans, and other mammals, pair bonds are developed via social interactions combined with the

biological activity of neurotransmitters and hormones such as oxytocin, vasopressin, dopamine, corticosterone, and others (On Marriage and Pair Bonds, n.d.)."

Judith Herman, a psychoanalyst, authored the influential book *Trauma and Recovery* in 1992, which recognized that women subject to a particular hostage situation, that is, domestic violence, often respond with traumatic syndromes that can be incapacitating and limit their ability to escape (Hadeed, 2021). While the physical consequences of violence are easy to identify, the most serious are psychological, which have profound consequences for the future of women: traces of physical aggression often vanish. At the same time, insults and humiliations leave indelible marks (Tullio et al., 2019). Linda Hadeed's article *Why Women Stay: Understanding the Trauma Bond Between Victim and Abuser Case Studies Were Written* reveals the following analysis:

"The current study applied object relations theory to explain the personality development of both victim and abuser stemming from childhood abuse, neglect or abandonment and the development of two defense mechanisms that influence women's decisions about staying. Using case studies with three women in a private practice setting, the research found that the childhood experiences of the three women included different levels of abuse, and that they all employed the moral and splitting defenses that influenced their decisions about staying (Hadeed, 2021)."

A more nuanced understanding of the phenomenon of domestic violence is obscured by two crucial factors:

1. There is an initial clinical focus on the reality of significant external obstacles to terminating these often-intense bonds, even in the face of foreseeable danger to the victim and children.

2. Perhaps more limiting are psychoanalytically based assumptions about "characterological masochism" that often reflect simplistic, moralistic, misogynistic assumptions about women that continue to inform psychoanalytic theory in the area of family life (Hadeed, 2021).

The authors of the article *Demonic Possession: Narratives of Domestic Abuse and Trauma in Malaysia* perception was quite intriguing to me as it relates to perpetrators' behaviors and survivors of intimate partner violence with trauma (Sahdan et al., 2021):

"The idea of demonic possession has utility because of its close fit both with perpetrators' behavior and the symptoms experienced by survivors with trauma. The research focuses on the intimate dynamics of abuse, including coercive control and intimate captivity, and the pivotal role of possession and trauma in the successful exertion of control and in extending the damaging effects of abuse. We argue that demonic possession reflects another way in which globally endemic practices of domestic abuse are justified and explained; it provides a means for perpetrators to evade responsibility for abuse, and a way in which the pernicious effects of both abuse and trauma on survivors, their families, and wider society are sometimes dismissed (Sahdan et al., 2021)."

As psychology and science see it, mating is the entire repertoire of behaviors that animals—including humans—engage in to find a partner for intimacy or reproduction (Mating | Psychology

Today, n.d.). Having an emotional connection means you can go to your partner and share anything with them (How Important Is an Emotional Connection in a Relationship | Marriage.com, 2017). It is the knowledge that both you and your partner have empathy for one another. Emotional bonds also have much to do with trust and security, knowing your partner will always be there for you regardless of the circumstances (How Important Is an Emotional Connection in a Relationship | Marriage.com, 2017). It promotes forgiveness and engagement and boosts morale (How Important Is an Emotional Connection in a Relationship | Marriage.com, 2017).

Prior research has suggested associations between cumulative childhood trauma, negative urgency, communication patterns, and psychological intimate partner violence, but no study has examined these links using a dyadic approach (Dugal et al., 2020). This dyadic type of violence has been recognized as emerging from the escalation of negative exchanges between two partners paired according to certain risk markers, for instance, if they both exhibit affect dysregulation.

The following suggestions or pathways are road maps to help you heal from trauma bonding (Alyssa, 2022) and intimate partner violence:

- Learn to grieve.
- Avoid self-blame.
- Practice self-care
- Cut off all contact.
- Establish a support group.
- Begin writing your emotions.
- Commit to practicing being in the moment.
- Write about what you noticed triggered the abuser.

Barriers to Leaving

L EAVING AN abusive relationship does not guarantee an end to the abuse; instead, the abuse often escalates at the time of separation (Domestic Violence Dynamics – What Domestic Abuse What It Does to Family, 2011). Nancy Grigsby and Brenda R. Hartman's 1997 Barriers Model was developed to understand women's domestic violence experiences at four different levels: (1) barriers in the environment; (2) barriers due to family, socialization, and role expectations; (3) barriers from the psychological consequences of violence; and (4) barriers from childhood abuse/neglect issues (Grigsby & Hartman, 1997).

Various empirically validated theories have explained the phenomenon of women in abusive relationships engaging in a repeated leave/return cycle when trying to terminate the relationship (Christman, 2009). Fewer treatment models have been empirically tested to work with couples who choose to stay together after violence, remaining committed to their relationship (Stith & Spencer, n.d.). The SAGE Journal article, *Future Directions in Intimate Partner Violence Research: An Intersectionality Framework for Analyzing Women's Processes of Leaving Abusive Relationships*, "theorized that the leaving processes are complex and shaped by intersections of various individual, familial, and sociocultural factors that affect one's access to resources and decision-making (Barrios et al., 2020)."

Hulley's SAGE Journals article provided the below illustration that attempts to capture drivers of unique challenges faced by Black, Asian, and Minority Ethnic (BAME) women in exiting violent relationships as developed through the synthesis of the 47 papers (Hulley et al., 2022).

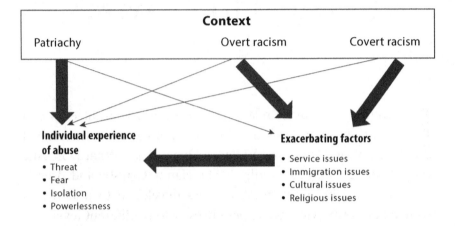

Figure 10. What are the drivers of unique challenges faced by Black, Asian, and Minority Ethnic (BAME) women in exiting violent relationships? Source: (Hulley et al., 2022)

The authors reported that barriers to escaping gender-based violence among ethnic minority and immigrant women operating at three interwoven levels: the 'individual experiences of abuse' category captures key features of control used by perpetrators of gender-based violence in intimate relationships (see Goodman et al., 2009; Refuge, 2017b; World Health Organization, 2012), irrespective of women's minority, ethnic, or immigration status.

Most survivors of intimate partner violence will leave a narcissistic abuser seven to 12 times before leaving the last time, and the victim may experience emotional deprivation. Studies reveal that leaving is typically not a single, sudden event but rather a slow process through several stages (Saunders, 2020). Daniel G.

Saunders, University of Michigan, remarks, "Counterintuitively, those married to an affluent, high-status abuser often encounter unique barriers." Ecclesiastes 7:8 KJV states, "Better is the end of a thing than the beginning thereof."

* * * *

Some people are in your life for a reason, season, or forever. We must decipher the category to place individuals in our sphere of influence. Some individuals are like trees or plants; eventually, we must prune the dead branches or leaves to stimulate growth, thrive, and flourish. Humans tend to hold onto things, including relationships, which need to be discarded. As seasons change from winter to spring, some plenteous homeowners or renters conduct spring cleaning of their premises. Spring cleaning is the annual deep cleaning tradition of your home, encompassing tasks beyond the standard weekly routine.

My toxic relationship with Maverick led me to no longer desire him. The late B.B. King's song said, "The thrill is gone, baby. The thrill is gone away." In professional boxing, contenders fight for a maximum of 12 rounds. A referee may terminate a bout for several reasons, including concern for a boxer's health, declaring a TKO (technical knockout) of an opponent in the ring, and a boxing contender sustaining an injury. I went through enough rounds with Maverick, decided to admit defeat, and stopped the match, ending my relationship.

Growing up, you may have heard your parents or elders say, "A hard head makes a soft behind," which happened to me. A former Texas pastor's deceased wife stated, "Every tube has to sit on its own bottom." How many times must we go through this merry-go-round because it is quite dizzying? God shows us that the individual is not the one, and our support network warns us out of concern for our well-being and safety, yet we go for rounds two, three, four, five, and six. It is heartbreaking to see how many times we have to hit our heads on the wall until leaving an abusive, toxic relationship makes sense. Unfortunately, this is easier said than done for victims of intimate partner violence relationships.

✶ ✶ ✶

Effective safety planning strategies reduce the risk of future revictimization. The first time an individual is victimized, they often take on the responsibility for the abuse (Revictimization: How Can This Keep Happening?, n.d.). When someone is victimized a second or third time (or more), research shows they are even more likely to feel guilt and shame and to judge themselves harshly. The fact that many victims do leave or seek help is truly remarkable considering the many barriers they face, including:

- Increased danger to victims and children;
- Fear of retaliation by the abuser;
- Lack of awareness of services;
- Lack of financial resources;
- Fear of losing custody of the children;
- Fear of not being believed;
- Religious, family, and societal pressures;
- Shame;
- Denial of the seriousness of the abuse;
- A belief that the abuser will change/hope for a continued relationship;
- Lack of support network; and
- Cultural and ethnic/racial barriers (Domestic Violence Dynamics – What Domestic Abuse What It Does to Family, 2011)

Trauma Bonding

The significant mediating effects of empathy on the association of intimate partner violence and dimensions of traumatic bonding mean that the subjective affective experiences of victims of intimate partner violence may play relevant roles in the decisions to leave or stay in an abusive relationship (Effiong et al., 2022). The author mentioned that "Empathy through guilt may more easily permit forgiveness through a reparative gesture, assuring the maintenance of the link with the partner and restoring an active position in the relationship by taking responsibility for the perpetrator's behavior." Forgiveness also has been shown to play a crucial role in the healing process of major relationship betrayals (Gordon et al., 2005).

Violence

Separation violence may occur when a victim tries to leave the abuser. Violence may increase based on experience, wherein one may endure severe bodily harm. One of the most heartbreaking types of violence is filicide-suicide: children murdered as an act of retaliation or revenge. The perpetration of child homicide by fathers seems to have a stronger association with intimate partner violence and retaliation or revenge as a consistent pattern (APA PsycNet, n.d.).

Various forms of separation violence tactics cause victims to fear being killed by the abuser: a) coercive-controlling violence, b) separation-instigated violence, c) situational couple violence, d) stalking, harassment, or monitoring, e) batterer will kidnap the victim, holding them hostage or harm another family member, f) abuser "teaching them a lesson" for trying to leave, g) economic abuse (blocking access to bank accounts and credit cards), h) legal abuse (court proceedings), and i) revenge porn or threats. The terminology legal abuse refers to using court proceedings and false reports of child abuse to control, harass, and impoverish the other parent or seek a change in custody to continue control over the other parent (8 Common Post-Separation Domestic Abuse Tactics, n.d.).

Guilt

Guilt can increase the risk of revictimization by focusing our attention, exaggeratedly, on our thoughts and feelings, leaving us vulnerable to missing external cues of danger (Revictimization: How Can This Keep Happening?, n.d.). A victim's guilt stems from the assumption of responsibility for the narcissistic abuser's emotional well-being; hence, it would be beneficial for them to work toward compassionately understanding why they had to assume it in the first place (How to Overcome Guilt after Leaving a Narcissistic Abuser, 2022).

Cultural Belief/Reasons/Norms

Cultural norms include acceptance of male violence toward women, which often prevents women from recognizing abuse (Hulley et al., 2022). To illustrate this, the Hulley article (2022) asserts:

- In South Asian culture, partner abuse is a private family issue and, as such, is largely overlooked or considered normal.
- In traditional gender roles within Mexican culture, men are entitled to harm their wives physically.
- African women highlighted their feelings of isolation and powerlessness experienced due to cultural acceptance of intimate partner violence.
- Sex is considered the husband's marital right, and sexual abuse is, therefore, not recognized in South Asian culture.
- Pakistani and Indian women: The role of culture in examining the women's conception of the abuse they experienced cannot be understated. Women were more likely to be able to identify physical and psychological abuse as violence than they were sexual violence as such.

Victims of intimate partner violence may feel they must be the perfect wife or mother as defined by their community or culture. Victims of this disturbing, psychological, and violent crime at the hands of their partner may not want to disturb or worry their relatives. Traditional customs or beliefs may influence someone's decision to stay in an abusive situation, whether held by the survivor or by their family and community (National Domestic Violence Hotline, n.d.).

Economic Hardship

Financial challenges (lack of resources) and instability may be considered barriers to leaving an abusive relationship.

Immigration Status

Individuals who are undocumented may fear reporting abuse will affect their immigration status, notwithstanding limited English proficiency concerns that can amplify a confusing and convoluted legal system and an inability to express their circumstances to others (National Domestic Violence Hotline, n.d.).

"Many of the women in the papers synthesized were undocumented immigrants, most of whom had relocated to their husband's host country. The threat of deportation was sometimes explicitly used against women without settled status by perpetrators and their families, illustrating how women's immigration status and 'tough' immigration policy served to deepen the ways in which violent partners and families could control their victims: 'My visa expired but (they) were not ready to apply for indefinite leave for me. His mother always used to say, "Deport her!" (Hulley et al., 2022)."

Normalization of Abuse

If your friend does not know what a healthy relationship looks like, perhaps from growing up in an environment where abuse is common, they may not recognize that their relationship is unhealthy (National Domestic Violence Hotline, n.d.).

Homelessness

Intimate partner violence (IPV) is a major cause of housing insecurity, causing severe consequences for women and their children, including mental health issues, economic instability, and social isolation. Often, they are forced to flee their homes with nowhere to go, or worse, evicted due to seeking crisis assistance by calling 911 emergency services. Addressing IPV comprehensively, including safe housing options, legal and financial aid, and awareness programs, is crucial. By doing so, we can create a society that values and protects the rights and dignity of all individuals. On May 14, 2019, the New York State Senate passed legislation A.2665-A (Lavine)/S.465-A (Hoylman) to prevent domestic violence survivors from being evicted for calling 911. The bill prevents landlords from evicting tenants who call the police for help with domestic violence and other crimes or emergencies, which happens in states across the country because of little-known laws known as nuisance ordinances (Michaels, n.d.). In a 2002 study, Gondolf found that more than half of women had negative views of shelters and programs for battered women because of negative experiences with those programs (Rakovec-Felser, 2014).

New York City's Comptroller Scott Stringer's *Housing Survivors October 2019* report determined that domestic violence is the primary driver of the City's Department of Homeless Services (DHS) shelter population. In Fiscal Year (FY) 2018, domestic violence accounted for 41% of the family population entering New York City's DHS shelters, with eviction the second-leading cause, accounting for 27%. That was a dramatic shift from FY 2014, when domestic violence accounted for 30% of the population and eviction 33%. In FY 2018 alone, 12,541 people entered a DHS shelter due to domestic violence. That includes more than 4,500 women and 7,000 children, more than half (56%) of whom were five years old or younger.

Emotional Entanglement or Attachment

There is a distinct difference between a true love connection and emotional attachment. Survivors of intimate partner violence hold unrealistic hope that their abuser will change and there will be a happily ever after. Amir Levine, a psychiatrist and neuroscientist at Columbia University, describes popularized attachment theory as the idea that early emotional bonds with our caregivers impact our future relationships. Three distinct attachment styles affect how we deal with relationship conflicts, our feelings toward sex, and our expectations of romantic intimacy (How Attachment Styles Influence Romantic Relationships, 2022).

Types of emotional attachment include (Jackson, 2021):

- *Secure attachment:* Secure attachment allows a person to feel comfortable, safe, and stable in a healthy relationship.
- *Anxious attachment:* Anxious attachments lead to problems with trust and worry as people react with a strong need for emotional reassurance.
- *Avoidant attachment:* With avoidant attachment, a person may have few relationships that are too much of a bother or numerous relationships without any real commitment.
- *Disorganized attachment:* Born from trauma and abuse, the disorganized attachment style is inconsistent and unpredictable.

Love is a multifaceted concept, marked by a combination of infatuation, attachment, and cognitive changes, with features including:

- Heart pounding (physiological effects)
- Caregiving (behavioral effects)
- Euphoria and anxiety (mixed feelings)
- Enhanced attention toward and memory of beloved-related details (cognitive affects) (Sosnoski, 2022)

According to Merriam-Webster's dictionary, emotional blackmail is an attempt to control someone with whom one has an emotional connection by tactics that make the person feel guilty or upset. Emotional extortion may become a tool the abuser could use to manipulate the victim of intimate partner violence entangled in their relationship.

We must get to the root cause of our unhealthy emotional attachment to be delivered. We must determine who hurt us in the past (childhood until present) so we can heal and enter a healthy relationship. Job 19:28 states, "But ye should say, why persecute we him, seeing the root of the matter is found in me?" Psychologist Daniela Beer-Becker's article on Psychology.com states, "In my clinical experience, clients who struggle with emotional dependence often have attachment wounds, and their needs have not been met sufficiently growing up. Frequently, they have experienced childhood trauma or child abuse (Beer-Decker, 2022)."

Defense Mechanism

Psychological defense mechanisms are ways of dealing with anxiety by unconsciously distorting one's perception of reality. For the three parts of the personality (id, ego, and superego) to function, constant conflict must be managed. Freud assumed that defense mechanisms were among the essential tools for dealing with the anxiety caused by this conflict (APA Dictionary of Psychology, n.d.).

In classical psychoanalytic theory, the ego employs an unconscious reaction pattern to protect itself from the anxiety that arises from psychic conflict. In more recent psychological theories, defense mechanisms are seen as ordinary means of coping with everyday problems and external threats. However, excessive use of anyone or immature defenses (e.g., displacement or repression) is still considered pathological.

Prominent defense mechanisms include the following:

- *Dissociation:* protects the individual by breaking up consciousness to avoid being overwhelmed by an experience, memory, or sensation (Revictimization: How Can This Keep Happening?, n.d.).
- *Denial:* refusal to recognize or acknowledge a threatening situation.
- *Repression:* pushing threatening or conflicting events or situations out of conscious memory.
- *Rationalization:* making up acceptable excuses for unacceptable behavior.
- *Projection:* placing one's unacceptable thoughts onto others, as if they belonged to them and not oneself.
- *Reaction formation:* forming an emotional reaction or attitude opposite to one's threatening or unacceptable thoughts.
- *Displacement:* expressing feelings that would be threatening if directed at the actual target onto a less threatening substitute target.
- *Regression:* falling back on childlike patterns to cope with stressful situations.
- *Identification:* trying to become like someone else to deal with anxiety.
- *Compensation (substitution):* trying to compensate for areas where a deficit is perceived by becoming superior in another area.

- *Sublimation:* turning socially unacceptable urges into socially acceptable behavior.

Family Dynamic Includes Children

The presence of children was related to a higher risk rating for imminent intimate partner violence revictimization and recommendations of more than standard levels of risk management strategies (Petersson & Thunberg, 2021). Those with children and with more traditional family norms face additional challenges (Saunders, 2020). Counterintuitively, those married to an affluent, high-status abuser often encounter more unique barriers (Saunders, 2020).

Healing Process

W HILE MANY emotional wounds take a while to resolve, psychic trauma may continue to linger (American Psychoanalytic Association, 2009). Victims can suffer physical, emotional, or mental health problems and experience detrimental social, psychological, and relational health effects on their families, especially children (Tullio et al., 2019) due to intimate partner violence. Adults subjected to domestic violence have PTSD, depression, panic states, substance abuse, somatization, dissociative disorders, and suicidality (Brandt & Rudden, 2020).

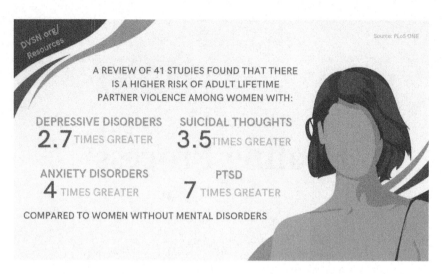

Figure 11. Domestic Violence Services Network, Inc. (DVSN) infographic on the risk factors of adult lifetime partner violence among women. Source: (Domestic Violence Services Network, Inc. (DVSN), 2023)

Steps to help victims of intimate partner violence through the healing process include:

- *Safety first.* The healing process begins when the victim of abuse is finally away from their abuser. Unfortunately, this step can take months or even years of planning and preparation before becoming a reality. Safety means the victim is physically away from their attacker and can sleep without fear. *After Nancy left, she had a hard time believing she was safe and needed the reassurance of others saying, "You are safe," over and over until it began to feel real.*

- *Stabilize the environment.* Therapists are tempted to dive into the healing process after a victim is deemed safe. However, doing this before stabilizing a new environment can retraumatize the victim. Instead, the victim needs rest to adjust to a new normal before the therapeutic work begins. The length of this necessary step is dictated solely by the victim and the amount of abuse endured. *It took several months before Nancy could breathe again as the confused fog of abuse lifted.*

- *Support unconditionally. Nancy felt unconditionally loved by her therapist and two close friends, even when she talked about how much she missed her abusive husband. It was as if Nancy was forgetting the trauma and only remembering the good times they shared. One of her family members became so frustrated with Nancy's sadness that they yelled at her and pulled away. This was so painful for Nancy, but the continued support of her two friends more than made up for the lack of family support.*

- *Share experiences.* One of the most helpful steps to recover from abuse is to find a support group with other victims of abuse. This shared common experience allows a person to realize they are not alone in their abusive encounters. Abuse is very isolating, personal, degrading, humiliating, and shameful. Knowing that other intelligent, beautiful, talented, and kind people have been abused is both saddening and relieving. *Nancy's support group gave her additional people she could lean on who understood from their own experience what she was going through.*

- *Settle incidents.* This is often the most difficult step from an awareness perspective. As the obvious abuse is recounted, new obscure abuse comes to light. Most victims do not even realize the extent of their abuse until they reach this step. When they do, it can be overwhelming and will likely restart the grieving process. *As Nancy examined each major traumatic incident, other types of abuse surfaced. She came to see that she was also mentally, verbally, emotionally, financially, spiritually, and sexually abused in addition to her physical abuse. Processing this information was hard at first, but it put a nail in the coffin of her abusive relationship for good. There was no turning back now for Nancy.*

- *Stitch wounds. To stitch the wounds of Nancy's abuse, she needed to rewrite her internal dialog of what happened. In the past, she would minimize his contribution to an incident and take excessive responsibility for his behavior. Things changed when she stopped doing this and instead held him responsible for his actions. Nancy no longer believed that she was worthless or deserving of his abusive treatment. As time progressed, she began to take pride in her scars as evidence of her strength, determination, fortitude, and perseverance.*

- *Set standards. The final step towards Nancy's healing was to set new standards for how she expected to be treated. These became the boundaries of what acceptable behavior was. Anytime a person violated one of her limitations, she would confront them. Nancy would remain in the relationship if they demonstrated respect by their actions and not words. If they did not, she would end things. These new standards helped reduce her fear that she would reenter another abusive relationship* (Lmhc, 2017).

In 1920, Freud published *Beyond the Pleasure Principle*, which identified repetition compulsion as a repeating and relieving of painful experiences instead of holding them in memory (Zamir et al., 2018). When applied more recently to revictimization, this theory, part of Freud's developing understanding of human instinct, places the bulk of responsibility squarely on the victim's psyche (Revictimization: How Can This Keep Happening?, n.d.).

A range of intense emotions may pop up when recovering from an abusive relationship — all of which are valid; moreover, you may experience some of the following thoughts or feelings:

- Missing your ex;
- Feeling lonely or isolated;
- Debating going back to the relationship;
- Feeling uncertain or unable to make decisions by yourself;
- Feelings of anxiety or depression;
- Finding it challenging to feel independent;
- A lingering fear or sense of being in danger; or

- Symptoms of PTSD (7 Tips to Heal after an Abusive Relationship, 2021)

Attachment Theory

According to Hazan and Shaver, the emotional bond that develops between adult romantic partners is partly a function of the same motivational system–the attachment behavioral system–that gives rise to the emotional bond between infants and their caregivers (Fraley, n.d.). Furthermore, "Hazan and Shaver noted that the relationship between infants and caregivers and the relationship between adult romantic partners share the following features":

- Both feel safe when the other is nearby and responsive.
- Both engage in close, intimate bodily contact.
- Both feel insecure when the other is inaccessible.
- Both share discoveries with one another.
- Both play with one another's facial features and exhibit a mutual fascination and preoccupation with one another.
- Both engage in "baby talk" (Fraley, n.d.).

Emotional Triggers

The emotional triggers that spark conflicts between intimate partners are well-known: he says he is going out with friends from work, his husband feels rejected, and his partner gets angry. She asks for more time to talk, her husband gets angry and defensive, and she feels guilty. She tells her wife she is disappointed in her, her wife bursts into tears, and her partner tells her she is overreacting (Edwards, n.d.).

"Triggers refer to any specific incidents, behaviours, or events that bring back traumatic memories or emotions. Trauma triggers can be incredibly intense and personal experiences, with sources ranging from seemingly harmless sensations or sounds to specific smells or even a tone of voice. The first step in this process is to gain awareness and understanding of what triggers you (Jhoydapsych, 2023)."

Now, whenever something happens that resembles, even subconsciously, those bad experiences, a part of your brain goes into overdrive, telling you that you are unsafe and about to get hurt again (Brenner & Letich, 2022).

"Recognizing and understanding emotional triggers is essential for fostering self-awareness and navigating relationships effectively. Common types of emotional triggers include abandonment, rejection, criticism, betrayal, and loss. Identifying these triggers allows individuals to gain insight into the underlying causes of their emotional responses, facilitating more targeted and effective interventions. Managing emotional triggers requires self-awareness, self-reflection, and the development of emotional regulation techniques. By cultivating self-awareness, individuals can recognize their triggers, understand their patterns, and make conscious choices in responding to them (Understanding Emotional Triggers and Building Healthy Relationships, n.d.)."

Shame

Due to gendered sexual and intimate crimes that violate social norms about what is appropriate and acceptable, survivors may experience stigma that includes victim-blaming messages from the broader society and specific stigmatizing reactions from others in response to disclosure. This stigmatization can be internalized among survivors as self-blame, shame, and anticipatory stigma (Kennedy et al., 2018). According to Merriam-Webster Dictionary, shame is a painful emotion caused by consciousness of guilt, short-coming, or impropriety. Most male survivors of intimate partner violence have become hesitant to seek help following victimization (Joseph-Edwards et al., 2020).

Shame permeates the experience of intimate partner violence and "can be a destructive harm that devastates a person's sense of self-worth (Camp, 2022)." People who perpetrate intimate partner violence commonly use tactics designed to cause shame in their partners, including denigrating their dignity, undermining their autonomy, or harming their reputation (Camp, 2022). Survivors typically experience societal stigma and internalized shame because of intimate partner violence victimization (Waller et al., 2022). Stigma and stigmatization play an important role in shaping survivors' thoughts, feelings, and behaviors as they recover, their risk of revictimization, and their help-seeking and attainment process (Kennedy & Prock, 2018).

Psychological Healing

"Psychological abuse leaves no bruises. There are no broken bones. There are no holes in the walls. The bruises, brokenness, and holes are held tightly within the target of the abuse."
— Shannon-Thomas

Letting someone abuse us so that they can work out their childhood trauma has a devastating and lasting effect on our physical, mental, emotional, spiritual, sexual, and financial well-being (NCADV | National Coalition Against Domestic Violence, n.d.). When operating optimally, the client-therapist relationship can be a powerful therapeutic agent and reflect and parallel other relationships in a person's life (Sprang, 2020).

Importantly, Ginny Sprang, Professor of Psychiatry at the University of Kentucky, mentioned, "The style of relating, combined with the methods of intervention used and received, becomes the catalyst toward recovery in trauma survivors (Sprang, 2020)." Effective interventions for survivors with mental and behavioral health issues included psychotherapeutic approaches and safety planning to address survivors' co-occurring healthcare needs (Sabri et al., 2021).

Psychotherapy is any psychological service in which a trained professional primarily provides communication and interaction to assess, diagnose, and treat dysfunctional emotional reactions, ways of thinking, and behavior patterns (APA Dictionary of Psychology, n.d.). Psychotherapy may be provided to individuals, couples (couples therapy), families (family therapy), or group members. However, this is not at odds with previous studies that found dissipated effects of psychotherapy on psychological well-being after one year or later (A Holistic Approach to Tackling Intimate Partner Violence among Marginalized Women in Urban Liberia: Guest Post by David Sungho Park, n.d.).

Post-traumatic growth is a positive psychological change caused by a person following severe difficulties and trauma (Bryngeirsdottir et al., 2022). The article's author suggests that "healing has been shown to be comprised of connecting with the self, others, and the world, while [post-traumatic growth] PTG also seems to involve that the person experiences increased spiritual maturity, discovers new opportunities in life, values life more, experiences increased personal strength and has better relationships with others (Bryn-geirsdottir et al., 2022)."

A victim's intense shame may defend against her dissociated/disowned awareness of her abuser's malignant behavior (Brandt et al., 2020). Moreover, the authors assert that recognizing coercive control in plain sight can challenge our fundamental ideas about intimate relationships. Bojack Horseman profoundly declared, "When you look at someone through rose-colored glasses, all the red flags just look like flags."

Introspection/Self-Reflection

Victims of domestic violence escaping their traumatic ordeal are experiencing complexities of emotions. Webster-Merriam Dictionary defines introspection as a reflective looking inward: an examination of one's thoughts and feelings. Self-care means taking the time to do things that help you live well and improve your physical and mental health (National Institute of Mental Health, 2021).

During introspection, ask yourself, "How did I get here?" The calm or complete separation period is a chance to gain more knowledge about yourself and how to make wise choices in the future. An individual could achieve awareness from lessons learned due to the lack of unhealthy relationship boundaries, an abusive partner's barrage of red flags seen but the victim negated, displaying deference to disregard his/her apparent controlling and manipulative conduct.

Know Your Value

The American Psychological Association's *Dictionary of Psychology* (n.d) defines value as "a moral, social, or aesthetic principle accepted by an individual or society as a guide to what is good, desirable, or important and the worth, usefulness, or importance attached to something." The Heavenly Father declares in Psalm

139:14 (AMP), "I will give thanks *and* praise to You, for I am fearfully and wonderfully made; Wonderful are Your works, And my soul knows it very well." Moreover, in Zechariah 2:8, the LORD of hosts declares, "for he that toucheth you, toucheth the apple of his eye."

"To attempt to love someone who cannot benefit from your love with spiritual growth is to waste your energy, to cast your seed on arid ground."—M. Scott Peck, M.D., The Road Less Traveled

---

If you struggle with self-worth, remaining in a romantic relationship where you are not valued will only exacerbate the problem. While you cannot control another's behavior, you can control your reaction and choices. This includes choosing to stay in a relationship that no longer serves you or walking away. As difficult and painful as it may be, sometimes walking away may be the greatest gift of self-compassion you can offer yourself (Does Your Partner Value You? | Psychology Today, n.d.).

I made it through the psychological aftermath of intimate partner violence trauma by the grace of God. Self-care, educating myself about relationships, viewing inspirational messages/posts, and restoring fellowship with Christ healed me after dealing with the despair and emotional toil of ungodly soul ties and shame, leading to social withdrawal and isolation, ridicule, embarrassment, and housing insecurity. Please do not become discouraged during your healing process because relapses, digressions, and highs and lows are common recovery aspects. In Christendom, there is a saying that "God is a God of second chances." Bishop Darius Nixon stated, "My comeback is a gonna be greater than my embarrassment." Jesus is not a respecter of persons. If He brought me out with His mighty power and an outstretched hand to overcome this vicissitude of life, He could do the same for you.

Every person needs to maintain independence or individuality within a relationship. What is God's divine purpose that He has designated for your life in this world? What is His perfect will for your life? What dream or ambition was abandoned due to dismal circumstances but must now be implemented to empower yourself? Jeremiah 29:11 (NIV) mentions, "For I know the plans I have for you,' declares the LORD, 'plans to prosper you and not to harm you, plans to give you hope and a future."

What are you enthusiastic about? What is your divine purpose that He called you to be here for such a time as this? What is the perfect will versus the permissive will of God for your life? I hope that during your self-reflection, you seek His wisdom and divine guidance as to your prophetic destiny and purpose on this Earth. May the gifts God has placed inside you become stirred up, bringing forth a fruitful and fulfilling life. Gospel artist Donald Lawrence and the Tri-City Singers song entitled, *Go Get Your Life Back,* chorus declares, "Go get your life back. Go and get it. Go get your life back. Everything the enemy stole from you, your life back. Go and get it. Go get your life. God said live."

Women sometimes lose themselves during the intimate partner violence process, being manipulated by their abuser's power and control. Eckhart Tolle said it best: "When you lose touch with yourself, you lose yourself in the world." What dreams or aspirations did you put down because of an abuser that you need to revisit (become resurrected)? One of the dreams I abandoned along the way is nearly accomplished as I will graduate, Lord willing, in the fall of 2024 with a degree in public and non-profit administration. Bishop Noel Jones preached a sermon, I've *Got to Get Myself Together*, and I am doing that now. I strongly suggest reading the book *Lady in Waiting: Becoming God's Best While Waiting for Mr. Right, Expanded Edition* by Jackie Kendall and Debby Jones to assist you in a journey to wholeness.

In aviation, an aircraft in a holding pattern awaits approval (clearance) from the airport's air traffic controllers to land safely on the runway; hence, it is a yes or no scenario that most pilots loathe. Cambridge Dictionary defines the phrase in a holding pattern as "temporarily unable to act because you are waiting for something to happen or be decided." A holding pattern for an airplane is a maneuver in which an aircraft flies a racetrack-shaped pattern in a designated area (Pilot Institute, 2022). They keep an aircraft in protected airspace while delaying its arrival later along its route (Pilot Institute, 2022). My dear sister, as God has you in a holding pattern, protecting you from unsuitable individuals, please wait for His best, specifically designed for you. While you are waiting, enjoy your singleness and life. I admonish you not to allow what you have been through to hinder where you are going — the perfect will of God for your life.

Military spouses are an understudied population concerning intimate partner violence perpetration (Park et al., 2021). Living with veterans with PTSD is associated with elevated distress in spouses; moreover, military spouses are at an elevated risk for domestic abuse, which might exacerbate their plight (Lahav et al., 2018). In the article, *Intimate Partner Violence and Abuse: A Qualitative Exploration of UK Military Personnel and Civilian Partner Experiences,* the author acknowledges, "The prevalence of Intimate Partner Violence and Abuse (IPVA) perpetration and victimization has been found to be higher in serving and ex-serving military samples compared to civilians (Lane et al., 2022)."

Using the frustration-aggression hypothesis and considering the possibility of mutual violence, the author examined (a) the direct effects of stressful events, marital discord, and work/family conflict on intimate partner violence perpetration among military spouses and (b) the indirect effect of anger arousal between stressful events, marital discord, and work/family conflict on intimate partner violence perpetration (Park et al., 2021). Bi-directional intimate partner violence refers to the co-occurrence of violence perpetrated by both partners (Hu et al., 2019).

I wonder how we begin ministering to this segment of the population with an authoritarian infrastructure. While overseas, one of my siblings became a victim of intimate partner violence at the hands of her ex-husband, who served in active duty within the U.S. Armed Forces.

Research on the effects of intimate partner violence on women demonstrates the significant physical, emotional, psychological, and spiritual consequences of this form of interpersonal trauma (D'Amore et al., 2018). The authors assert, "However, a small, predominantly qualitative body of research exists on women's experience of and capacity for healing from the effects of IPV, but more research is needed to advance theory and practice in this important area." AWAKE, a comprehensive hospital-based intimate partner violence advocacy program collocated at a children's hospital, represents an innovative example of how pediatric healthcare settings can provide healing-centered care through healthcare provider training and direct support for intimate partner violence survivors (Ragavan & Miller, 2022). The authors further affirm, "Healing-centered engagement is a strength-based approach, which focuses on connecting survivors with support that helps them meet their unique needs."

There are three overarching themes and six sub-themes of healing and posttraumatic growth in women's narratives: Awareness and Insight (subthemes: Discerning the Self and Understanding Relationships), Renewal and Reconstruction (subthemes: [Re] building the Self and Redefining Relationships), and Transformation and Meaning (subthemes: New Perspectives and Finding Purpose Through Helping Others) (D'Amore et al., 2018).

Risk Factors of IPV

A CCORDING TO the World Health Organization (WHO), "[t]he most widely used model for understanding violence is the ecological model, which proposes that violence results from factors operating at four levels: individual, relationship, community, and societal (Understanding and Addressing Violence against Women BOX 1. FORMS of INTIMATE PARTNER VIOLENCE (2), n.d.)."

Individual Factors

"Some of the most consistent factors associated with a man's increased likelihood of committing violence against his partner(s) are:

1. Young age;

2. Low level of education;

3. Witnessing or experiencing violence as a child;

4. Harmful use of alcohol and drugs;

5. Personality disorders;

6. Acceptance of violence (e.g., feeling it is acceptable for a man to beat his partner); and

7. History of abusing partners (Understanding and Addressing Violence against Women BOX 1. FORMS of INTIMATE PARTNER VIOLENCE (2), n.d.)."

"Factors consistently associated with a woman's increased likelihood of experiencing violence by her partner(s) across different settings include:

1. Low level of education;

2. Exposure to violence between parents;

3. Sexual abuse during childhood;

4. Acceptance of violence; and

5. Exposure to other forms of prior abuse (Understanding and Addressing Violence against Women BOX 1. FORMS of INTIMATE PARTNER VIOLENCE (2), n.d.)."

Relationship Factors

"Factors associated with the risk of both victimization of women and perpetration by men include

1. Conflict or dissatisfaction in the relationship;

2. Male dominance in the family;

3. Economic stress;

4. Men having multiple partners; and

5. Disparity in educational attainment (i.e., a woman has a higher level of education than her male partner) (Understanding and Addressing Violence against Women BOX 1. FORMS of INTIMATE PARTNER VIOLENCE (2), n.d.)."

Community and Societal Factors

"The following community and societal factors were found across studies:

1. Gender-inequitable social norms (especially those that link notions of adulthood to dominance and aggression).

2. Poverty

3. Low social and economic status of women.

4. Weak legal sanctions against intimate partner violence within marriage.

5. Lack of women's civil rights, including restrictive or inequitable divorce and marriage laws.

6. Weak community sanctions against intimate partner violence

7. Broad social acceptance of violence to resolve conflict.

8. Armed conflict and high levels of general violence in society (Understanding and Addressing Violence against Women BOX 1. FORMS of INTIMATE PARTNER VIOLENCE (2), n.d.)."

Psychological Impact

"Limited research exists on the impact of psychopathy within romantic relationships (Forth et al.)", which is a significant risk factor for engaging in intimate partner violence. Psychopathy is a neuro-psychiatric disorder marked by inadequate emotional responses, lack of empathy, and poor behavioral controls, commonly resulting in persistent anti-social deviance and criminal behavior (Anderson & Kiehl, 2014). The *Sage Journal* article, *Toxic Relationships: The Experiences and Effects of Psychopathy in Romantic Relationships*, reveals a comprehensive meta-analysis by Robertson et al. (2020) that identified psychopathy as one of the strongest predictors of intimate partner violence compared to other known risk factors (e.g., aggression, anti-social behavior, alcohol use).

Moreover, "[s]everal studies have found that polyvictimization is associated with more negative outcomes (e.g., attachment dysfunction, sexual problems, and negative mental health symptoms) than experiencing a single type of abuse in adolescents and adults. The author notes that out of the 475 former and current intimate partners of individuals with psychopathic traits recruited from online support groups. Victims reported various abusive experiences and a myriad of adverse symptomatology involving emotional, biological, behavioral, cognitive, and interpersonal consequences (Forth et al., 2021).

"Intimate partner violence (IPV) victimization is associated with a wide range of mental and physical health problems, but little is known about the effect of intimate partner violence on cognitive decline (Williams et al., 2017)." A case study examining neuropsychological impairment in women who have experienced intimate partner violence using DSM 5 criteria for mild and severe cognitive impairment was written in the *Journal of Forensic Psychiatry & Psychology* (Daugherty et al., 2018). A total of 108 females in Spain were included in one of three groups: psychological abuse (n = 24), physical and psychological abuse (n = 45), and no abuse (n = 39). Significantly, "there were differences between the control and IPV groups in attention and executive functioning. Furthermore, approximately 25% of women experiencing intimate partner violence suffer mild neuropsychological alterations and 5% severe, mainly in memory and executive function domains. The study's evidence supports the growth in research that suggests psychological violence is as strongly related to poor health outcomes as physical violence in intimate partner relationships (Daugherty et al., 2018)."

An *International Journal of Environmental Research and Public Health* article entitled *Acceptability of Intimate Partner Violence among Male Offenders: The Role of Set-Shifting and Emotion Decoding Dysfunctions as Cognitive Risk Factors* revealed that intimate partner violence against women offenders with deficits in attention switching, set-shifting, and emotion decoding abilities demonstrated greater acceptability of intimate partner violence against women (Romero-Martínez et al., 2019).

The article further asserts, "Although the question of how cognitive impairments may facilitate violence expression remains unanswered, exploring these basic cognitive processes may help to explain why individuals who present cognitive dysfunctions are more prone to violence than normative individuals (Romero-Martínez et al., 2019)." "Men experiencing relational violence, both physical and non-physical, are most likely to present with PTSD and depression, not to mention additional mental health concerns for this population, including anxiety, insomnia, and social dysfunction (McLeod et al., 2021)."

"Battered Woman Syndrome, a theory developed in the 1970s that is now associated with Post Traumatic Stress Disorder (PTSD), is sometimes used in court cases as mitigation in homicide cases where a battered woman kills her abuser (Strucke & Hajjar, 2009)." Battered Woman Syndrome is composed of the following symptoms:

- Re-experiencing the battering as if it were reoccurring even when it is not;
- Attempts to avoid the psychological impact of battering by avoiding activities, people, and emotions;
- Hyperarousal or hypervigilance;
- Disrupted interpersonal relationships, 'I' body image distortion, or other somatic concerns; and
- Sexuality and intimacy issues (Walker, 2006)

April Rose Wilkens' former partner beat and sexually assaulted her for hours until she could take his gun and fire multiple times, killing him (Bishop, 2023). She became the first woman to use the Battered Woman Syndrome defense.

Children's functioning is indirectly impacted by intimate partner violence exposure prenatally, partly because of the mental health consequences experienced by their mothers (Howell et al., 2016). The *National Library of Medicine's* article *Developmental Variations in the Impact of Intimate Partner Violence Exposure During Childhood* further stated, "Mother's level of distress during pregnancy affects parental warmth, caregiving, and the development of healthy attachment patterns (Howell et al., 2016)."

For more than 25 years, researchers worldwide have studied the impact of intimate partner violence on diverse areas of children's development, including emotional and behavioral adjustment, cognitive functioning, structural brain development, school performance, and physical health. (Howell et al., 2016). According to the Centers for Disease Control and Prevention (CDC) website, "adverse childhood experiences, or ACEs, are potentially traumatic events that occur in childhood (0-17 years) (Centers for Disease Control and Prevention, 2023)."

Children exposed to intimate partner violence scenarios most likely deal with ACEs. Students come to school with toxic stress from their home environment and constantly adjust during critical brain development. Toxic stress is a term used to describe childhood traumatic experiences that threaten healthy brain development (cognition) and are associated with lifelong health and social problems. "Adverse outcomes from exposure to IPV in childhood include an increased risk of psychological, social, emotional, and behavioral problems, including mood and anxiety disorders, PTSD, substance abuse, and school-related problems in children and adolescents (Wathen & Macmillan, 2013)."

A study examined the relationship between exposure to intimate partner violence, non-violent angry verbal conflict, and adjustment difficulties for one to three-year-old children. The results revealed that children exposed to intimate partner violence had significantly higher levels of adjustment problems, particularly regarding atypical or maladaptive behaviors (e.g., making odd sounds and repetitive movements) (Howell et al., 2016).

The impact of exposure to domestic violence on children adopted from the National Child Traumatic Stress Network (Children and Youth Exposure to Domestic Violence, n.d.) states the following:

"Newborn to 5 years old

1. Sleep or eating disruptions.
2. Withdrawal/lack of responsiveness
3. Intense/pronounced separation anxiety.
4. Inconsolable crying.
5. Developmental regression, loss of acquired skills.
6. Intense anxiety, worries, or new fears.
7. Increased aggression or impulsive behavior.

Ages 6 to 11 years old

1. Nightmares, sleep disruptions.
2. Aggression and difficulty with peer relationships in school.
3. Difficulty with concentration and task completion in school.
4. Withdrawal or emotional numbing.
5. School avoidance or truancy.

Ages 12 to 18 years old

1. Anti-social behavior.
2. School failure/impulsive or reckless behavior.
3. School truancy.
4. Substance abuse.
5. Running away.
6. Involvement in violent or abusive dating relationships.
7. Depression.
8. Anxiety.

9. Withdrawal (Children and Youth Exposure to Domestic Violence, n.d.)."

Medical Impact

Past studies mainly focused on the physical and structural brain injuries in women survivors with a history of intimate partner violence. However, little attention has been given to the biological impact and cognitive dysfunction resulting from such psychological stress (Wong et al., 2013). "Eve M. Valera, an associate professor of psychiatry at Harvard University and a leading researcher on traumatic brain injuries among survivors of domestic violence, estimated that the number of annual brain injuries among survivors of domestic abuse is 1.6 million (Hillstrom, 2022)."

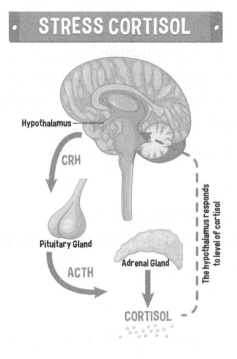

Figure 12. The biological impact and cognitive dysfunction resulting from psychological stress. Source: Freepik.com

"In 1990, [British physician Gareth] Roberts was teaching neuroanatomy at Imperial College London with one of the world's leading groups investigating Alzheimer's. A colleague requested his assistance evaluating the autopsy of a 76-year-old woman who died after years of abuse from her husband. The letter described rib fractures, bruises, and abrasions to the head. She had a history of stroke and, it was reported, had become "demented" in her later years — mostly in the form of memory loss and confusion. What Roberts found in her brain was similar to what he saw in brains with Alzheimer's — tangles of tau and beta amyloid proteins associated with neurodegeneration. Her autopsy revealed a brain that had deteriorated to a degree comparable to boxers suffering from chronic traumatic encephalopathy, or C.T.E., once known as "punch-drunk syndrome." It was the first time the literature had connected abused women with neurodegenerative disease (Hillstrom, 2022)."

"Cortisol, a stress hormone, mobilizes energy from the storage site or nonessential organs to exercise muscles for the "fight-or-flight" response (Wong et al., 2013)." However, prolonged stimulation may cause either cell death or shutdown of the neurogenesis processes in the amygdala and hippocampus because they are recognized as nonessential brain regions during the "fight-or-flight" response (Wong et al., 2013). "Individuals who have experienced [traumatic brain injury] TBI from strangulation may experience outcomes secondary to hypoxia, such as seizures, coma, or even brain death (Costello & Greenwald, 2022)."

"Research on traumatic brain injury (TBI) from domestic violence has greatly increased in the past decade, with publications addressing the prevalence, diagnosis, evaluation, and treatment (Costello & Greenwald, 2022)." The *National Library on Medicine* article *Update on Domestic Violence and Traumatic Brain Injury: A Narrative Review,* further emphasized, "Battered woman syndrome was first described in 1975, at which point it was described as more of a social and psychological issue than a medical issue. Since then, research on TBI due to domestic violence has increased. It has now been estimated that the number of women who have experienced TBI secondary to domestic violence is 11–12 times greater than the number of TBIs experienced by military personnel and athletes combined (Costello & Greenwald, 2022)." "A large proportion (44–75%) of women who experience intimate partner violence appear to sustain repetitive mild traumatic brain injuries from their abusers (Valera et al., 2019)."

"Healthcare costs ranged between 2.3 and 7.0 billion, particularly for the following twelve months post-injury (Monahan, 2019)." Notably, the *Journal Of Aggression, Maltreatment & Trauma article Intimate Partner Violence (IPV) and Neurological Outcomes: A Review for Practitioners* asserts that the number of women experiencing intimate partner violence-related traumatic brain injuries is staggering. It is now estimated that women who receive at least one intimate partner violence-related traumatic brain injury are approximately 31,500,000 in the United States. For instance, the article indicated that women report punches to the jaw, mouth (broken teeth), cheekbone, and eyes (Matteoli et al., 2016), their head slammed into the wall or dashboard of the car, and blunt force trauma injuries to the head (Monahan, 2019).

I suffered from memory retention, and perhaps a traumatic brain injury was the cause, from the multiple punches received to my head and face over months with Maverick and previous physical assault from my ex-husband. I remember on December 9, 2009, amid the excruciating pain in my head, I erroneously did not seek medical attention to assess for a concussion.

The article entitled *Intimate Partner Violence (IPV) and Neurological Outcomes: A Review for Practitioners* was quite alarming, citing The Centers for Disease Control and Prevention report that 156,000 TBI-related deaths, hospitalizations, and emergency department visits per year are assault-related (Langiois et al., 2004). Women experiencing intimate partner violence and traumatic brain injuries experience difficulties from mild negative sequelae to a host of serious trauma resulting in cognitive, psychological, physical, and emotional issues that may go undetected by medical personnel (St. Ivany et al., 2018a; Valera & Kucyi, 2017) (Monahan, 2019).

A 2006 study found that relational violence took a significant physical toll on survivors, and results determined that women studied had an increased risk of stroke, heart disease, and asthma (McLeod et al., 2021). According to *The Model of Systemic Relational Violence: Conceptualizing IPV as a Method of Continual and Enforced Domination*, "[a]dditional health consequences of relational violence for victims include chronic pain, gastrointestinal disorders, and chronic disease. Furthermore, gynecological issues, including sexually transmitted infections, chronic pelvic pain, and urinary tract infections, are also common among survivors of relational violence (McLeod et al., 2021)."

Multiple known and suspected adverse health outcomes of family and domestic violence exist (Huecker & Smock, 2023). The National Library of Medicine (NIH) website reports the health outcomes of long-term consequences of broken bones, traumatic brain injuries, and internal injuries. Patients may also develop multiple comorbidities such as:

1. Asthma
2. Insomnia
3. Fibromyalgia
4. Headaches
5. High blood pressure
6. Chronic pain
7. Gastrointestinal disorders

8. Gynecologic disorders

9. Depression

10. Panic attacks

11. PTSD (Anderson & Kiehl, 2014)

"Children exposed to IPV are also at increased risk for physical, sexual, and emotional abuse and neglect. In extreme cases, children face acute harm and even death, with up to 20% of filicide (especially paternal) cases involving a history of domestic violence. Children experience significant loss and harm in the context of interparental domestic homicide (Wathen & Macmillan, 2013)."

Alcohol Consumption Contributor to IPV

"Heavy drinking and alcohol use disorders are well-established risk factors for perpetuating intimate partner violence (IPV) (Clements & Schumacher, 2010)." The article, *Perceptual Biases in Social Cognition as Potential Moderators of The Relationship Between Alcohol and Intimate Partner Violence: A Review*, states, "psychopharmacological effects of alcohol intoxication may escalate the risk of violence directly by impairing cognitive function and facilitating aggressogenic processes by distorting perceptions of social cues and lowering inhibitions (Clements & Schumacher, 2010)."

Community Engagement/ Involvement

To COMBAT intimate partner violence, we need community involvement, not bystander engagement, to challenge or address social norms and prevent this behavior. Several services are available to women who sustain intimate partner violence (e.g., shelters, advocacy, legal protection), and the combination of these services has been termed a coordinated community response to intimate partner violence (Shorey et al., 2014). Shorey and fellow researchers of this peer-reviewed article enlighten readers by expounding further, suggesting that, "Although there is no standardized protocol for implementing a [coordinated community response] CCR (Klevens et al., 2008), these programs involve an ecological approach to helping victims of IPV, which includes community-wide agencies such as the police, legal system, social service providers (e.g., victim advocates), government, health care systems, and educational and vocational programs (Sullivan, 2006) (Shorey et al., 2014)."

I concur and love this statement that Tonya, a former police officer at Abbotsford Police Department, points out, "Not everyone experiencing IPV wants to end a relationship, and the collaborative work helps us tackle some of those real-life challenges (Dyal, 2022)."

The Institute for Community Peace Model emphasizes mobilizing for community peace versus actions contributing to violence. The Institute for Community Peace Model believes that violence prevention is sustainable only when communities address violence in the broader community and within families. As times change, enculturation plays an essential role in shaping the family and violence within the family; therefore, paradigm shifts in policy and programs regarding the interventions are necessary for a more fluid and suitable response by the government and community-based organizations to cater to modern society (Mahapatro & Prasad, 2021).

The status of interpersonal violence as a public issue is the product of moral transformations and political actions. Furthermore, the author believes "social movements and victims' advocates played a great role in redefining as morally intolerable some kinds of violence that were previously tolerated, as much as in making public what was considered a private matter (Pache, 2020)."

Prevention Institute's Adverse Community Experiences and Resilience (ACE|R) Framework explains the need to understand trauma at the population level (Prevention Institute, n.d.).

The Production of Trauma from Violence

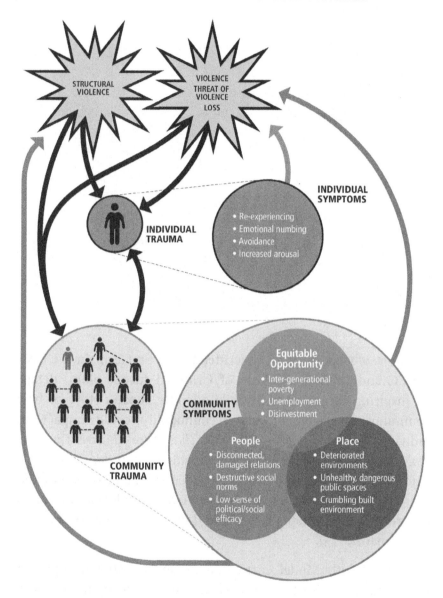

Figure 13. The Production of Trauma from Violence infographic. Trauma at both the individual and community level increases the likelihood of further adverse community experiences, thus creating a mutually reinforcing production cycle in which trauma and violence are produced and reproduced in communities and across generations. Source: (Prevention Institute, n.d.)

"The Framework advances the understanding that adverse community experiences – structural violence and violence — contribute to trauma at the individual and community levels. Trauma manifests as symptoms within individuals and across communities, such as in disconnected social relations and networks. Trauma at both the individual and community level increases the likelihood of further adverse community experiences, thus creating a mutually reinforcing production cycle, in which trauma and violence are produced and reproduced in communities and across generations. Supporting community healing and building community resilience fosters communities that can thrive, even in the context of future adversity and creates conditions for effective collective action by communities to find solutions that improve community wellbeing (Prevention Institute, n.d., pp. 5-6)."

Stone of Hope: A Memoir, written by Jim St. Germain, a CUNY BMCC and John Jay College of Criminal Justice alum, details an inspiring incarcerated juvenile offender success story of how community engagement and accountability could impact an individual's life. *Falling for the Ones That Were Abusive: Cycles of Violence in Low-Income Women's Intimate Relationships*, an article study "serves as a call to action to widen sampling strategies and examine abuse in ways that better fit victims' understandings and experiences of intimate partner and domestic violence (Cervantes & Sherman, 2019)."

"The Duluth Model curriculum is an educational approach grounded in feminist theory that focuses on changing attitudes toward women and unlearning power and control motivations (Zarling & Russell, 2022)." Ellen Louise Pence, a scholar and housing, anti-war, civil rights, and feminist movements activist, "moved to Duluth, MN, in 1980, where she and a small group of activists organized the Domestic Abuse Intervention Project, commonly referred to as the 'Duluth Model' *(Obituary for Ellen Louise Pence, n.d.)*." The Duluth Model includes the Domestic Abuse Intervention Project, or Pence's model, and is a controversial model that brings agencies together to solely reduce domestic violence against women (Wikipedia contributors, 2023). "The model, which has been adapted for use throughout the world, employs an interagency approach to shift responsibility for confronting domestic violence from the victims of the violence to the community, based on the idea that women (and their children) have as much right to be safe at home as all people have to be safe on the street (Obituary for Ellen Louise Pence, n.d.)."

"This practice employs a feminist psychoeducational approach with group-facilitated exercises to change abusive and threatening behavior in males who engage in domestic violence. The practice is rated **Effective** *[Crime & Delinquency – Violent offenses] for reducing recidivism with respect to violent offenses and* **Promising** *[Victimization – Domestic/intimate partner/family violence] in reducing victimization. The results found fewer partner reports of violence in the intervention group relative to the comparison groups (Practice Profile: Interventions for Domestic Violence Offenders: Duluth Model, n.d.)."*

Please note: *The Practice Profile: Interventions for Persons Who Committed Intimate-Partner Violence: Duluth Model was created and posted on September 13, 2013, nearly ten years ago, on the United States Department of Justice (DOJ) Office of Justice Programs National Institute for Justice Crime Solutions webpage and I am unable to locate or verify DOJ's updated stance regarding its effectiveness.*

Acceptance and Commitment Therapy with the Duluth Model curriculum took place in community-based corrections to treat men convicted of domestic violence (Zarling & Russell, 2022). "[Acceptance and Commitment Therapy] ACT is a third-wave cognitive–behavioral approach that utilizes experiential methods to foster psychological flexibility (Zarling & Russell, 2022)."

Services for Victims of Intimate Partner Violence

The Victims of Crime Act (VOCA) legislation was signed by President Ronald Reagan on October 12, 1984, establishing the Crime Victims Fund (the Fund). On July 22, 2021, President Joseph R. Biden, Jr. signed the 117th Congress' VOCA Fix to Sustain the Crime Victims Fund Act of 2021 (VOCA Fix). The Fund assists with victim services throughout the country, supporting millions of survivors through hundreds of direct services organizations such as domestic violence shelters, rape crisis programs, victim services programs, child abuse programs, and more (Victims of Crime Act (VOCA), n.d.).

"As domestic violence cases increasingly enter the court system, and consequences of aggressive accidents threaten the functioning, well-being, and health of victims in the family or external systems, it is crucial to describe the extent and nature of this phenomenon (Rakovec-Felser, 2014)." The National Domestic Violence Hotline, local district attorney's domestic violence bureaus, local victim services units at local police precincts, Safe Horizon, and the Domestic Violence Resource Center are vital resources for victims or their support networks. A victim could acquire information on providing safe escape planning or placement in a domestic violence shelter.

For your convenience, below are valuable resources to aid intimate partner violence victims:

National Domestic Violence Hotline 1-800-799-7233 (SAFE) https://www.thehotline.org/	**Safe Horizon** *Moving victims of violence from crisis to confidence* 1-800 621-4673 (HOPE) https://www.safehorizon.org/
Domestic Violence Resource Center 1-866-469-8900 (24-hour Crisis Line) https://www.dvrc-or.org/	**New York State Office for the Prevention of Domestic Violence** https://opdv.ny.gov/help/fss/contents.html

Table 5. Resources for Intimate partner violence victims, survivors, and their support network.

Support Network/Sphere of Influence

"Public attitudes, such as victim-blaming, are essential for understanding differences in the occurrence of IPVAW, as they contribute to its justification (Ivert et al., 2017)." "Victim blaming is the tendency to hold someone responsible for their victimization, instead of the perpetrator (Weiss, 2020)." I suffered victim-blaming/shaming by relatives and friends after the December 2009 intimate partner violence incident, showcasing a lack of empathy and compassion following the tragic experience that hurt me physically. I received chastisement from family and a friend for allowing the intimate partner violence incident to transpire. It is a heartbreaking experience for a victim to go through the trauma of intimate partner violence, go through great shame after the occurrence, and immediately have family and friends in their support network ridicule them for what happened. In a service, Bishop Darius Nixon stated, "My comeback is gonna be greater than my embarrassment."

"Assessments of victim-blaming attitudes in high-income countries have included justifications such as infidelity or women "asking for it" (United States of America) and women's provocative behavior (European countries) (Gracia, 2014)." Gracia's article, *Intimate partner violence against women and victim-blaming attitudes among*

Europeans, emphasizes my point on why victim-blaming is harmful to intimate partner violence survivors, "Public attitudes that place the responsibility for violence on the victims' shoulders often conceal a lack of sympathy or insensitivity towards victims that creates a psychological distance between victims and their observers." Significantly, the author suggests, "Blaming the women who are treated with violence by their intimate partners is a form of the second victimization that can undermine their mental health and hinder their recovery and psychosocial adjustment (Gracia, 2014)."

The bystander effect is something a victim of intimate partner violence should not experience from her support network of family and friends, medical professionals, and neighbors. According to Britannica, the bystander effect is an "inhibiting influence of the presence of others on a person's willingness to help someone in need (Blagg, 2019)." In other words, it is "a phenomenon in which people fail to offer needed help in emergencies, especially when other people are present in the same setting (APA Dictionary of Psychology, n.d.)." "In 1964, a woman named Catherine "Kitty" Genovese was attacked and repeatedly stabbed by a serial killer named Winston Moseley despite calling for help in her apartment courtyard. As many as 38 people were said to have witnessed her murder (Clicktivism Is Not Enough: What to Do about the Bystander Effect, 2021)."

Intervention and Advocacy

"A 2021 review of 18 studies relying on data from police, domestic violence hotlines, and health care providers found that reports of intimate partner violence increased by 8% after [the COVID-19 pandemic government-mandated] lockdown orders were imposed (Community-Based Response to Intimate Partner Violence during COVID-19 Pandemic – Bill of Health, 2021)."

"The pandemic showed that community-based supports, like pod mapping, mutual aid, and community accountability, originally developed by activists critical of law enforcement responses to violence, can foster safety and accountability without requiring state intervention. The pandemic could spur advocates seeking to distance themselves from state-based responses to expand their services. (Community-Based Response to Intimate Partner Violence during COVID-19 Pandemic – Bill of Health, 2021)."

Effective interventions incorporating safety planning were empowerment and advocacy-focused (Sabri et al., 2021). Furthermore, the author asserts, "elements included were comprehensive assessments of survivors' unique needs and situations, educating them about IPV, helping them identify threats to safety, developing a concrete safety plan, facilitating linkage with resources, providing advocacy services as needed, and conducting periodic safety check-ins."

In addition to essential relationships, a comprehensive strategy to prevent intimate partner violence involves community and policy-level approaches such as creating protective physical environments in schools and communities and increasing economic and work-related support to families (e.g., paid family leave and child tax credits) can have a broader public health impact (The National Intimate Partner and Sexual Violence Survey Report on Sexual Violence, 2016).

Role of Mass Media

Abnormalizing abuse also sets the stage for later abuse within intimate relationships to be downplayed (Cervantes & Sherman, 2019). A strategic showcasing of films and television series with powerful fathers or family decision-makers addressing a vital supportive role in opposing domestic violence will reinforce moral values, attitudes, and practices (Mahapatro & Prasad, 2021). *Fifty Shades of Grey*, a best-selling novel and 2015 romance drama film, has intimate partner violence scenarios: emotional abuse and sexual violence. Anastasia becomes disempowered and entrapped in the relationship as her behaviors become mechanized in response to Christian's abuse (Bonomi et al., 2013).

"Racial trauma manifests when folks report re-experiencing a particular event, so if there was a direct incident of racism, racial harassment, or discrimination, they think about the event constantly. Watching [police shooting people of color, racial violence, and discrimination] videos and taking in all the images, taking in the news, or looking at social media timelines and activated by the messages received undoubtedly contribute to racial trauma (Navigating Racial Trauma in the Aftermath of Police Killings | the Takeaway, 2021)."

The article, The *Contribution of Social Media Toward Racial Trauma And Post-Traumatic Stress Disorder In Black Americans: A Forensic Perspective,* uses a literature review "to investigate why Black Americans can be significantly impacted by exposure to police brutality videos (Isen, 2022)." The article includes a case study of a Black American male who developed PTSD in response to such videos in the context of a forensic evaluation (Isen, 2022).

The author asserts that some individuals may also experience difficulties with executive functioning, memory, and decision-making. Likewise, women victims or survivors of intimate partner violence may become re-traumatized by viewing movies, television shows, or drama series airing batterers displaying acts of aggression and physical harm to an individual with whom they are in romantic relations.

Prosecuting the Abuser

Domestic violence courts only handle cases with criminal domestic violence charges. Recognizing that an intimate partner relationship does not necessarily require cohabitation, a romantic status, or a continuing relationship is essential. Even if the relationship has ended, abuse can still occur. It is crucial to understand and acknowledge these nuances to address and prevent intimate partner violence effectively. An individual can have an intimate partner relationship if they do not reside with the abuser, the relationship is not sexual, or the relationship is over. Factors the court may consider when deciding if a relationship is an intimate relationship include:

1. The nature or type of relationship

2. How often do you see/saw each other?

3. How long has the relationship gone on?

Filing a domestic incident report with the local police department is critical in documenting abuse. The domestic incident report documents intimate partner violence-incident(s), shows the behavioral pattern of the abuser, and assists with prosecuting the perpetrator. Amendments to domestic incident reports after filing are allowed. Victims should also obtain a restraining or protective order from the court. Some counties have special courts that focus only on domestic violence cases. The judge and staff will have specialized training on domestic violence issues. These domestic abuse cases can come before criminal, family, or divorce courts. The Victims' Protection Amendment Act of 2021, Bill 24-0116, was introduced by Mayor Muriel Bowser. This legislation creates a felony offense of strangulation and an offense for violating a post-conviction stay away or no contact order, which would protect victims— particularly victims of intimate partner violence (Domestic Violence Basics | NY CourtHelp, n.d.).

According to the National Domestic Violence Hotline website's calendar year 2020 intimate partner violence impact report, they received the following reports:

1. 182,784 reports of emotional and verbal abuse

2. 122,953 reports of physical abuse

3. 51,826 reports of economic and financial abuse

4. 33,261 reports of digital abuse

5. 23,418 reports of sexual abuse (A YEAR of IMPACT, 2020)

According to the National Network to End Domestic Violence (NNEDV) 15th Annual Domestic Violence Counts Report May 2021:

1. "The COVID-19 pandemic reduced options for survivors because temporary closures, social-distancing measures, and strains on staff and resources meant fewer available services and interventions. Many shelters limited their capacities to keep residents safe from the virus (24-HOUR SURVEY of Domestic Violence Shelters and Services Domestic Violence Counts Report, 2021)."

2. On September 10, 2020, tragically, there were 11,047 requests for services that participating programs could not provide due to a lack of resources (24-HOUR SURVEY of Domestic Violence Shelters and Services Domestic Violence Counts Report, 2021).

"Most inhabitants of small communities have quite extensive knowledge of the lives of others in their community. In the case of IPV, this knowledge can amplify hurtful community gossip, generate retribution by one family against another or within families, increase the marginalization and stigma faced by victims of IPV, and may serve to silence victims of violence as a form of self-protection (Moffitt et al., 2020)."

It is essential to provide victims and survivors of intimate partner violence with a supportive community that can aid in their healing journey. They have experienced a traumatic event that has left a lasting impact, and we must show them compassion and understanding throughout their recovery process. Their children also require our strengthening and attention during this challenging time. Let us come together as a community to provide a safe and nurturing environment for those affected by intimate partner violence. "Although most survivors note they have experienced rejection and anticipatory stigma as barriers to their help seeking, African American women additionally experience racism and racial discrimination as obstacles that may further preclude their help-seeking (Waller et al., 2021)." Over the past 50 years, programs serving survivors of intimate partner violence have expanded nationally; however, despite program growth, service gaps remain, particularly for the most marginalized and vulnerable survivor populations (Kulkarni, 2018).

Researchers have explored factors that reinforce the silencing of women who experience intimate partner violence, however, an integrated understanding of how factors at each level of an ecological subsystem interact to reinforce the silencing is missing (Pokharel et al., 2020). Sadly, secondary trauma occurs when mental health professionals counsel victims of intimate partner violence. "Human service professionals offering psychosocial services to people who have experienced intimate partner violence (IPV) report multiple impacts on their physical and psychological well-being (Brend et al., 2020)." Brend et al. report, "These impacts have been described and investigated through multiple concepts including vicarious trauma, secondary traumatic stress disorder, compassion fatigue, and post-traumatic stress disorder (Brend et al., 2020)."

Although I cannot fulfill my SMART goal of establishing a domestic violence shelter in New York City, I remain committed to supporting those affected by intimate partner violence. To this end, I am thrilled to recommend my informative book on intimate partner violence to anyone interested in advocating for victims and creating a safe haven for them and their children. This resource is an excellent tool for anyone seeking to make a positive impact in their communities, and I hope it proves valuable to all who utilize it

A Broken System

Figure 14. Justice infographic with a handcuffed prisoner on Lady Justice scale and other scenarios. Source: Freepik.com

Criminalization of Domestic Violence Survivors

THE UNITED States criminal justice system has criminalized women for murdering or assaulting their abusers. Nearly 60% of people in women's prisons nationwide, and as many as 94% of some women's prison populations, have a history of experiencing physical or sexual abuse before being incarcerated (FREE MARISSA NOW, n.d.). Former New York State Governor Andrew M. Cuomo signed the Domestic Violence Survivors Justice Act (S.1077/ A.3974) into law on May 14, 2019. The bill codifies more meaningful sentence reductions for survivors of domestic abuse in the criminal justice system (Governor Cuomo Signs the Domestic Violence Survivors Justice Act, Longtime Bill Sponsored by Senator Persaud, n.d.).

"The vast majority of incarcerated women have experienced physical or sexual violence in their lifetime, and too often these women wind up in prison in the first place because they're protecting themselves from an abuser," Governor [Andrew] Cuomo said. He further asserted, "By signing this critical piece of our 2019 women's justice agenda, we can help ensure the criminal justice system takes into account that reality and empowers vulnerable New Yorkers rather than just putting them behind bars (Governor Cuomo Signs the Domestic Violence Survivors Justice Act, Longtime Bill Sponsored by Senator Persaud, n.d.)."

Marissa Alexander was convicted of aggravated assault charges in 2012 for firing a warning shot at her husband, who she said had abused her. Marissa, an African-American woman, resided in Jacksonville, Florida, which has a stand-your-ground law. Marissa was prosecuted and threatened with 60 years in prison for defending her life from her abusive husband. Marissa eventually pleaded guilty in November 2014, which she had refused to do during her first trial. Marissa was released on January 27, 2017, after serving three years of a 20-year sentence behind bars. She spent two years in house detention while being forced to wear and pay for a surveillance ankle monitor. Marissa's release occurred after a successful *Free*

Marissa Alexander campaign to drop charges against her (FREE MARISSA NOW, n.d.).

Congresswoman Corrine Brown's statement on May 11, 2012, regarding the Florida criminal justice system's dual messaging to the people: "One is that if women who are victims of domestic violence try to protect themselves, the "Stand Your Ground Law" will not apply to them. Secondly, the system will treat you differently if you are Black *(Fla. Woman Marissa Alexander Gets 20 Years for "Warning Shot": Did She Stand Her Ground?, n.d.).*

The Stand Your Ground Law is a Florida statute for the justifiable use of force-home protection, use or threatened use of deadly force, or presumption of fear of death or great bodily harm. Under the more restrictive castle doctrine, a citizen was only justified in using deadly force when defending against a deadly threat inside his or her home. A person must at least consider retreating outside of one's home (and rule it out) before fighting back with deadly force (Understanding Florida's Stand Your Ground Defense, n.d.).

Cyntoia Brown, who served 15 years of a life sentence for killing a man when she was 16, who for years has maintained that the 2004 killing was an act of self-defense, was released from a Nashville prison on August 7, 2019, by then-Governor Bill Haslman who commuted her sentence (Allyn, 2019). Cyntoia, whose life entailed a traumatic adolescence of drug addiction, rape, and sex trafficking that led to a murder conviction (addressed in her book *Free Cyntoia*), provided the following remarks in a statement on her clemency, "I am thankful for all the support, prayers, and encouragement I have received. We truly serve a God of second chances and new beginnings. The Lord has held my hand this whole time and I would have never made it without Him. Let today be a testament to His Saving Grace (Staff report, Knoxville News Sentinel, 2019)."

Brown's release contributed to her supporters' efforts, prominent lawyers fighting for her defense, a PBS documentary, and the backing of Kim Kardashian and Rihanna (Allyn, 2019). "Statistics cited by the American Civil Liberties Union (ACLU) and the Women's March suggest a wide gender gap in sentencing. The average prison sentence for men who kill their female partners is two to six years. By contrast, women who kill their partners are sentenced on average to 15 years (Chalabi, 2019)." Studies have shown that there is a clear gender bias in the criminal justice system when it comes to convictions related to intimate partner violence, with women often being treated more harshly than men for the same crimes.

"In 2017 in North Carolina, a man convicted of stabbing his pregnant wife to death in their bedroom was released from prison after only 7 years. Last May, a New Jersey man was sentenced to 15 years for the June 2017 murder of his wife, who died of blunt force trauma and was found floating in the couple's backyard pool. Her online search history showed she was planning on leaving her husband. In Nebraska, a man who was found guilty of severing his wife's head has been allowed to reenter the community, with supervision, after spending only five years in a psychiatric hospital. Kim Dadou received 17 years for fatally shooting her boyfriend after he climbed on top of her in his car and threatened to kill her. This was also after she endured four years of his abuse. Crystal Potter, interviewed recently for This is Life with Lisa Ling in an episode called, "Women Who Kill," served 20 years in prison for shooting her husband after he got out a gun and aimed it at her head. Again, this was following Potter living through his weekly beatings (Kippert, 2020)."

Healthcare System

The healthcare systems, such as primary care, emergency departments, and other medical subspecialties, are often the first point of contact for survivors of intimate partner violence (Langhinrichsen-Rohling et al., 2020). The authors point out that a "reduced sense of stigma and increased privacy afforded by health settings uniquely positions the healthcare system as a safe space for IPV inquiry, detection, and early prevention and intervention efforts (Langhinrichsen-Rohling et al., 2020)." However, both lifetime and current experiences of intimate partner violence victimization are often underreported by survivors and overlooked by providers in healthcare settings (Langhinrichsen-Rohling et al., 2020).

Estimates of the prevalence of intimate partner violence among women seeking medical care vary according to the study location (an inner-city health clinic vs. an integrated health delivery system), survey methods (anonymous survey vs. clinic screening), and time frame (lifetime vs. recent) and are higher than the estimated prevalence in the general population, especially in primary care, emergency, obstetrics and gynecology, mental health, and addiction services (Miller & McCaw, 2019). The authors further assert that "[Q]ualitative studies indicate that women experiencing such violence want health care providers to talk to them about the violence in a safe and private setting, to be prepared to ask multiple times without pushing for disclosure, and to offer tangible medical and social resources for support (Miller & McCaw, 2019)."

"In September 2016, the Health Resources and Services Administration (HRSA) Office of Women's Health launched an agency-wide initiative, The HRSA Strategy to Address Intimate Partner Violence ("the Strategy"). The impetus was to move HRSA beyond pilot projects and isolated initiatives in order to make a systems-level impact on IPV awareness, screening, and

treatment across the health care and public health sectors. The Office of Women's Health led the planning, bringing together HRSA's Bureaus and Offices that play a role in directly funding or otherwise supporting program delivery. The Strategy is the culmination of a year-long process in which Bureau and Office representatives from across the agency collaborated to identify partnerships, strengthen existing programs, and create new initiatives to address IPV (THE HRSA STRATEGY to ADDRESS INTIMATE PARTNER VIOLENCE, 2017)."

The adoption of an initiative-taking stance in addressing intimate partner violence (IPV) during the medical intake or screening portion is a non-threatening approach. If my abuser had not accompanied me to the hospital following my assault, the environment would have been a safe space to inform medical staff of what happened to me. Patients may be annoyed by the probing questions on whether they are experiencing physical abuse at home or with a partner during a doctor visit's screening process. However, it may save the life of a victim of intimate partner violence.

I applaud the Health Resources and Services Administration's (HRSA's) efforts in "implementing a multiyear strategic framework to improve the response of health care systems to intimate partner violence (Miller & McCaw, 2019)." *The HRSA Strategy To Address Intimate Partner Violence 2017-2020* publication's executive summary describes that "The Strategy's objectives are organized within four priorities describing how HRSA's employees and programs can address IPV" (The HRSA Strategy to Address Intimate Partner Violence, 2017):

PRIORITY	STRATEGIC OBJECTIVES
Train the nation's health care and public health workforce to address IPV at the community and health systems levels	**1.1:** Create or adopt a range of culturally competent, evidence-based, and trauma-informed educational materials and technical assistance on IPV for health care and public health professionals in the field. **1.2:** Expand IPV technical assistance and training opportunities for the health care workforce through HRSA Bureaus' and Offices' national and regional grant programs and training networks.
Develop partnerships to raise awareness about IPV within HRSA and HHS	**2.1:** Leverage existing mechanisms to promote awareness of IPV as a public health issue among HRSA employees. **2.2:** Establish within-HRSA and interagency partnerships on IPV.
Increase access to quality IPV-informed health care services across all populations	**3.1:** Highlight the importance of IPV as a topic that HRSA grantees can propose to address. **3.2:** Increase awareness of IPV among HRSA's key external stakeholders. **3.3:** Improve the delivery of IPV-related services for economically disadvantaged (poor) and geographically isolated communities. **3.4:** Establish a model of collaboration among federal, state, and local health care leaders to strengthen systems of care for IPV.
Address Gaps in knowledge about IPV risks, impacts, and interventions	**4.1:** Contribute to the evidence based on the risk factors and impacts of IPV. **4.2:** Support the continuous review and evaluation of federal IPV-related activities and legislative priorities.

Table 6. Health Resources and Services Administration's (HRSA) Strategy to Address Intimate Partner Violence infographic. Source: (The HRSA Strategy to Address Intimate Partner Violence, 2017)

Law Enforcement

"Beginning in the 1980s, advocates and legal scholars sought to criminalize intimate partner violence by implementing pro-arrest and mandatory arrest policies, supporting preferred prosecution policies, enforcing protective orders, or requiring intervention programs for those convicted of abuse (New Approaches to Policing High-Risk Intimate Partner Victims and Those Committing the Crimes, n.d.)." "In 2015, the Police Executive Research Forum (PERF) found that 42% of surveyed law enforcement agencies reported using a structured risk assessment to determine if a victim is in danger of future violence. Furthermore, the "PERF report also indicated that 39% of U.S. agencies use a risk-assessment approach to identify persons who repeatedly commit crimes (New Approaches to Policing High-Risk Intimate Partner Victims and Those Committing the Crimes, n.d.)."

"Gender plays an important role in everyday life for everyone, including men. For instance, gender-based violence reinforces gender-based inequalities like the male role that is hard to understand beyond gender norms, social structures, and reinforcing roles (Galla, n.d.)."

To illustrate the importance of intimate partner violence abusive temperament, "currently two victim-focused models of IPV risk assessment are used in the United States: The Lethality Assessment Program (LAP) and the Domestic Violence High-Risk Team (DVHRT) model (New Approaches to Policing High-Risk Intimate Partner Victims and Those Committing the Crimes, n.d.)." According to the National Institute of Justice Journal *New Approaches to Policing High-Risk Intimate Partner Victims and Those Committing the Crimes*, LAP is a police-led model that follows the Lethality Assessment Program–Maryland Model, created in the early 2000s, through a collaboration of advocates, researchers, and law enforcement practitioners. The journal reports, "LAP assessment is based on Dr. Jacquelyn Campbell's Danger Assessment instrument, which she developed with the support of NIJ and other federal agencies to determine the likelihood that a man would kill his female intimate partner." The DVHRT, or high-risk team approach, has also gained traction across the country over the past decade, wherein law enforcement personnel seek to identify victims at high risk for lethal-like violence using the Danger Assessment–Law Enforcement tool (New Approaches to Policing High-Risk Intimate Partner Victims and Those Committing the Crimes, n.d.).

Where are ambiguities or loopholes in our system regarding victims of intimate partner violence? The question remains why many victims are murdered despite the enormous efforts of law enforcement agencies because the new approaches are not antiquated policies. According to reporting by *Newsweek,* a Florida man killed his pregnant, transgender partner in a murder-suicide. "Riley John Groover, 26, of Winter Haven, Florida, allegedly shot and killed himself after shooting his pregnant fiancé 'multiple times' in front of witnesses outside of their home last week, according to a statement from the Polk County Sheriff's Office (Zurick, 2023)."

David Keegan Riotto Haigh drove from Pennsylvania to visit a friend in New York City and stabbed James Koron Johnson in his residence, whom he connected with on a gay hookup app (Foldy, 2018). A Brooklyn man accused of stabbing his wife and her new lover to death when he caught them having sex in a car was acting in self-defense, according to a *New York Daily News* article articulating the lawyer's statement (Brooklyn Man Accused of Fatally Stabbing Wife, Her New Lover Was Acting in Self-Defense: Lawyer, 2014). Intimate partner violence can and has occurred in many places.

According to *How Domestic Violence Perpetrators Manipulate Systems Why Systems & Professionals Are So Vulnerable & 5 Steps to Perpetrator-Proof Your System,* "Domestic violence perpetrator manipulation of systems is a critical problem that undermines responses to family violence and deeply impacts adult and child survivors in many ways (How Domestic Violence Perpetrators Manipulate Systems Why Systems & Professionals Are so Vulnerable

& 5 Steps to Perpetrator-Proof Your System, n.d.)." The article notes two tiers of systems targeted by perpetrators:

- *Tier 1 Entities*, comprised entirely of government systems, have the most obvious and profound impact on the lives of adult and child survivors due to their legal authority to arrest, monitor, incarcerate, remove children from parents, and determine child custody and access. 1st Tier Systems – Systems such as police, child protection, and family courts have the most power to directly affect adult and child survivors.

- *2nd Tier Systems*, including mental health and substance abuse providers, legal professionals, and evaluators, feed into 1st Tier Systems and contribute to their information gathering and assessments. Tier 2 entities consist of private professionals and agencies that provide services to families and other organizations like faith institutions (How Domestic Violence Perpetrators Manipulate Systems Why Systems & Professionals Are so Vulnerable & 5 Steps to Perpetrator-Proof Your System, n.d.).

Below are examples of manipulation behaviors in law enforcement and criminal court:

- Calling the police and making allegations against the survivor.

- Committing crimes, like fraud, in the name of the survivor.

- Pretending to be the victim and painting the survivor as the perpetrator.

- Coercing survivors into committing crimes, taking the blame for criminal behavior, or getting into debt.

- Calling the police on a child or family member who intervenes to protect the survivor.

- Harassing or intimidating survivors or children under the guise of "help" or "support" by asking law enforcement to do wellness checks (How Domestic Violence Perpetrators Manipulate Systems Why Systems & Professionals Are so Vulnerable & 5 Steps to Perpetrator-Proof Your System, n.d.).

Examine Underlying Factors Batterers Commit Intimate Partner Violence

Research has established a relationship between ecological contexts and intimate partner violence. However, little is known about how environmental factors affect childhood development over time and culminate into intimate partner violence perpetration from the perspective of men who perpetrated intimate partner violence (Voith et al., 2020). A *Science Digest* peer-reviewed article used grounded theory to study employed focus groups with 32 low-income, African American men in batterer intervention programs to explore factors and processes through which families, neighborhoods, and policy influence men's development, contributing to their use of intimate partner violence (Voith et al., 2020). The authors report that "Three core categories emerged from focused and axial coding: adverse childhood experiences (ACEs) and trauma, structural forces, and systemic forces (Voith et al., 2020)."

Role of Institutionalized Racism in the Destruction of the Family Dynamic

Brittanica.com declares institutional racism as perpetuating discrimination based on race by political, economic, or legal institutions and systems (Britannica, 2023). There is a difference between intrinsic institutional racism, which holds that institutions are racist by their constitutive features, and extrinsic institutional racism, which holds that institutions are racist by their negative effects (Matthew, 2022). "Racially segregated housing creates racial isolation, with disproportionate costs to Black Americans' opportunities, networks, education, wealth, health, and legal treatment

(Banaji et al., 2021)." Most importantly, "These institutional and societal systems build in individual bias and racialized interactions, resulting in systemic racism (Banaji et al., 2021)."

"In truth, Black people are sicker and die earlier than their white counterparts because they are more likely to encounter those things that we know compromise health–like inaccessible or biased health care providers, inadequate schools and education systems, unemployment, hazardous jobs, unsafe housing, and violent, polluted communities (Bridges, 2020)." Ta-Nehisi Coates wrote an article in October 2015 for *The Atlantic* entitled *The Black Family In The Age Of Mass Incarceration*, in which she expresses:

"American politicians are now eager to disown a failed criminal-justice system that's left the U.S. with the largest incarcerated population in the world. But they've failed to reckon with history. Fifty years after Daniel Patrick Moynihan's report "The Negro Family" tragically helped create this system, it's time to reclaim his original intent (Coates, 2015)"

In assessing the article, *The Transmission of Violence and Trauma Across Development and Environmental Contexts: Intimate Partner Violence from The Perspective of Men with Histories of Perpetration*, we can ascertain that systemic racism or environmental stresses are considered a potential root cause of intimate partner violence in marginalized communities. "Cross-sectional and prospective studies have highlighted links between violence exposure in early life or chaotic family life (e.g., low parental monitoring) and intimate partner violence perpetration in later life (Voith et al., 2020)." Researchers examining social disorganization theory uncovered community violence and social disorder as key mechanisms that partially explained the neighborhood-intimate partner violence link (Voith et al., 2020).

"Findings reinforce the notion that environmental stress not buffered by protective adults profoundly affects development and behavior. From the perspective of male perpetrators, our results help identify those stressors and how they might contribute to male-to-female IPV (Voith et al., 2020)."

Systemic Racism

Enslaved African families were severely ascribable to malicious and heinous actions of their owners (masters), selling off family dynamics (children, siblings, parents, and spouses) like cattle. This elimination and breakdown of the enslaved family dynamic was a cruel part of American history that should not be concealed from students of all nationalities.

"A decontextualized family systems theory (FST) approach would ignore the elephant in the room (i.e., race and racism) that often serves as a catalyst for culturally sanctioned parenting practices and parent–child interactions within Black families. The racial identity of families (level of racial consciousness of the family unit) and of its members (e.g., parents, extended family) drives the need to engage in practices to help children develop in a racialized society. Turning a blind eye to racism or how a color-blind ideology may affect some Black families would prevent scholars and practitioners from completely understanding reasons that some Black families tend to be structured the way they are and reasons they engage in certain patterns of behaviors (James et al., 2018)"

The African American family dismantlement began when their enslaved ancestors "[s]eparated from their families and cultures, captives endured a long trek to the coast, where they were often imprisoned for months before embarking on the horrifying transatlantic voyage (White et al., 2016 p. 132)." After that, enslaved Africans dealt with South Carolina's adoption of the Barbadian Slave Code, discouraging rebellion and runaways. This Slave Code has a provision that three-time offenders could be castrated, which cuts procreation, affecting the family dynamic expansion and men's psychological well-being.

The Emancipation Proclamation of 1863 declared that "all persons held as slaves" were free in rebellious states. Concluding the bloody Civil War, a new type of enslavement arose called prison "Chain Gangs," aka slave labor, still affecting the family dynamic. "The egregiousness of the violence and corruption of the system began to turn public opinion against convict leasing (Chain Gangs | Slavery by Another Name Bento | PBS, 2017)."

During the Reconstruction Era in American history, structural forces and trauma intertwined when "Black codes attempted to economically disable freed slaves, forcing African Americans to continue to work on plantations and to remain subject to racial hierarchy within the southern society (Black Codes (Article) | Reconstruction | Khan Academy, n.d.)." African-Americans dealt with Jim Crow Era laws, including lynchings, which exacerbated more structural forces. College-educated and classically trained Black performers years ago were frequently offered a limited range of roles or played stereotypical roles.

Currently, institutional racism consists of the school-to-prison pipeline and recidivism, wherein some ex-felons find, upon release, difficulty securing employment and housing discrimination (bias or stigma). Countless narratives could be presented as to why African-American men (inexcusably) become abusive to their partners while living with frustration, breakdown, or destruction of the family dynamic. Deconstructing institutional racism at the academy's core is integral to decolonization (Lazaridou & Fernando, 2022).

Due to the pervasive nature of structural racism in the United States, no Black person in America (regardless of their country of origin or ancestry) is immune from the effects of racism (Federal Policies Can Address the Impact of Structural Racism on Black Families' Access to Early Care and Education – Child Trends, 2021). Systemic racism is so embedded into systems that it is often assumed to reflect the natural, inevitable order of things (Braveman et al., 2022). "Among the root causes of domestic violence in Black communities specifically, 72.6% of participants in the 2017 *Black Leaders Survey on Domestic Violence* cited systemic racism, a factor ranking slightly behind economic stress (85.6%), childhood trauma (84.9%), and substance abuse (72.6%) (Kippert, 2020)."

Slavery—explicitly supported by laws—endured for 250 years in the United States and was followed by almost 100 years of Jim Crow laws—often enforced by terror—that were deliberately designed to restrict the rights of African Americans, including the right to vote, work, and earn an education (Braveman et al., 2022).

"Unconscious inferences, empirically established from perceptions onward, demonstrate non-Black Americans' inbuilt associations: pairing Black Americans with negative valences, criminal stereotypes, and low status, including animal rather than human. Implicit racial biases (improving only slightly over time) imbed within non-Black individuals' systems of racialized beliefs, judgments, and affect that predict racialized behavior. Interracial interactions likewise convey disrespect and distrust (Banaji et al., 2021)."

Systemic and structural racism are forms of racism that are pervasively and deeply embedded in systems, laws, written or unwritten policies, and entrenched practices and beliefs that produce, condone, and perpetuate widespread unfair treatment and oppression of people of color, with adverse health consequences (Braveman et al., 2022). A large body of scientific research documents racially unequal outcomes and racial bias in virtually all aspects of the criminal legal system. Black people experience harsher outcomes concerning police encounters, bail setting, sentence length, and capital punishment than White people (Bailey et al., 2021).

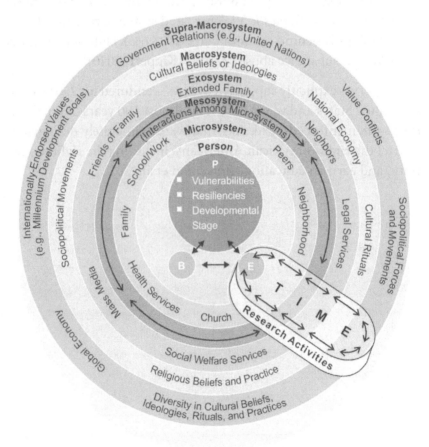

Figure 15. What does the ecological system look like?

"Intimate partner violence (IPV) disproportionately affects marginalized women in the United States (Sabri et al.)." "Although African American women are at disproportionate risk for domestic violence, [a] review of the literature suggests that traditional law enforcement, criminal justice, and advocacy efforts may be ineffective with this population due to (a) Black female victims' experiences of systemic racism and oppression, which prevents disclosure of abuse and access to resources, and (b) utilization of culture-blind approaches in the development and administration of interventions (Hampton et al., 2008)." For a Black survivor, oppression, implicit/explicit bias, and racial loyalty/collectivism directly impact how female survivors perceive, react to, and report intimate partner violence (Rice et al., 2020).

In 1979, Urie Bronfenbrenner developed *Bronfenbrenner's Ecological System Theory,* "one of the most accepted explanations regarding the influence of social environments on human development to explain how their immediate and surrounding environment affects how children grow and develop. This theory argues that the environment you grow up in affects every facet of your life. Social factors determine your way of thinking, the emotions you feel, and your likes and dislikes (Santa Clara University, 2022)."

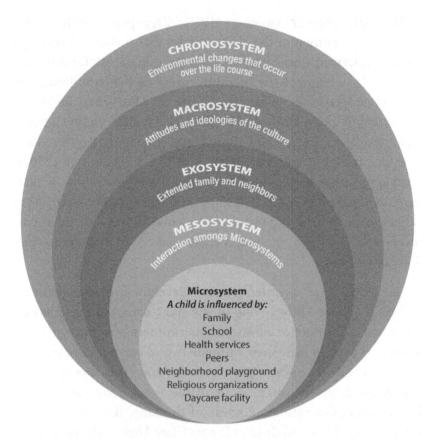

Figure 16. Bronfenbrenner's Ecological System Theory dynamics.
Bronfenbrenner's Ecological System Theory expounds on the influence of
social environments on human development to explain how their immediate
and surrounding environment affects how children grow and develop.
Bronfenbrenner's theory consists of the following systems dynamics: *1*. The
Microsystem, *2*. The Mesosystem, *3*. The Exosystem, *4*. The Macrosystem, and *5*.
Chronosystem. Source: (Guy-Evans, 2023)

Bronfenbrenner's Ecological System Theory consists of the following
systems dynamics:

1. *The Microsystem*: The Microsystem is the first level of Bron-
    fenbrenner's theory and includes things/people that have
    direct contact with the child in their immediate environ-
    ment, such as parents, siblings, teachers, and school peers.

Relationships in a microsystem are bi-directional, meaning other people can influence the child in their environment and change other people's beliefs and actions (Guy-Evans, 2023).

2. *The Mesosystem*: The Mesosystem encompasses the interactions between the child's microsystems, such as interactions between the child's parents and teachers or school peers and siblings. The Mesosystem is where a person's microsystems do not function independently but are interconnected and assert influence upon one another (Guy-Evans, 2023).

3. *The Exosystem*: The Exosystem incorporates other formal and informal social structures, which do not contain the child but indirectly influence them as these social structures affect one of the microsystems. Examples of exosystems include the neighborhood, parents' workplaces, parents' friends, and the mass media. These are environments in which the child is not involved and are external to their experience but affect them anyway (Guy-Evans, 2023).

4. *The Macrosystem*: The Macrosystem is a component of Bronfenbrenner's ecological systems theory that focuses on how cultural elements, such as socioeconomic status, wealth, poverty, and ethnicity, affect a child's development. Thus, the culture that individuals are immersed within may influence their beliefs and perceptions about events that transpire in life. The Macrosystem differs from the previous ecosystems as it does not refer to the specific environments of one developing child but the already established society and culture in which the child is developing (Guy-Evans, 2023).

5. *The Chronosystem*: This system consists of all the environmental changes that occur over the lifetime that influence development, including major life transitions and historical events. These can include normal life transitions, such as starting school, and non-normative life transitions, such

as parents getting divorced or moving to a new house (Guy-Evans, 2023).

Societal-Level Factors

"Crenshaw (1994) argues that it is inadequate to understand intimate partner violence against women of color solely based on one dimension, such as gender; rather, it is imperative to analyze the intersection of these dimensions (race and gender are featured in her essay) and how they shape the structural and political aspects of violence against women of color (Cramer & Plummer, 2009)." The four critical systemic inequities may allow intimate partner violence to thrive:

1. Rigid and imbalanced gender expectations and norms
2. Poor-quality education and low education attainment
3. Economic hardship and poverty
4. Lack of inequitable response to intimate partner violence by law enforcement and the criminal justice system (Grady et al., 2019)

Sexual Orientation

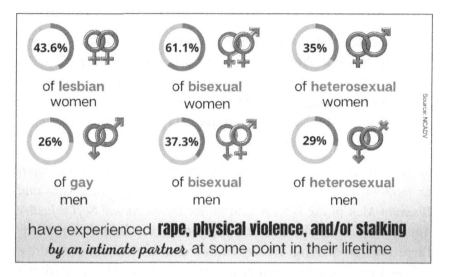

Source: NCADV

Figure 17. Sexual orientation infographic percentage statistics depict lesbian women, bisexual women, heterosexual women, gay men, bisexual men, and heterosexual men experiencing rape, physical violence, and stalking by an intimate partner at some point in their lifetime. Source: (Domestic Violence Services Network, Inc. (DVSN), 2023)

Lesbian, gay, bisexual, and transgender (LGBT) college students experience disproportionate rates of intimate partner violence compared with their heterosexual and cisgender counterparts (Whitfield et al., 2018). We cannot overlook intimate partner violence among Black gay and bisexual men (BGBM) in the United States.

> *"Lovelace explains further, 'There are gender issues at play, for both Black women and Black men, and at the intersection of LGBT communities, trans communities, and gender non-conforming individuals who are Black. There are very specific circumstances and experiences that each of those genders have as Black people and across other identities as* well. There are multiple identities that people live in, and the idea that any service

that only serves one piece of that identity doesn't really fully see us (Kippert, 2023)."

"By centering the intersectional needs of BGBM and the role that racism, homophobia, and heteronormativeness have played in shaping intimate partner violence-related services, this article challenges the intimate partner violence field to advance a social justice orientation to address the unmet needs of BGBM who experience intimate partner violence (Brooks et al., 2020)."

The article, *Gaps in Science and Evidence-Based Interventions to Respond to Intimate Partner Violence Among Black Gay and Bisexual Men in the U.S.: A Call for an Intersectional Social Justice Approach,* admonishes "More specifically for BGBM, currently there are no existing evidenced-based interventions to address IPV and the interconnected health disparities that IPV exacerbates and/or produces. To advance the field and become more inclusive, we must:

- Move away from a color-blind heteronormative framework and adopt an Intersectional Social Justice approach that addresses racism, homophobia, and heteronormativity to effectively meet the IPV needs of BGBM.

- Systematically collect qualitative data on the IPV needs of BGBM and other sexual and gender minorities to understand the unique social and cultural contexts in which IPV is occurring.

- Increase funding and opportunities for integrating IPV into substance use, mental health, and HIV prevention and treatment programs.

- Create culturally responsive programs and interventions along with increasing the capacity of providers to serve this key population.

- Create community-level campaigns and mobilization efforts to address the interconnections of IPV and other health disparities.

- Intentionally create policies that address the unique needs of this subgroup (Brooks et al., 2020)."

"Black gay and bisexual men (BGBM) IPV Victims: Sheldon Timothy Herrington Jr., a University of Mississippi graduate, was arrested in August 2022 for the July 2022 murder of Jimmie "Jay" Lee, a 20-year-old gay, Black student known for performing in drag, whom he had been in a sexual relationship with (Niemeyer, 2022). A Black man burned his gay lover's corpse to hide their relationship (Padgett, 2022)."

Healthcare System

In the healthcare system, explicit and implicit provider bias makes African Americans less likely than Caucasians to receive medical attention (Grady et al., 2019). "One study found that among young Latino adults, racial/ethnic discrimination was a risk factor for self-reported bidirectional IPV perpetration and that the effect of discrimination on bidirectional IPV perpetration was stronger for immigrants than for U.S.-born Latinos (Maldonado et al., 2020)." Black lesbians intersecting identities "may simultaneously experience racism, classism, homophobia, and discrimination based on her perceived mental disability as she navigates her daily life, including how she contends with IPV and attempts to access services and systems (Rice et al., 2020). "

"Critical race theory (Donovan & West, 2015) and Black feminisms in social work (Bent-Goodley, 2004, 2005) have provided a powerful vocabulary with which to understand and counter the inequalities and barriers experienced by Black women in leaving abusive relationships – for example, the response of child welfare services and the criminal justice system to Black women in US and European contexts (Hulley et al., 2022)."

"The synthesis found that these women faced additional barriers because of institutional racism, immigration laws, culture and religion, and issues of cultural competence, and lack of diversity within frontline services. Such barriers, from a range of formal and informal resources, services, and other mechanisms of support, served to exacerbate feelings of fear, threat, isolation and powerlessness. The barriers were also further weaponized by perpetrators to extend their reign of terror and control. As a result, women were caught in a double-bind – stay in an abusive relationship or face further threats and consequences if they attempted to leave. Whilst our search criteria focused on barriers to help-seeking, many of the papers included in our synthesis also explored facilitators to help-seeking, which are included in our findings and overwhelmingly relate to informal support from females.
(Hulley et al., 2022)"

Law Enforcement

Law enforcement plays a strong role in intimate partner violence as a buffer to deter escalation, help victims escape safely, and punish the perpetrators. Factors like offender reprisal, past experiences with police, and community-reinforced perceptions of law enforcement may influence women's police engagement in intimate partner violence (Holliday et al., 2019). "Mandatory reporting laws can affect help-seeking by requiring some sources of support to report survivors to formal systems (Lippy et al., 2019)." Reasons for non-report of abuse, specifically among Black women, include institutional racism, self-blame, and socio-cultural norms that mandate protecting same-race perpetrators from retribution (e.g., incarceration), non-disclosure of private matters, and stereotypical strength (Holliday et al., 2019).

African-American women survivors of intimate partner violence disproportionately experience homicide due partly to the racism and racial discrimination they experience in the process of seeking help (Waller et al., 2022). Research has shown that Black women report more severe injuries and mental health consequences, are less likely to report intimate partner violence, and receive fewer services related to victimization than White women (Kelly et al., 2020). "Structural influences on police reporting included police discriminatory police misconduct, perceived lack of concern for citizens, power disparities, fear of harm from police, and IPV/SV-related minimization and victim-blaming (Decker et al., 2019)."

As an African American woman, my first 911 emergency service call seeking police assistance with intimate partner violence was demoralized. My assertions of abuse were minimized on the initial incident report (actual assault vs. perceived harassment documented by the officer). No wonder there is historical mistrust of the justice system. After this interaction with the police, I received more empathy from the victim services division, and the assistant district attorney who interviewed me demonstrated empathy and concern. During the petition for a restraining order, the interviewer who transcribed my statement was attentive. After I returned to the police station to amend the initial report, officers were armed with an arrest warrant. When the officers arrived at my residence, they shielded me from harm as I unlocked the door for them to enter and took my abuser into custody.

"So, while slavery in its most heinous form was banned 156 years ago, the Jim Crow era and the systematic oppression

that it fostered has yet to be removed from the fabric of the United States. From this realization, Dr. Joy DeGruy (2017) created the concept of post-traumatic slave syndrome (PTSS) to address the multigenerational transmission of trauma for Black Americans trying to survive in a country that never intended for them to do so. In this article, we focus on the term the first author has coined, toxic Black femininity, which is the internalized and dominant message that, as a Black woman, one must be rigidly strong, hypersexual, and primary caregiver to all, before acknowledging or taking care of one's own needs and desires. The components of PTSS that contribute to toxic Black femininity also contribute to the barriers Black women face when experiencing IPV (Kelly et al., 2020)."

The Women of Color Network's domestic violence fact sheet was certainly accurate on some commonalities "which may account for the under-reporting of DV by women of color and a failure to seek appropriate help services:

- A strong personal identification based on familial structure/ hierarchy, patriarchal elements, and cultural identity (e.g., role as wife, mother, and homemaker).
- Religious beliefs that reinforce the woman's victimization and legitimize the abuser's behavior.
- Fear of isolation and alienation.
- A strong loyalty to both immediate and extended family and to race and culture (the "yoke of silence").
- Guarded trust and reluctance to discuss "private matters."
- Fear of rejection from family, friends, congregation, and community.
- Individual needs often defer to family unity and strength.

- Distrust of law enforcement (fear of subjecting themselves and loved ones to a criminal and civil justice system they see as sexist and/or racially and culturally biased).

- Skepticism and distrust that shelter and intervention services are not culturally or linguistically competent.

- For immigrant and undocumented women, in particular, there is a fear or threat of deportation or separation from children (Women of Color Network, n.d.)."

"Despite the criminal legal system's purported goal of securing justice for crime victims, survivors of domestic violence and trafficking are instead often arrested, prosecuted, and imprisoned," said Liz Komar, Sentencing Reform Counsel at The Sentencing Project, and a co-author of Sentencing Reform for Criminalized Survivors. "Confronting the many drivers of criminalization is essential for justice. A fair and proportional criminal legal system should account for the multitude of factors that led to an offense, including abuse (Bishop, 2023)."

Disabilities affect more than one in four women and one in five men in the United States and have been associated with a greater risk of experiencing violence compared to people without a disability (Sexual Violence and Intimate Partner Violence among People with Disabilities |Violence Prevention|Injury Center|CDC, 2021). "Current research suggests that women with disabilities are at a significantly higher risk of experiencing violence throughout their lifetime (Cartrine Anyango et al., 2023)."

A literature review by Smith (2008) explained the higher rates of intimate partner violence among women with disabilities. The authors describe their contention:

For example, those with physical disabilities may need help with replacing the battery on a wheelchair, toilet operations, or dressing, among other intimate actions. This kind of dependence may lead to perpetrators taking advantage of the women's vulnerability for instance, demanding a kiss before assisting, withholding medication, and removing the battery from the wheelchair are some examples of disability-related abuse experienced by women with disabilities (Cartrine Anyango et al., 2023).

"Linear explanations for why some abused persons of color with disabilities may be reluctant to call the police or why some people with disabilities refrain from calling domestic violence hotlines fail to examine how social, economic, political, and cultural contexts influence the construction of multiple identities/selves (Cramer & Plummer, 2009)."

"Women with disabilities have been reported to experience multiple forms of violence (psychological, physical, and sexual) for more extended periods than women without disabilities (Cartrine Anyango et al., 2023)."

"Chenoweth (1996) discusses the marginalization, exclusion, and overall vulnerability of disabled women. The author addresses these issues by concentrating on the concepts of silence and paradoxes surrounding them. Silence is based on the societal denial and control of the disabled population. These paradoxes include overprotection, segregation, trained compliance, and simultaneous asexual and promiscuous expectations of disabled women (Cramer & Plummer, 2009)."

Future research should clarify and extend our understanding of racial/ethnic differences in police reporting for intimate partner violence. This work will require quantifying the social and structural influences identified through qualitative research yet unmeasured in the National Crime Victimization Survey (NCVS) (Holliday et al., 2019). As a member of a devalued racial identity, some women of color, particularly African-American women, may fear that calling the police will subject their partners to racist treatment [and the danger of police brutality] by the criminal justice system as well as confirm racist stereotypes of Black people as violent (Sokoloff & Dupont, 2005).

I am quite emotional thinking about a vulnerable segment of the population, people with disabilities, becoming victims of intimate partner violence and failing to consider them falling prey to such a repulsive crime. The research for this book has truly been a revelation for me. If I have an innate inability to conceptualize the disabled class of our population as victims of intimate partner violence, what about other spheres of society, including law enforcement or medical professionals during office visits?

Domestic Violence Shelters

When people in positions of power hold oppressive beliefs, their beliefs shape and become solidified in our legal system, government, schools, and even in social service agencies, making it harder for survivors to seek support to heal, receive justice, and ultimately live lives free from violence and oppression (The Correlation of Domestic Violence & Systemic Oppression, 2020).

As an individual displaced (housing insecurity) due to intimate partner violence, I did experience an economic impact in my life. At the same time, my human resource governmental assistance benefit (social service agency) was dramatically cut while inside the Department of Homeless Services (DHS) transitional women shelter. According to Colsaria Henderson, Executive Director of Community Overcoming Relationship Abuse (CORA) in San Mateo, California, the systems put in place to help survivors were not created with Black people's needs in mind and have been working toward more inclusionary services (Kippert, 2020). It has been a struggle, she says,

---

"There are higher rates of Black and brown survivors being labeled as aggressive and being exited from shelter as a result. There's a different idea that happens when someone with brown skin gets upset than someone with white."
(Kippert, 2023)

The racial justice lens is a solution to dismantle systemic racism and intersectionality of intimate partner violence because "women of color, who experience domestic violence at high rates, continue to encounter barriers when trying to access supportive services (Why Is It Important to Bring a Racial Justice Framework to Our Efforts to End Domestic Violence?, 2018)."

What is racial justice, and why is there an interconnectivity between political, social, and economic forces?

"Racial justice is the systematic fair treatment of people of all races, resulting in equitable opportunities and outcomes for all. Racial justice initiatives address structural and systemic changes to ensure equal access to opportunities, eliminate disparities, and advance racial equity—thus ensuring that all people, regardless of their race, can prosper and reach their full potential. Racial justice and equity are not achieved by the mere absence of racial discrimination or the perceived absence of harmful racial bias, but rather through deliberate action to dismantle problematic and build positively transformational systems – action must be carried through with the conviction, commitment, and dedication of advocates (Racial Justice, n.d.)."

Personal Testimony of Intimate Partner Violence

Figure 18. A graphic depiction of the anguish and fear of an intimate partner violence victim when her abuser is about to attack her physically.
Source: Freepik.com

I N THIS portion of the book, I provide my candid, first-hand account of intimate partner violence that I have experienced since childhood. I share the emotional turmoil and challenges I faced as a victim of intimate partner violence, which can be difficult for those who have not experienced it to comprehend fully, hence providing valuable insights into the complex dynamics of this type of trauma. During my childrearing years and as a young adult, I did not receive sit-down discussions on toxic or healthy relationships from, as Bronfenbrenner's Ecological System Theory states, my microsystem (e.g., family, peers, school/work, neighborhood, church, health services) or socialization (Guy-Evans, 2023). I must take responsibility for my failure to take the initiative to read books on toxic or healthy relationships to safeguard myself and other support network members against individuals who may cause potential harm. I have encountered various vicissitudes of life; the one that affected me the most was intimate partner violence.

I hope that my vulnerability and honest descriptive outline in this book will help individuals and family members recognize the warning signs of intimate partner violence early, and victims or survivors of this horrid crime become enlightened to know they can also soar above the circumstances and survive the trauma from victim to victor.

School-Aged Exposure to IPV

Children are often considered the hidden victims in families where domestic violence occurs, and studies have estimated that 3.3 – 10 million children witness domestic violence yearly (Domestic Violence Information, n.d.). My first exposure to domestic violence happened in junior high or high school when I watched my biological mother become physically abused by her then-husband. To shield her children, my mother sent us to our bedrooms so we would avoid seeing the abuse she suffered. My mother sent my siblings and me to our late maternal grandmother's apartment, and we never returned to our residence. Thankfully, my mother acquired enough courage to leave this relationship and move on, eventually becoming divorced.

My First Experience with Intimate Partner Violence-My Ex-Husband, John

In the mid-1980s, while working at a financial institution in midtown New York, I met a handsome young man also employed there. John was an inspiring minister at a multi-ethnic, multi-generational, faith-believing church in Brooklyn, New York. On the contrary, I was no longer actively involved in church after getting saved at 15 years old, baptized, and filled with the Holy Spirit. John eventually proposed marriage within a couple of months of dating.

The importance of adhering to Godly counsel and your spiritual covering was revealed to me regarding marriage. Proverb 11:14 (NKJV) states, "Where there is no counsel, the people fall; But in the multitude of counselors there is safety." 1 Corinthians 10:23 (AMPC) states, "All things are lawful [that is, morally legitimate, permissible], but not all things are beneficial or advantageous. All things are lawful, but not all things are constructive [to character] and edifying [to spiritual life]."

While riding the escalator at work, I heard in my spirit, "no" regarding marriage. My ex-husband, John and I attended the same church and went to the pastor's study to request that he marry us. Our pastor told us to wait and not marry, but we did against his counsel, which was a huge mistake. Warning truly comes before destruction. Psalm 103:13 (AMP) says, "Just as a father loves his children, So the LORD loves those who fear and worship Him [with awe-filled respect and deepest reverence]."

John and I intermittently resided at a saint's home with her children. I purchased a sharp-looking Italian silk suit for his birthday and prepared a cake for the celebration. Instead of staying with me for the occasion, he left. I started to cry uncontrollably due to the continual hurt I endured by this man. The person I stayed with, like a mother to me, called my biological mother due to my emotional state and inability to stop crying. Nothing compares to the genuine consolation of a mother's love, a warm embrace, and comfort.

I recall Thanksgiving Day, during our first year of marriage; we delivered a meal to my mother's home. I held the dish in my hand, walked to the building door, turned to my left, and John punched me in my back. He assumed I was looking for an ex-boyfriend, although that was false.

I mentioned the situation to a brother-in-law, David, who had been interested in me for quite some time, but I did not give in to his cues. David escorted me to the car to bid farewell and looked at John. I motioned to David (who may have had a weapon) not to harm my then-husband. This scenario sets the stage for non-intimate partner violence, family feuds, and bloodbaths.

I found a picture of a female church member inside John's clothes closet. When he returned home, I confronted John about the item and wrongfully (without thinking) slapped him in the face. Then, I was punched in the mouth and started bleeding. John tried to console me in the restroom by wiping my lips, but I rejected the concern. I was tired of being neglected by John, who did not help me around the home but always seemed to want to be at church.

Having a nice figure at the time (in my 20s), I adorned myself with a tight-fitting dress one night. John came home, saw it on, and refused to let me wear the outfit outside.

I told him, "Since you do not want me, I will find someone who does."

John removed my attire, responded, "I see what you want, and I will give you what you are looking for," and proceeded to engage in marital rape.

According to the United States Department of Justice website, sexual assault means any nonconsensual sexual act proscribed by Federal, tribal, or State law, including when the victim cannot consent. Later that day, I placed a hammer underneath my pillow as protection against my then-husband but decided not to use it.

John and I separated often during the marriage. He insisted on having his lover remain inside our apartment against my objection. The woman stayed with him in the living room while I remained in the bedroom.

One day, after commuting from work at the Brooklyn District Attorney's Office, I saw an ex-boyfriend, Jerome, whom I had not seen in a while. We conversed, and then emotions kicked in. Bam, a hickey appeared on my neck (just from kissing). I went home, John saw the hickey, and he punched me. I responded with a rebuttal slap; he was surprised. At the time, his brother was in our residence and confronted and reprimanded John for assaulting me, considering he had already disrespected me by having another woman residing in our marital home.

I eventually moved out of the apartment, and Jerome picked me up to escort me to my mother's residence. John came downstairs while I walked to the vehicle and told Jerome to "take care of his wife." I had a divorce attorney draw up papers due to his infidelity, yet John did not sign the document. After my hickey incident, his signature was inscribed on the divorce paperwork, finalizing the uncontested dissolution of our marriage.

John and I did not listen to the advice of our pastor, and our union lasted less than two years. We were separated most of that time. 2 Corinthians 13:1b (AMP) states, "...Every fact shall be sustained and confirmed by the testimony of two or three witnesses." My ex-husband, John, and I participated with other couples in a marriage tag-team sermon delivery at our local church, and our assigned topic was *Wait*. John preached and tagged me, and I did the teaching portion of the message. This scenario of doing a sermon on *Wait* was absurd as we did not abide by this principle when we married against spiritual guidance and advice from our pastor. Decades in the making, John said the Holy Spirit had placed in his spirit to apologize to me. There was a heart-to-heart conversation, and forgiveness acquiesced; thereinafter, we became friends.

Frequently, we place ourselves in precarious situations, ignoring innate survival instincts and rational decision-making, leading to self-inflicted wounds. The disparaging circumstances are perhaps due to a lack of integrity, non-compliant with business ethics and moral principles, disobedience, not learning from prior lousy experiences or observing someone else's, which is the best teacher, non-conformity or unwillingness to listen to wise counsel, stepping outside the perfect will of God, no growth-mindset just a know-it-all attitude, disregarding intuition or common sense, and failure to read red flags or warning signs. Experience, one often hears, is the best teacher, but that is true only if one learns from it (Bolman & Deal, 2021, p. 13).

Intimate Partner Violence Experience-Ex-boyfriend, Charles

In the 1990s, while residing in Texas, I began dating Charles, whom I cared deeply about, but this person hindered my walk with Jesus Christ. I was a single, self-sufficient, African-American young woman employed at a large oil company, earning an excellent salary, and actively involved in church. There is a difference between being alone and lonely; I was far from either, although my life lacked a male partner. I succumbed to a relative's proclamation that "God does not want you to be alone." Psalm 1:1 (AMPC) declares, "Blessed (happy, fortunate, prosperous, and enviable) is the man who walks and lives not in the counsel of the ungodly [following their advice, their plans and purposes], nor stands [submissive and inactive] in the path where sinners walk, nor sits down [to relax and rest] where the scornful [and the mockers] gather."

When I first met him, my handsome, light-skinned African-American Charles had a Holy Bible in his vehicle's windshield and eventually showed me his minister's license. Charles cooked delicious meals for me and transported me to and from work in his Lincoln Town Car. Charles eventually became possessive and sexually abusive, displeased with me speaking my mind, and physically threatened me by choking me in the car. Charles and I participated in ways not consistent with a holy lifestyle as a born-again believer should adhere to — fornication [Isaiah 35:8; Romans 12:1; 1 Corinthians 6:18, 7:2, 10:8; Galatians 5:19; Colossians 3:5; 1 Thessalonians 4:3].

I was so distraught after committing these acts of sin that I prayed (repented to God) afterward. As I walked to Charles' residence one day, and "...neither be partaker of other men's sins [1 Timothy 5:22 KJV]" came up in my spirit. I stopped in my tracks and proceeded to go in a different direction, but Charles called my name more than once (with a pitiful sound), and I reluctantly went to see him. I eventually broke off the relationship with Charles and provided a farewell letter. I tried to end the relationship nicely with kind words in the letter. One day he asked me to come over and read the document to him, yet in return, Charles attempted to rape me in his apartment. Upon calling on the name of Jesus in the bathroom, Charles uttered a few words after laying his hand on my head (similarly to praying for someone at the altar) and then allowed me to leave his residence. I moved out of the complex to another part of the city to escape Charles.

Charles worked on something in my apartment one day at the request of my mom. I came home, saw him, spoke, and gave Charles the cold shoulder. My failure to interact warmly probably disturbed him because he left my apartment. Afterward, my mom reprimanded me for not being polite to Charles and told me to go after him. I went to his apartment to check on him and was surprised/ shocked that the door was open. I went inside and spoke with him to calm him down. I recall one day, he proposed to me in his car with an engagement ring, but I rejected it.

When he came home, I remember he would park his car in front of my apartment unit. Unfortunately, after moving out of the apartment complex, I saw Charles seated behind the wheel in his vehicle when I visited a sister-in-Christ, a resident there. Charles had a delighted expression and wanted me to get inside the car. I declined because I assumed unwanted intimate contact was something he was pursuing. Charles followed me in his vehicle, and when I crossed the road median, he almost ran me over.

I exclaimed, "The Blood of Jesus," and he left me alone, eventually driving away.

I forewent reporting Charles' harassing action to the police of an assault with a deadly weapon, a car, whether playful or not. The statute states that usage of this instrument may cause an individual significant, substantial bodily harm, injury, or death. I did not consider filing a criminal complaint with local law enforcement and left the vicinity. I had difficulty getting over Charles, as my former pastor's wife told me, "You let him go in your head but not your heart." As Ravi Zacharias said, "Sin will take you farther than you want to go, keep you longer than you want to stay, and cost you more than you want to pay." By the grace of God, I overcame this knot, or entanglement, in my heart toward Charles and was determined to live for Christ.

Intimate Partner Violence Experience-Ex-boyfriend, Maverick

Insanity, they say, is defined as doing the same thing repeatedly and expecting different results. In the early 2000s, I relocated to my birthplace, New York, and eventually became the victim of intimate partner violence through trauma bonding methods and the cycle of abuse.

Women need to follow their intuition. In 2008, I met my abuser, Maverick, while commuting to work on an elevated New York City mass transit train platform. I initially tried to get away from Maverick, even disembarking the train to avoid his pursuit, even though Maverick was a handsome young man with brown sugar skin, a muscular build, and naturally wavy hair. I was saved and filled with the Holy Spirit and endeavored not to get entangled with a man but eventually dated him.

Maverick and I started dating on August 29, 2009. God sends a warning before destruction; I experienced it personally regarding my relationship with this abuser. Job 19:28 (KJV) says, "But ye should say, Why persecute we him, seeing the root of the matter is found in me?" I must take accountability for what happened to me because I ignored frequent red flags?" I did not clearly define personal boundaries in our relationship, enabling the abuser to isolate me from neighbors, friends, and family due to a lack of interaction and isolation.

Background Check

One effective way to break the cycle of abuse is to do a background check on potential partners. Still, it is essential to remember that criminal history is not the only indicator of abusive behavior. I have to be honest. I did a background check on Maverick and discovered that he has a bit of a checkered past. My last abuser, Maverick, has been associated with criminality, admitted to crimes, and has a lengthy rap sheet. It is essential to be aware of these things when making decisions about being with someone, as they can give insight into their past behavior and potential future actions. Being aware of a person's history is critical when entrusting your heart to someone.

Maverick was always very protective of me. He shielded me from potentially dangerous situations [oxymoron-with him being my intimate violence partner abuser], including not introducing me to his friends, especially those who had a criminal background. Maverick ensured my safety and well-being by protecting me from potential harm and danger in case disagreements or threats arose. I'm grateful for his concern for my well-being in this scenario. His thoughtfulness in not introducing me to violent parties was a testament to our "friendship" established at the beginning of the relationship. This aspect is why the dynamic of intimate partner violence is so complicated, complex, or perplexing for a victim. An abuser shows care and consideration (loving behavior), and conversely, the individual can be abusive to you as well.

Maverick, my soulmate, the individual I have an emotional attachment to, and the one I ironically had a unique spiritual connection with, is now nonexistent in my life. Our connection was exceptional, and I could finish his sentences. Although there was a connection, sometimes we get ahead of God's timing to be in a relationship. An individual may have to undergo emotional surgery (removal of past hurts, traumatic experiences, and wounds of the heart), or God may need to work on their character, integrity, etc., for you to have a healthy relationship.

Bishop T.D. Jakes stated years ago, "A half a man and half a woman make half a marriage; a whole woman and a whole man make a whole marriage." Women often take the position of a savior or mother in a relationship and try to fix a man or man-babies. We are not God, and the romantic relationship with a mother-child dynamic is a dysfunctional scenario.

I tried talking with Maverick about attending church. Maverick had a way with words and interacted with people from all walks of life (Jewish community, formerly incarcerated individuals, law enforcement, restaurant patrons). Maverick fasted weekly and prayed daily, faithfully to God while we were together. If he truly surrendered his life to God and became a born-again believer receiving the baptism of His Holy Spirit and power, he could be a fantastic soul winner; appealing to individuals from the streets or criminal mindset would be awesome.

I received a word of prophecy from a Woman of God (whom I had never met or spoken with before) inside the laundromat who proclaimed to me, "God said, whatever you are about to do – do not do it." The warning comes before destruction, and God will not have us ignorant of Satan's devices (2 Corinthians 2:11-13 KJV). I did not adhere to the alarm and allowed Maverick to move into my single-room occupancy premises even though the scriptures enlightened me in Romans 13:14 (KJV), which declares, "But put ye on the Lord Jesus Christ, and make not provision for the flesh, to fulfil the lusts thereof."

Biblical knowledge admonished me about being unequally yoked. I read books on relationships (*Act Like a Lady and Think Like a Man* by Steve Harvey and *If You Want Closure in Your Relationship Start with Your Legs* by Big Boom) and should have implemented the knowledge I received. At my church, there is a saying, "Knowledge is power when applied."

"Knowledge is not power, it is only potential. Applying that knowledge is power. Understanding why and when to apply that knowledge is wisdom!" — Takeda Shingen

Maverick and I eventually shared the same residence; he became psychologically, sexually, and emotionally abusive and extremely jealous. Maverick physically assaulted me from September 2009 to December 9, 2009, and we had just started dating in August 2009. Maverick was leery when I interacted with anyone. Isolation plays a significant role in domestic violence cases alongside other tactics that separate victims from their loved ones (Kupferman & Golden Family Law – the Role of Isolation in Domestic Violence, n.d.).

Maverick and I had 'brain dates' conversing for hours on the telephone. On September 20, 2009, Maverick had me listen to the song by Drake entitled *Best I Ever Had*, which implied how he felt about me. Later that day, Maverick called, saying, "I am in love with you." I replied that I loved him. Then, he asserted, "I love you more." In a whisper on September 21, 2009, Maverick said, "I would like to marry you." As an individual who loves writing, I captured notes from September 7 through 22, 2009, of our telephone conversations:

- He was dreaming about me when he first met me.
- Being his wife is inevitable.
- He loves the woman I am.
- We really connect.
- I am definitely a queen.
- I am "truly a treasure, not just something special."
- I'm what he likes and do it for him in a crazy way.
- Not abusive
- We do not own the other party. Distance ourselves. Give the person breathing room.
- Consciously look at the relationship and always remember you are dealing with a human being with feelings – have compassion.
- Every party is allowed to flow (happen) naturally, which is a benefit.
- He wants us to grow together.
- He could "really appreciate me."
- I am amazed and should always know that.

Maverick had two personalities: the sweet side everyone sees and the narcissistic, manipulative side. My abuser ridiculed how I managed flirtations from men towards me or disrespectful connotations compared to his downplayed female acquaintances' interactions. I confided in him that a male building resident liked me, and he would not allow me to wear anything that revealed my figure, sanctioning me only to sport a loose-fitting lounger.

One day, Maverick arrived home after work and saw I had on a pair of jeans. Consequently, he stripped my clothes down to my undergarments and attempted to drag me out of the room. Maverick's message through this encounter suggested that since I want people to look at me (be appealing/alluring), I should go in this manner just to let male residents see my body exposed. In this psychological coercion scenario, I learned to think twice about wearing jeans or anything that showed my figure, which was problematic considering I am a curvy, full-figured woman.

Abusive partners do not like it when their victim talks back. I received the first punch to my face after speaking words that Maverick was displeased with on the telephone. This incident shocked me. How could he do this to me? Here I am, a citizen of the United States, in my mid-forties, with the right and privilege of freedom of speech, and a boyfriend punches me in the face because he did not like what I said in my own residence. No individual deserves this type of treatment as a human being. This disposition by Maverick displayed aggression, anger issues, lack of control, and conflict resolution skills. The aggressive behavior gets a victim into a submissive position and says her ideas and thoughts are not valued. Maverick may have thought he was my father or parent because he also used a belt on me.

One day, he punched me in the face, and I decided to seek medical attention at a King County Hospital due to the severe pain and swelling. Maverick ironically insisted upon commuting on mass transit with me to the facility to prevent me from pointing the finger at him, and out of genuine concern. It took a while to acquire medical treatment at the hospital due to triaging and insurance financial counseling, so I just left with Maverick in tow. He expressed something about my innocent disposition and appeared to regret physically assaulting me.

One day, Maverick ascertained my blood pressure was elevated because my conversation with him entailed slurred speech, and he knew I was an individual who did not consume alcohol. He immediately instructed me to take some apple cider vinegar, a routine I do to bring the level down. Maverick rushed back from his job or wherever he was to see how I was doing. Maverick pointed out that he did not even visit his ex-girlfriend while she was in the hospital but left work for me. My relationship with Maverick was quite stressful, which led to increases in my blood pressure levels.

I recall commuting with Maverick on the train one day, and a male passenger stepped on my foot without uttering an apology. With his eyes closed, Maverick gave the passenger standing against the door a look. The individual expressed his regret for offending me by stepping on my toes. With his stern face, Maverick had a demeanor that denoted to others not to mess with him.

I received criticism from Maverick, pronouncing that I was not good at anything except computers, which was far from the truth as he eventually found out years later. I was even forbidden to speak with anyone in my building. I was an avid football and basketball fan for years until I met Maverick, who felt my enjoyment of the sport was only for viewing players in their uniforms. I can no longer consider it as enjoyable as before due to the brainwashing and belittlement I received during my time with him.

An identity crisis had arisen in my life due to Maverick's ill-conceived perception that I did not know how to manage myself when interacting with others. Maverick frequently compared how I dealt with men flirting with me against females he knew and instructed me how to behave. Maverick's insistence on my adherence to his narrow conception of femininity led me to live a lie. Imposter syndrome is defined as a personality pattern characterized by pathological lying, which fabricates an identity or a series of identities to gain recognition and status (APA Dictionary of Psychology, n.d.). The National Library of Medicine states, "Imposter syndrome is a behavioral health phenomenon described as self-doubt of intellect, skills, or accomplishments among high-achieving individuals (Anderson & Kiehl, 2014)."

Maverick restricted my movement by having me use a laptop a girlfriend purchased for his entrepreneurial business (so he claimed), although the login was her name. I was scheduled to start a free Internet and Computing Core Certification course with male students. Maverick did not want me to attend my first day of class, pretending to desire to spend the day with me. He eventually went to work, and I missed an incredible opportunity to better myself.

Maverick's obsession with keeping tabs on me was over the top, and I had to take my cell phone to the bathroom each visit, or he would think I was conversing with men. One day, when we were not officially dating, I went to a real estate office to acquire an apartment. He stayed on the phone and would not release the call, and while walking away, he talked until I reached my destination and still wanted to remain on the line.

I find the situation outlandish because Maverick constantly conversed with ex-girlfriends and female acquaintances and even stated that he would be there if they needed him. Due to my upbringing and Christian belief, I have embedded grace, forgiveness, a smiling face, an approachable demeanor, love for others, and kindness towards humanity. Maverick had straightforwardness, sometimes an unapproachable cold demeanor, a street mindset, and was a smooth talker.

Maverick called me to meet around 42nd Street to go to the movies together. It was late in the afternoon. After waiting for this date for hours, my feet started to bother me due to the shoes I wore that day. Maverick declined my request for a Popeye's Chicken meal and insisted I make dinner late in the evening instead. I was walking slower due to not feeling well, and Maverick hastened to the residence ahead of me. The following day, karma indeed appeared because he awoke with a cold.

In November 2009, Maverick and I had another argument over the telephone on his birthday. Maverick indicated upon returning to the residence that he would punch me in the face, which was a threat he decreed. I left and went to stay at my oldest sibling's place in another state for a while. Maverick made numerous calls at my sibling's residence to convince me to return home. My abuser returned to our residence (actually mine) and noticed I had left. He lost his composure [as a man with a threatening demeanor, but I have seen him contrariwise-gentle caring side] against a vehicle by crying but did not want anyone to see him.

I left Maverick on his birthday, and an intimate partner violence incident happened days later. After my foolish return to my residence, Maverick verbally abused and threatened me, stating I could die. I had no idea what might happen to me, but I knew he could kill me with his violent nature. Although it may seem like a nonsensical threat, after all, how could he hurt me, a person who's been kind to him and assisted with his business and abode, I knew the possibility was there.

Maverick placed a long knife on the floor beside his side of the bed. Maverick kept this deadly instrument as a preventive protection against burglars, posing great harm to any victim. Maverick stated he knew where to locate me. He further asserted, "This is how people get killed, playing with people's hearts." I saw a furious look in Maverick's eyes and felt he could do anything.

On December 9, 2009, a few days after reconciling, I gave Maverick a three-week deadline to save funds, vacate my premises, and acquire his own apartment. He abruptly ended the call. Maverick called me again to converse while I was cooking and preparing to eat, but I refused to answer. At approximately 7:35 p.m. that evening, Maverick arrived home to question why I refused to answer his call for an hour. After explaining why, he became highly enraged and punched my face and head.

After months of dealing with the abuse, I stated, "Oh, we're going there again?"

Maverick responded, "Yes."

I tried fighting this burly man and pleaded with Maverick, "Don't hit me." I unlocked the door, ran out of the unit, and yelled in the hallway for any neighbor who could hear me to call 911.

A male neighbor on my landing (who desired a romantic relationship with me, and Maverick thought we were messing around) opened the door to assess what was happening with his lady guest present. Maverick used his fist to punch me in the face and head repeatedly in front of him. After such a barrage of punches, openly embarrassing me in front of the resident of my building, Maverick returned to the apartment, retrieved his coat, and left the premises.

After the incident, I returned to my apartment. I contacted 911 to report the abuse that led to assault charges against Maverick. While on the call with the 911 operator, Maverick returned then fled the scene. The two officers who responded to my call asserted that I was the only individual who called 911, although one of my neighbors witnessed the assault. I filed an incident report with the police department regarding the attack, but the officer listed the occurrence as harassment, not assault.

Maverick had the potential to access firearms because of his affiliation with gang members or individuals who were involved in criminal activities. He refused to introduce me to these friends because he feared they were the type of people that would go through me to get to him if they could not get directly to him. I contacted my best friend to see if I could stay at her home because I was highly fearful for my continued safety and life and was seeking immediate relief. Family members and friends arrived at my residence in several vehicles, concerned about my well-being, and then transported me to a safe place to reside.

I returned to my residence with uniformed police officers possessing Maverick's arrest warrant. The officers requested that I open the door and step aside. As I unlocked the door to my modest living quarters, Maverick greeted me with a smile. It was as if he expected me to return to the unhealthy situation I had recently left. However, to my surprise, the police arrived and asked me to step aside for my safety. They quickly apprehended my former partner without any resistance to arrest.

While being escorted in handcuffs to the police cruiser, Maverick cried out, "Do not do this to me," and that he loved me.

As my abuser sat inside the police cruiser, I couldn't help but notice Maverick's gaze on me. It may appear to be a look of deep concern or sadness, one that conveys a sense of melancholy and poignancy.

A Kings County Family Justice Center representative was enraged that the police officers responding to my 911 call wrote the complaint as harassment instead of physical assault. The other insult was that, as a person of color, my bruising did not appear immediately; hence, the officer wrote my complaint as harassment. The victim services unit representative took photos of the bruises on my face, instructed me to amend the police report at the precinct, took me to a district attorney in the bureau, offered domestic violence shelter information, and provided a referral. The representative stated that police officers do not like taking the day off to appear in court, causing them to lose their regular earnings. I returned to the police precinct to amend my initial incident report by law enforcement.

One of my cousins came to the police precinct concerned about me. He informed me to stay away from unsaved men. While dating Maverick, I did a New York State Department of Corrections inmate search, and it confirmed his criminal record of drug dealing, attempted robbery, robbery, and assault. The State proceeded to oversee the case with my victim's statement documentation, although I was not keen on doing it. The district attorney interviewing me regarding my assault case informed me of Maverick's lengthy criminal record and the necessity to proceed. Although warranted, it bothered me that Maverick was imprisoned. Maverick wasn't just another Black man behind bars (incarcerated), but this one was an individual I loved.

"A prosecutorial No-Drop Policy in domestic abuse cases indicates that a victim does not have the power to withdraw the complaint once the charges are filed. Instead, the district attorney has the sole freedom to pursue a case, even if the victim is no longer on board (Re-Traumatizing Domestic Violence Victims | Psychology Today, n.d.)."

The photo taken of my injuries at the Victim Services Unit showed the physical, psychological, and emotional trauma I endured.

Physical abuse: I had a black eye. Bruising was a visual and highly embarrassing sign of intimate partner violence.

Psychological: The person I loved and adored punched me with his fist as though fighting with a man. I received chastisement from family and a friend for allowing this to occur on the day of the incident. While conducting academic research for human services in the spring of 2021, scholarly papers demonstrated the appropriate way a support network should have handled the situation, with what a survivor needs after trauma. Trauma-informed services from a therapist or psychiatrist are essential after an intimate partner violence incident, and I acquired them.

Emotional: My love hurt me to this depth, although I have tried solely to help him. The ridicule received from individuals in my support network, and the appearance of indifference or lack of empathy by a close relative regarding the traumatic event I endured was disheartening. Shame and my being a private person allowed the abuser to repeatedly treat me repugnantly for months, as I did not reveal the intimate partner violence to my support network and large family.

* * * *

While at the location of the incident, two of my older male cousins arrived by car to check on my well-being and observed my black eye. Naturally, there was concern from my family members and resentment towards the person who did this to my face, knowing my character as someone who does not bother anyone and is always willing to help others.

My family was concerned for my safety in New York following the intimate partner violence due to Maverick's incarceration, criminal background, and potential retaliation from those with whom he was acquainted. My sister presumed departing New York was a better solution for me; hence, I stayed in another state nearby.

After observing my mental state as void of life, my eldest sister presented me with my evangelist bio newsletter (created years prior while I was a Texas resident) as a gentle reminder of who I am. My eldest sister's interventions in my psychological state finally relieved a distraught mindset with outings and the display of empathy. My confidant, friend, and protector (ironically enough, from individuals who would harm me) was no longer part of my life. I was very detached and held limited conversations or interactions with my sister, with whom I resided. I was at a loss without him, even though Maverick abused me emotionally, physically, psychologically, and sexually. Maverick taught me many things about men and how to handle coworkers who mistreated me because I did not establish boundaries or take a stand. Maverick had to attend a court-mandated anger management program. This behavioral remediation had a drawback as my abuser obtained a physician's note furnishing an excuse to circumvent crucial session(s) to deal with or tackle issues that provoke violent tenacities.

Maverick was charged and convicted of third-degree assault, and I received a seven-year order of protection from the Kings County Criminal Court. The New York State Penal Law Section §120.05 Assault in the second degree would have been appropriate, considering I received numerous punches to my face from my abuser, as it states, "With intent to cause serious physical injury to another person (Assault in the Second Degree, 2021)." Maverick's public defender worked out a plea deal.

According to the journal article entitled *I'm Not A Victim, She's An Abuser: Masculinity, Victimization, and Protection Orders,* "Three themes related to gender and victimization emerged from the men's narratives:

1. First, the men's descriptions of the violence they had experienced focused on their power and control over their intimate partner.

2. Second, the men described their active resistance to the abuse but were careful to note that their actions were not 'abusive' and that they were not the 'abusers.'"

3. Finally, although most of the men described both verbal and physical abuse, most did not express a fear of their partner (Durfee, 2011).

My Barriers to Leaving

Ungodly soul ties: "The mind replays what the heart cannot delete." I tried to get over Maverick but was unsuccessful. Even though Maverick perpetrated numerous blatant, despicable acts of intimate partner violence, I could not rid the memory of him from my mind and heart. The inability to cut ties with someone who destroys you or your life is a complexity of intimate partner violence. Going through this world in a relationship with other people inevitably creates connections in our inner being called soul ties ("Breaking Toxic Soul Ties: Healing from Unhealthy and Controlling Relationships," n.d.).

The most compelling argument by the author Tom Brown is "if the relationships become abusive or manipulative, or cause rejection, they create a toxic brokenness within our soul that we carry with us, even long after the relationship ends. If these toxic inner soul ties are not severed, we will experience failure, fractured relationships, and even health problems."

One of the reasons so many individuals have difficulty ending intimate romantic relationships is that they unknowingly become one flesh after sexual intercourse. 1 Corinthians 6:16 (NLT) expounds this verse: "And don't you realize that if a man joins himself to a prostitute, he becomes one body with her? For the Scriptures say, 'The two are united into one.'" 1 Corinthians 6:16-20 The Message (MSG) Bible defines this passage in greater detail.

"There's more to sex than mere skin on skin. Sex is as much spiritual mystery as physical fact. As written in Scripture, "The two become one." Since we want to become spiritually one with the Master, we must not pursue the kind of sex that avoids commitment and intimacy, leaving us more lonely than ever—the kind of sex that can never "become one." There is a sense in which sexual sins are different from all others. In sexual sin we violate the sacredness of our own bodies, these bodies that were made for God-given and God-modeled love, for "becoming one" with another. Or didn't you realize that your body is a sacred place, the place of the Holy Spirit? Don't you see that you can't live however you please, squandering what God paid such a high price for? The physical part of you is not some piece of property belonging to the spiritual part of

you. God owns the whole works. So let people see God in and through your body."

Genesis Chapter 34 tells the story of Dinah, the daughter of Jacob and Leah, raped by Shechem, who loved and was attracted to her. Genesis 34:3 (AKJV) expounds about Shechem's reaction after the defilement: "And his soul clave unto Dinah the daughter of Jacob, and he loved the damsel, and spake kindly unto the damsel." The terminology of soul ties is not stated explicitly in scripture, but there are instances where it occurred.

Housing Insecurity

After escaping an intimate partner violence incident in December 2009, I went from one traumatic ordeal to another. My experience with homelessness included a domestic violence shelter, overnight stay at BronxWorks' Housing Works' 24-hour drop-in center for homeless adults, intake homeless shelter, transitional shelter, supportive housing, a studio apartment at an extended stay hotel, and couch-surfing family or friend's residences across four states.

I was classified as chronically homeless because I was in the New York City Department of Homeless Services for over two years. While staying at a New York City Department of Homeless shelter intake facility in 2010, the food looked like something served to inmates in jail or prison. Food quality was an issue as I saw expired dates on food given for resident consumption. Fights are common in the shelter system; several residents threatened me, and one fought with me.

The conditions of these intake facilities at this time were horrible as well. All residents at the intake facility received limited sanitary products and toiletries. If an individual missed the 10 p.m. curfew (no matter the reason), their bed was reassigned to another person.

Homeless shelter residents had to wait to see if they could remain at the facility because beds were on a first-come, first-serve basis after the 10 p.m. curfew.

I had worked for years, had good jobs (with salary) and nice apartments, and never stayed in a shelter. I asked a relative for two dollars to get some soap for personal hygiene and was informed the money she had was lunch money. It was hurtful that I only requested two dollars for body wash, and knowing I resided in a shelter, my relatives refused to help me. Here is the irony: I helped my relative numerous times financially, and she never gave me back the money.

Re-victimization and entanglement-Maverick

During a reconciliation period, while I resided at a women's transitional shelter, Maverick revictimized me. One day, while walking in Harlem, I heard someone shout out my name, and it turned out to be Maverick, whom I still loved and missed after years of separation. He beckoned me to come over. Maverick, who was on probation due to my criminal case against him, humbly requested to speak with me. While apologizing to me, I fell into his arms on the street and started to weep. Maverick looked up to the sky and later told me he prayed to God about me. The lyrics from R&B artist Alicia Keys, "If I Ain't Got You," which I often sang, conveyed my mindset about Maverick:

"Some people want it all But I don't want nothing at all If it ain't you, baby If I ain't got you, baby Some people want diamond rings Some just want everything But everything means nothing If I ain't got you, yeah."

One day, I saw weird-looking bugs on the wall next to the shower at a transitional women's shelter facility. I called Maverick because I was disgusted, and he welcomed me to his residence in a men's scattered site apartment. At that time, Maverick was diagnosed with a severe heart condition. I researched and acquired a cardiologist at New York Presbyterian Hospital who performed a procedure that saved his life.

Once, during this reconciliation period, Maverick locked me out of his residence due to his unfounded jealousy because I had a conversation with a male staff member at the medical office. I wandered the streets for hours without funds or a MetroCard to commute anywhere. I slept at the New York Times Squares McDonald's restaurant, where I asked patrons to help me purchase something to eat. I stayed awake and slept a few hours inside Grand Central Terminal or 34th Penn Station's waiting room area. I used to freshen up inside hotel restrooms, restaurants, or coffee shops.

I recall working a second shift schedule (3 p.m. – 11:00 a.m.) at a transportation company during that time and decided to leave early from one shift. I contacted Maverick to alert him of my arrival, and he assured me he would come shortly. The scattered site apartment was solely for male residents, so Maverick hid me from other residents in the building. Consider a woman alone after 11 p.m. in an urban section of New York City on a pitch-black night, seated inside a park with men around and observing the scene. One of the gentlemen stated he would not have me outside like that if I were his woman. Maverick did not appear at the residence until the wee hours of the early morning while I waited for him on a bench.

* * * *

Maverick's jealousy and smothering were overwhelming, and there was no validity to his assumptions of my infidelity in our relationship. Merriam-Webster's Dictionary describes obsession as a persistent disturbing preoccupation with an often unreasonable idea or feeling broadly: compelling motivation. I carried my cell phone to the shared bathroom at the single-room occupancy whenever Maverick called me. Failure to answer Maverick's calls often resulted in hearing: "Why didn't you pick up?" "Who were you talking to?" "What took you so long to pick up?" Or, "What were you doing that you couldn't answer my call?" The individual accusing another partner of infidelity is sometimes the person being unfaithful in the relationship. A cheating gaslighter may blame or accuse their partner of cheating to distract them (Why Gaslighters Accuse You of Gaslighting | Psychology Today, n.d.).

Maverick told me he thought women liked men to show jealousy. Unfortunately, this type of unhealthy jealousy was not something I was accustomed to or desired to have in a partner. On one occasion, Maverick and I visited a medical practice near his residence. While there, I spoke with a male staff member about something (medical documentation for myself). Maverick thought I was interested in the individual and left me at the medical office. Maverick took my laptop and MTA MetroCard with him, and I had no funds because I was unemployed. I called out to Maverick, even using his full name since he refused to acknowledge me as he walked to the local train station. Maverick left me stranded, and I had to wait inside Burger King's restaurant.

Once, Maverick took my bag, which had food inside, to his doctor's appointment in Manhattan, leaving me with nothing. I eventually commuted there to retrieve my personal belongings. He informed me that I would not be allowed to come to his place that evening.

I was a customer service representative for a black car transportation company. One day, at the end of an eight-hour work shift, I innocently laughed with one of my male co-workers while walking out of the building. This interaction triggered Maverick's jealous reaction because I smiled while leaving. Maverick had a jealous outburst. Subsequently, observing my mindset, he tried to calm me down because I was distraught and personally ready to leave Earth due to his unjustified treatment of me.

If I did not answer his calls promptly, the assumption was that I was talking with a man. One day, Maverick called the call center, and one of the male representatives answered. Of course, this, being on a call with a client, and not picking up the line right away, did not sit well with him. I informed Maverick that our conversation was being recorded, yet he disregarded my warning and continued to harass me on the line. I told him I would contact him on the non-recorded line in the office's hallway. The harassment and jealousy that day led me to resign from the company. I asked him, "Are you happy now?" To be unhappy at work and unhappy at home was horrible.

While commuting on the subway, Maverick did not want to be near or converse with me. I sat away from him, pulled out my cell phone, and called one of my female cousins. Maverick immediately came over to inquire about whom I was on the phone with. I called one of my male cousins, and he deducted that the individual was interested in me. In a conversation with another male cousin, Maverick abruptly ended the call, yet he could speak with another woman in my presence without any reservations. When I attended a Microsoft Office Suite Certification course, Maverick thought my instructor and I were in a relationship. If he called me during class and I did not pick up, he was suspicious that I was with another man. Individuals in scenarios such as these should run from the toxic relationship. I did not, at the time, but I hope that you can.

I tried numerous times to break up with Maverick, but he refused to move on. I even prayed for God to send another woman into his life so he would leave me alone. He was upset about that. I once told Maverick about my decision to leave him and that I needed to take my items to storage. He purposely delayed returning to the residence, causing me to miss the timeframe for placing my things in the storage unit by the close of business. I had to take my shopping cart of items to my Microsoft Office Suite training facility. Due to the situation, the security guards, understandably so, were hesitant to allow me to come inside. I spoke with the officials, explained the problem, and provided my order of protection against Maverick. I was given a one-time exception.

I recall Maverick saying very hurtful words when I had nowhere to go, which is why he could do things to me. One day, Maverick poured syrup on my cart full of clothes that I was taking to the laundromat. I was so distraught and in disbelief over this despicable act that I cried because I was homeless and going through so much. Unbeknown to Maverick, I could still return to a women's transitional shelter and transfer to a better facility in another borough.

One day after Christmas, Maverick started mistreating me, and I left. The irony of what he said turned out to be false. Tearing down my self-esteem, Maverick said, "Look at you, I don't want you," or "Look at you, nobody wants you." My response to him was, "One man's trash is another man's treasure." Unbeknownst to him, before we reconnected, I was dating someone who loved me, brought me around his circle, and gave me the title of being his woman, which Maverick did not. We were not intimate then, as I could not bring myself to be. Maverick made that statement unaware that the ex-boyfriend still wanted me back and purchased a Christmas gift.

✶ ✶ ✶ ✶

I recently learned about Othello syndrome and cannot attest that Maverick had this condition as a non-medical professional. However, I can see some of the symptoms in Maverick's behavior towards me. Othello syndrome is a psychotic disorder characterized by the delusion of infidelity or jealousy; it often occurs in the context of medical, psychiatric, or neurological disorders (Cipriani et al., 2012). Symptoms of delusional jealousy include:

- False but certain belief that a partner is being unfaithful.
- Persistent delusions about a partner's infidelity

- Preoccupation with a partner's infidelity
- Paranoid and irrational thoughts and emotions
- Unacceptable or extreme behavior (Obsessive Love Disorder: Symptoms and Treatment, 2019)

In a close analysis of homicides in five cities, The *Washington Post* found that more than one-third of all men who killed a current or former intimate partner were publicly known to be a potential threat to their loved one ahead of the attack. Many victims are killed even after police and courts have stepped in ("How Domestic Violence Leads to Murder," 2018).

"A young mother killed by her 'obsessive' partner feared social services would 'take her baby away' if she kept reporting his 'controlling' and violent behaviour to police, her aunt told an inquest. Raneem Oudeh, 22, was murdered outside her mother's home in Solihull, West Midlands, shortly after midnight on August 27, 2018. She was killed alongside her mother Khowla Saleem, 49, by her ex-partner Janbaz Tarin, then aged 21, who the jury heard had once carved her name into his arm with a razor. (Carr, 2022)"

An estimated 45,000 women and girls were killed by their intimate partner or a family member last year (Armstrong, 2022). Furthermore, an article from Statista asserts, "This bleak figure forms part of a new report by the United Nations, drawing attention to the unacceptable threat faced by females around the world each day: based on this estimate, more than five women and girls were murdered by their partner/family every hour in 2021." Looking regionally, an enormous amount of these homicides were committed in Asia (17,800) and Africa (17,200) (Armstrong, 2022). When comparing per 100,000 of the female population, however, the view changes: a) Africa stands out from the rest of the world in this regard, with 2.5 such homicides per 100,000 population, b) compares to 1.4 in the Americas, c) 1.2 in Oceania, d) 0.8 in Asia and e) 0.5 in Europe, which has the lowest rate (Armstrong, 2022).

According to The World Economic Forum's *Global Gender Gap Report 2020*, "The Middle East and North Africa has the highest rate with 45% of women being harmed (Broom, 2020)." The report also suggests that "The problem persists across the world. In North America, the rate was 32% and in Western Europe 22%. And in the UK, a new first-of-its-kind report from the Femicide Census shows that a man kills a woman every three days in the country – a statistic unchanged across the 10 years studied." A graphic embedded in the report points out shares of women who suffered intimate partner physical and/or sexual violence origins: 45% from the Middle East and North Africa, 38% from South Asia, 32% from North America, 31% from Sub-Saharan Africa; 27% Latin America and the Caribbean; 23% East Asia and the Pacific; 22% Western Europe; 19% Eastern Europe and Central Asia; and 31% globally (Broom, 2020).

Healing Process

A healthcare provider diagnosed me with PTSD. I experienced separation anxiety from Maverick because he was my world, my everything. I had emotional triggers and panic attacks while inside the train station in Harlem. I was greatly concerned that I might cross paths with Maverick, wherein I sometimes experienced panic in that station or the Harlem area in general. I stayed away from the train tracks and vigilantly observed my surroundings.

I received mental health treatment following the intimate partner violence incidents. I visited a Safe Horizon facility, spoke with a representative regarding placement at a domestic violence shelter, and broke down inside her office while discussing my circumstances. A Licensed Clinical Social Worker provided a letter for me and stated this assessment: "Please be advised that Ms. [Grace] was seen on **/**/13 for the last session. She scored severe on both anxiety and depression. Pt. was referred for long-term treatment and medication management."

Healing from such a traumatic experience as intimate partner violence took time due to the emotional and psychological damage that occurred throughout my time with Maverick. I saw more than one psychologist and mental health therapist and received prescription medication for treatment. My therapists in the Brox were personable and provided a safe communication space for me to release what I held inside.

✶ ✶ ✶ ✶

After reading my personal testimony, you may wonder why I stayed with Maverick and maintained an emotional attachment to him. Dr. Lenore Walker explains the complexity and co-existence of abuse with loving behaviors and describes intimate partner violence's cyclical nature in her cycle of violence. Maverick was, paradoxically, protective of me, including with my family members. He also demonstrated a caring nature when I experienced mobility issues due to severe back pain.

One day, Maverick called me to see how I was doing. As previously mentioned, after hearing my slurred speech due to my elevated blood pressure, Maverick told me to take some apple cider vinegar and rushed back to the apartment to ensure I was okay. I almost fell inside the shower, and he panicked. Later, he stated that he would be sent to jail if something happened due to the order of protection (restraining order) I had against him.

I had urgently requested my relative to restock my breakfast items as I had nearly run out and was dealing with mobility issues. To my dismay, in our telephone conversation, my relative informed me she had forgotten to buy the items and subsequently did not purchase them. This situation has left me in a difficult position. I had hoped she would rectify the problem as soon as possible, considering the decrease in my pantry was attributed to helping her household's needs. This happened before the COVID-19 pandemic when I could barely walk two blocks without stopping to rest due to the pain in my back.

Maverick, who had a one-bedroom residence across town, had come to my rescue by purchasing food or groceries for me. Maverick escorted me to my rheumatology appointments, helped me onto the medical office examination bed, helped cook meals following my direction or guidance (though I got up to check on the food), purchased outside food, etc., while family members did not. Truth be told, Maverick benefited from assisting me because my abode was near various train lines, where I could commute to Manhattan quickly.

This complexity is why I had struggled to break ties with him — the nurturing side versus the physical, emotional, and psychological abuse. The mind replays what the heart cannot delete — memories of our time together. I tried to get over Maverick but could not, even though Maverick did heartless things to me. I could not get him out of my mind and heart.

＊＊＊＊

God is so merciful that He sustained me throughout a horrific ordeal despite my disobedience to Him and forewarning. Since I returned to New York, my prayer life has been lacking, and my walk with God has not been at its optimal peak. An old hymnal declares, "He was there all the time, waiting patiently in line. He was there all the time." Isaiah 30:18 (AMP) says, "Therefore the LORD waits [expectantly] and longs to be gracious to you, And therefore He waits on high to have compassion on you. For the LORD is a God of justice; Blessed (happy, fortunate) are all those who long for Him [since He will never fail them]." I can honestly say that Carolyn Traylor's song expounds "Can't Nobody Beat God Being God" because I could have lost my mind, experienced premature death due to stress (heart attack), or been killed due to the abuse.

I thank my Heavenly Father for the mercy and grace shown toward me during my folly of indulgence in sin. Sin will take you farther than you want to go and keep you longer than you wish to stay. Hebrews 12:6 (KJV) says, "For whom the Lord loveth he chasteneth, and scourgeth every son whom he receiveth." God is a God of a second chance, a third chance, etc. Psalm 103:13 (KJV) says, "Like as a father pitieth his children, so the Lord pitieth them that fear him."

I gave up on life and stated something to the Lord years ago, which caused me to wonder if my medical ailments contributed because we must be careful about for which we pray. I asked God to end my life. But God, Jesus, who is a Great Shepherd! Psalm 34:18 (AMPC): "The Lord is close to those who are of a broken heart and saves such as are crushed with sorrow for sin and are humbly and thoroughly penitent."

From Victim to Victor

Genesis 50:20 NLT states, "You intended to harm me, but God intended it all for good. He brought me to this position so I could save the lives of many people."

As I described above, my bout with homelessness was indeed a struggle. The shelter system wanted to reduce the population by forcing residents to go into single-room occupancies. I told my caseworker I was not interested. I believed God for an apartment, and she mocked me, asking how I could get an apartment with $250 a month from welfare. A supportive housing program accepted my application, providing a large, two-bedroom apartment with the assistance of HRA and a stipend from the organization for utilities. The transitional supportive housing staff placed me in a supportive housing apartment with a recently released felon.

Due to poor housing conditions in the apartment, I submitted complaints to the New York City 311 Complaint Line. The supportive housing agency placed me in another apartment with an individual released from a drug addiction program. My housing situation went from bad to worse due to this scenario because I have no criminal background or drug addiction.

On November 3, 2012, I attended a New York Southeast Ecclesiastical Jurisdiction service at Salvation & Restoration Church of God in Christ in Brooklyn, New York. During the altar call, I went up for prayer. Pastor James Thompson prophesied to me, "The Lord is gonna bless you beyond your wildest dreams." The Word of the Lord came to pass in 2014. The Lord has blessed me to have gone from living in homeless shelters for years to residing in a newly developed, multi-faceted building with a door attendant. My current residence has 24-hour security, a free and paid fitness facility, penthouse access for tenants and guests, a grilling area, a children's play area, a stackable washer and dryer in the unit, a dishwasher, and holiday functions. My rent, at that time inside a studio apartment, was below what I paid for my single-room occupancy unit ($600 a month) at the time of my intimate partner violence incident.

As Carolyn Traylor's song proclaims, "There's a story behind my praise." As she said in one of her videos, "You see the glory, but you just don't know the story." I am grateful to God for His grace and those who stood beside me through the storms of life — chronic homelessness and intimate partner violence. I must express my gratitude to the God of glory for sustaining me and keeping me safe while unhoused for over two years and living in a shelter system. He is genuinely a waymaker (Isaiah 43:16) and provider (Jehovah Jireh-Genesis 22:14).

There are always three sides to a story: his side, her side, and the truth, I frequently say. I remember when I was younger, everything seemed so new and exciting. While young, an individual's perspective is filled with wonder and curiosity as one explores the world around them. As I matured into adulthood, my lens shifted to responsibility and duty. I had to navigate school, work, and relationships with maturity and purpose. In my later years, my lens has moved again, this time to one of reflection and appreciation. I am grateful for the experiences that have shaped me into the person I am today, and I try to live each day with a sense of gratitude for the grace of God. It is incredible how our lenses and perspectives on life can shift and evolve.

According to a Psychology Today article, "Perspective is the main factor in determining how an event resonates with you, how you feel about a situation, and how you will remember what happened" (Perspective: The Difference Maker in Memories & Experiences, 2017).

"Mindsets are a culmination of all the experiences we have had. Bad experiences tend to generate a negative mindset and good experiences tend to generate positive mindsets. However, experiences can be both good and bad. Bad experiences can make a person see things in a way that makes them hurt people. It makes them 'see red' and they need someone to tell them that what they are doing is not right (How Experiences Shape Who We Are, 2020)."

A male family member sexually assaulted Maverick's ex-girlfriend. He handled our relationship in correlation to what happened to or with his girlfriend(s). His propensity to shield me from men (even family members), possessiveness, and extreme jealousy was overwhelming. I must admit that while walking through Prospect Park one evening, a friend's attractive relative tried to rape me, and I ran from the scene with one sneaker to a cousin's home in the Flatbush section of Brooklyn, New York. Similarly, there was an occasion for an attempted molestation by a family member.

I have a tight-knit family with whom I grew up closely. For Maverick to prevent me from communicating with family members was something other individuals I dated did not do. One of my cousins, Doug, and I talked on my mobile phone, and Maverick ended the conversation abruptly. Another first cousin, Kev, called me, and Maverick accused him of liking me romantically.

One day in his single-room occupancy after we had reconciled, Maverick said, "You too." I turned to the window as he cried. I had seen or spoken with an ex-boyfriend, and Maverick thought I had cheated on him. The scene was quite heartbreaking, and I went to comfort him. The irony is that Maverick told me that if any of his female friends needed him, he would be there, yet I could not communicate with anyone I had formerly dated.

The Pareto principle centers on the idea that one person cannot meet your needs 100% of the time (The 80/20 Rule: Dating Using the Pareto Principle Rule | ReGain, n.d.). The 80/20 relationship rule helps couples to expect only 80% of their romantic desires and wants to be fulfilled by their partner; for the remaining 20%, one should try to meet for themselves (Pace et al., 2022). In Tyler Perry's movie, *Why Did I Get Married*, one of the male actors conversing with others at the pool hall remarks, "In marriage, you only gonna get 80% of what you need. This woman offering 20% looks really good when you ain't getting it. But the problem is you're gonna leave 80 thinking you're gonna get something better and you end up with 20 (Tyler Perry - 80/20 Clip, n.d.)." This statement is well said because some individuals do not know what they have until they lose it or do not miss the water until the well runs dry.

Following my breakup with Maverick, I lost a great deal of weight, but he gained a significant amount in his face due to prescribed medication. While together that day, I heard him mention karma. I have a saying, "You will need me before I need you," and Maverick contacted me seeking financial assistance (carfare). In February 2014, I weighed 300+ lbs. At the beginning of 2017, I dropped to 195 lbs. under the medical care of an exceptional endocrinologist and weight loss guru. In 2017, Maverick saw me walking down the street and began shouting my name. I ignored it. He was astonished at my weight reduction and slender waistline.

Lessons Learned

I take accountability for my part in the relationship by allowing continual abuse and falling in love with Maverick and others who did not deserve me. I permitted Maverick to treat me the way he did, causing intimate partner violence to exist. Maverick abused me in my residence after I gave him the door key. I ignored warning signs. I failed to allocate time for my support network due to his objection, which led to isolation, preventing a sense of community. I constantly returned to Maverick and accepted his apologies. I did not avoid being unequally yoked.

Wise counsel was given, but I did not take heed. Proverbs 24:6 (KJV) states, "For by wise counsel thou shalt make thy war: and in multitude of counsellors there is safety." My middle sister offered to change the locks on my room, preventing Maverick from entering the premises. I contacted a male cousin who was a mover to help me extract my items, but they remained in the unit. A male friend somehow knew Maverick abused me and instructed me to make police reports. By dismissing what Kev stated, I hampered efforts to upgrade my New York City Housing Authority (NYCHA) application to N1 PRIORITY – Victims of Domestic Violence (VDV).

I should have established and maintained boundaries in my romantic relationships from the beginning, distinguishing between toxic and healthy personalities and relationships.

I stayed in relationships without real connection, chemistry, or shared interests, providing false hope to my demise. I remained in a relationship with Maverick, although the chemistry dissipated. Eventually, romantic interest no longer existed. Maverick reasoned that I had him imprisoned. For me, the abuse and mistreatment endured at his hands warranted unresponsive emotions. I must admit that Maverick provided companionship, a place to shelter at the risk of him losing housing and freedom [becoming incarcerated for violation of the final order of protection] preventing proximity to me (the victim of intimate partner violence) and friendship.

I did not adhere to self-care during my relationships. As women, we tend to be nurturers, putting others before ourselves. We must always ensure a life outside our relationships and not make an individual (intimate relationship) the center of our world. Bishop T.D. Jakes disclosed there are five people you need in your life: 1) The Caretaker, 2) The Couple, 3) The Adventurer, 4) The Planner, and 5) The Honest Friend (5 Types of Friends You Need to Have in Your Life, n.d.).

Affirmations are great to decree and declare aloud into the atmosphere daily because our words create our environment. Reciting affirmations daily to yourself is a compelling way to cultivate a positive and uplifting environment. However, there have been times when I neglected my prayer, scripture reading, and church attendance. Studies have proven that affirmations can assist with maintaining healthy self-esteem despite challenging circumstances, such as dealing with threats or a harsh or critical boss (A Guide to Affirmations and How to Use Them | Psychology Today, n.d.).

Affirmations are a valuable tool for promoting overall well-being. If I had consistently practiced affirmations of self-worth and reminded myself of my identity and belonging, I could have avoided negative thought patterns and strengthened my self-esteem. That is why I am grateful to include the words of affirmations in this book's appendix – they have the potential to heal those who have been hurt and support anyone who wants to utilize them.

"People use affirmations for a variety of purposes. Generally speaking, affirmations are used to reprogram the subconscious mind, to encourage us to believe certain things about ourselves or about the world and our place within it. They are also used to help us create the reality we want—often in terms of making (or attracting) wealth, love, beauty, and happiness (Affirmations: The Why, What, How, and What If?, 2014)."

One hit is too many. When a man/woman physically places their hands on you the first time, they will undoubtedly do it again. There is a saying, "hurt people, hurt people." Maverick's portrayal of his family dynamic made me aware that he comes from a dysfunctional home and has no contact with his brother. Maverick's mother passed away, and I was unaware of his relationship with his father; hence, insight into the family dynamic is opaque. I must embrace self-acceptance and not allow anyone to belittle or physically abuse me. I learned after the December 2009 intimate partner violence incident that there are times when men cheat and cannot be with the other woman. The abuser physically assaults their intimate partner. Men unable to acquire employment are frustrated about how they will survive and physically abuse their partner.

I must remain a strong, robust Black woman despite a man who is intimidated by this demeanor or attribute. Victims of intimate partner violence must always file a police report after the incident to lay the groundwork for legal prosecution. I remember Zechariah 2:8 (KJV) said, "For thus saith the Lord of hosts; After the glory hath he sent me unto the nations which spoiled you: for he that toucheth you toucheth the apple of his eye." Bishop Noel Jones' sermon on June 18, 2010, during the Higher Ground Holy Convocation held at The Potter's House in Dallas, Texas, entitled *I Am Not Vulnerable Anymore*, pronounced, "No one can hurt you when you are walking in the perimeters of God's word." Nonetheless, there shall be glory after this!

Stop being so secretive. I did not want to involve my family or friends in my intimate partner violence experience. When a victim tells family members or friends about their significant others and then decides to return to the abuser, their relatives will have ill feelings for the individual. My best friend, Velma, called to check on me. I did not pick up. After being remorseful for negating to answer, I decided to go to a male neighbor's house and call my friend, Velma, from there. I think Maverick was home, and something prevented me from contacting her from my house. After I returned upstairs to my single-room occupancy, Maverick thought I called the police. After finding out I did not call law enforcement but contacted Velma, he punched me and said hurtful words about no one being there for me. Our family and support network solely keep our best interests at heart and can sometimes prevent a fatal outcome.

Was Maverick protective, an obsessive, jealous partner, or both? Maverick's obsession was so crazy that I had to take my cell phone to a shared bathroom every time I used it. According to Collins Online Dictionary, the word daddy, my term of endearment for Maverick and how I addressed him, was an informal word for father. Maverick, I venture to say, assumed the role of an overprotective father due to my innocent personality as an individual who had been in church for a long time and not from the streets. Maverick was protective and a defender of all his female friends. I knew he would hurt someone when it came to me. One day, I was in a precarious situation while separated from Maverick, and I thought of "Daddy." I became accustomed to Maverick protecting me, ironically, considering I was in an intimate partner violence relationship with him.

Was my friendly demeanor a contributing factor to Maverick's jealousy? There is a distinct difference between flirting and friendliness. Over the years, men have misconstrued friendly, cordial conversation as me having an interest in them. Subsequently, these individuals provided unwanted advances. I must ponder why individuals misinterpreted my friendly demeanor as flirting and body language cues of fondness towards them. Do I stand too close to men while conversing? Was it my speech, a gaze that suggests or appears a spark in my eyes indicating interest? What about my behavior is causing this misconception? If there is a recurrence, I must evaluate my condition and correct how I interact with men to eliminate false hope of a potential romantic relationship. It's important to remember that being friendly is not the same as flirting, and it's not your responsibility to manage other people's expectations or emotions. That said, it's also worth reflecting on your own behavior and body language to see if there are any signals you may be sending unintentionally. It's up to each person to determine what they are comfortable with when interacting with others. I must appraise how I conducted myself in Maverick's presence, which warranted his protective or overly obsessive jealous behavior. Every partner must contemplate what part or role they played in the demise of a relationship.

Love with your Head and Not your Heart. It can be challenging to reconcile the idea of someone who has hurt us in the past becoming a source of support later on. Coming to terms with the possibility of receiving support from someone who has caused us harm (e.g., psychologically, emotionally, physically, socially, and financially) in the past can be a challenging experience. However, it is crucial to understand that forgiving someone does not necessarily mean staying in an unhealthy, unsatisfying, toxic, or unfulfilling relationship.

Comedian Deon Cole aptly points out that we often marry individuals for their strengths, but that does not necessarily mean they can handle all facets of life. In Deon Cole's Netflix stand-up special, the comedian profoundly stated, "See, you married on a level you should have been passing in life…What you should have remembered is he was good at the level but not life [because he is stuck on that level where you meet and has elevation] (Watch Deon Cole: *Cole Hearted* | Netflix Official Site, n.d.)."

Acknowledging or recognizing when a relationship is not working and moving on is acceptable. In 1980, American R&B group LTD featuring Jeffrey Osborne released a smash hit entitled *Where Did We Go Wrong*, a great love ballad (portion of the lyrics below):

"(Where did we go wrong), Now tell me what went wrong with love, And maybe we can fix it, (What's wrong between us), (Where did we go wrong), Now tell me what went wrong with

> love, It doesn't matter who is right or wrong, It doesn't matter
> who's to blame, We both have to swallow our pride, To make
> this love strong, ooh, baby. And we can conquer anything, hey,
> baby Together, together, together, together and if our love was
> meant to be, oh, girl We'll find a way to save it We'll build a
> road of love, oh, baby."

The lyrics of the R&B hit *Where Did We Go Wrong* are a poignant reminder that sometimes love is not enough to maintain a relationship. It is crucial to approach love with your heart and mind and make choices that prioritize your well-being and happiness. Although I can forgive the abuser as a foundation of Christian belief, it does not mean I must remain in the predicament. Unfortunately, sometimes you cannot fix what went wrong in a relationship, especially when intimate partner violence is involved, and you just need to move on.

I believe Maverick cared about me, but there are some hurdles you can't cross. In my short-term memory is the abuse suffered, the belittlement, the destruction that did not belong. Displeased by its content, he tossed my computer, which could have become damaged in the process; he poured syrup on my laundry clothes out of spite. He left me stranded in the wee hours of the morning outside his house in a park for over an hour after I arrived after a second shift of working non-stop as a customer service representative at a call center.

I could not have peace of mind or happiness with his jealous tendencies. It's important to prioritize my well-being and safety and to surround myself with people who treat me with kindness and respect. It's not always easy to leave a toxic relationship, but having peace of mind and happiness in the long run is worth it. Remember, Grace, you deserve to be treated with love and care.

I remember my friend and former co-worker giving me invaluable advice years ago. She said to always "love with your head, not your heart," and as I could tell with Maverick, leopards never change their spots. It's something that has stuck with me ever since. It's something that has stuck with me ever since. This advice has stayed with me for decades, reminding me to be mindful and wise in matters of the heart, although I did not utilize that advice with Maverick.

Follow my intuition and pay attention to red flags. The red flag has been used throughout history as a signal that there is a problem or danger—encouraging people to stop and take notice (Brown, 2019). Confirmatory factor analyses provided support for a 25-item five-factor structure (i.e., Monitoring Behaviors, Controlling Behaviors, Demeaning Behaviors, Threatening and Aggressive Behaviors, and Jealous and Possessive Behaviors) (Kearney & O'Brien, 2018).

What is the root cause of revictimization in an intimate partner violence relationship?

Sir Winston Churchill was a British statesperson, writer, and orator famous for this quote, "Those that fail to learn from history are doomed to repeat it." In my prior intimate partner violence relationships, there were patterns of:

Submissiveness	My world encircled that individual	Infrequent interaction with family and friends	Imbalance in affection
Self-esteem destroyed by abuser	Failure to follow my gut feelings or intuition about an individual	Flagrant disregard of red flags	Compromises
Allow myself to be manipulated, coerced, and controlled by others	Lowered my standards	Forsaking my Christian principles and foundational teachings	Being passive and not having an assertive demeanor
In relationships with men who were substance abusers (alcoholic, beer, or illegal drugs)	Dating individuals with criminal backgrounds	Tolerating individuals who took my kindness for weakness	Avoidance of confrontation or conflict
Prioritizing other individuals' feelings ahead of my own	Assisting partners with entrepreneurial aspirations	Incompatible personalities	Unequally yoked in belief or personality

Table 7. Patterns of behaviors Smiley Grace exhibited that may have emboldened her abusers.

Church and Intimate Partner Violence

The manipulative and controlling, at times, authoritarian environment of male leadership figures within the church setting may play a role in intimate partner violence. Discussion on religious/spiritual abuse in the context of intimate partner violence and abuse has been limited within academic literature (Davis & Johnson, 2020). Spiritual abuse is often misunderstood or unrecognized as it is often not discussed within the context of abuse (Training Curriculum for Intimate Partner Abuse Prevention and Intervention Among American Evangelical Keralite Women - ProQuest, n.d.).

"Tracy (1999) describes spiritual abuse as the "Phariseeal" art of utilizing scripture to manipulate and control others with the perception of it being spiritual in nature. Although spiritual abuse can occur within a family context, when it extends from leaders of a faith community, it may create more confusion and psychological damage to victims. Tracy (1999) outlines four distinct characteristics of spiritual abuse: (1) power posturing, where leaders express their authority by constantly reminding others of it; (2) performance preoccupation, where spirituality is viewed as an outward performance; (3) unspoken rules, such as never being able to disagree with pastors/elders, which is seen as an unspiritual act of disloyalty, and (4) lack of (spiritual) balance (i.e. "the Lord spoke to me, and you must receive this message") (Training Curriculum for Intimate Partner Abuse Prevention and Intervention Among American Evangelical Keralite Women - ProQuest, n.d.)."

Underlying and contributing factors to violence against women and the means of prevention lie in a range of environments (such as schools, sports settings, and faith-based institutions) and at multiple levels of influence – individual/relationship (including families), community and organizational, and societal (Preventing Violence before It Occurs a Framework and Background Paper to Guide the Primary Prevention of Violence against Women in Victoria, n.d.). Abused Christian women are more likely to remain in or return to unsafe relationships, citing religious beliefs to support such decisions (Westenberg, 2017).

The article *When She Calls for Help—Domestic Violence in Christian Families* states, "Christian women who suffer domestic violence display a tendency to use Christian symbolism and religious language to explain or tolerate abuse, and to remain in or return to marriages that contain domestic violence (Westenberg,

2017)." Although many mainline denominations have directly addressed the church's intolerance of intimate partner violence, it is still perpetuated covertly due to ingrained patriarchal beliefs and the use of scripture as a weapon toward women (Lynn, n.d.).

Psalm 55:12-13 (ESV): "For it is not an enemy who taunts me— then I could bear it; it is not an adversary who deals insolently with me— then I could hide from him. But it is you, a man, my equal, my companion, my familiar friend." The words sung by the psalmist David may capture the sentiments of many of the victims of intimate partner violence, which is defined as "physical, sexual, or psychological harm by a current or former partner or spouse (Lynn, n.d.)." According to Lynn's article, *Understanding Intimate Partner Violence in the Church: A Call for Church Leaders to Engage in Dialogue*, a study conducted with a large conservative church sample (N=1431) found that

- 10% of women suffered from extensive physical and emotional harm.
- 29% of women experienced sexual violence.
- 47% of women reported non-deadly physical/emotional abuse.
- 68% of women reported being a victim of controlling and demeaning behavior (Lynn, n.d.).

In her article, Leonie Westenberg of the School of Philosophy and Theology at the University of Notre Dame Australia outlined how the Christian language can unintentionally promote violence. According to Westenberg's analysis from 2017, certain phrases and concepts within Christian discourse can contribute to normalizing aggression and harm. It is important for individuals and communities to critically examine the language they use and consider the potential impact it may have on those around them (Westenberg, 2017).

1. *Women's Submission and Male Leadership.* While studies have demonstrated that Christian men are no more likely to

be abusers than men in the general population and that religious affiliation according to denomination and/or liberal/conservative Christian views does not predict the likelihood of domestic violence (Wang et al., 2009), there remains the fact that Christian women who have suffered domestic violence cite the use of religious language to accept abuse (Knickmeyer et al., 2016).

2. *The Sanctity of Marriage.* Many pastors, for example, cited the statement "God hates divorce" to support the intervention and counseling that should occur within families that experience domestic violence rather than advocating separation or divorce (Ware et al., 2003).

3. *The Value of Suffering and the Virtue of Forgiveness.* Christian language often presents the concept of mercy with the association of forgiveness as a virtue (Westenberg, 2017).

Religious leaders are influential in orchestrating gender norms within society in ministerial sermons preached to parishioners of their congregation, conventions, or during premarital and marital counseling sessions. In Nigeria, most of the mainline churches forbid divorce and remarriage, and one of the passages most popularly quoted in support of this doctrine is 1 Corinthians 7:10–11 [traditional interpretation teaches that marriage is 'for better, for worse'] (Ademiluka, 2019).

What is the difference between husband or pastoral covering when an abuse of power utilizes scriptures as a foundation?

"Religious and spiritual abuse in the context of IPV occurs across multiple religious traditions (Jayasundara et al., 2017), through various tactics. This behavior has been cited as occurring within Jewish, Christian, and Muslim communities (Jayasundara et al., 2017). R/S abuse has been noted as occurring within Orthodox Jewish communities when an *abusive husband engages in get-refusal (e.g., refusing to grant his wife a Jewish divorce), mocks and criticizes acts of prayer, or refuses to buy necessary ingredients to prepare challah (a special kind of bread that women are required to make by religious commandment; Arowojolu, 2016; Dehan & Levi, 2009; Starr, 2017). Within the Christian community, R/S abuse may encompass acts described as "proof-texting," which involves misinterpreting or twisting specific scriptures in order to fit a pre-conceived idea (Ross, 2013). In an Islamic context, R/S abuse may occur when Islamic marriage contracts are manipulated by abusive husbands or when "abusers cite God-given authority to discipline their wives." Dena Hassouneh explains R/S abuse in the lives of Muslim women as "disabling their defenses and adding yet another layer of suffering to their lives" (Hassouneh-Phillips, 2001, p. 944), a description that resonates across various religious traditions (Davis & Johnson, 2020)."*

I have attended the Pentecostal church since childhood, and during this time, I embraced Jesus Christ as my Lord and Savior. In those days, most Black churches were led by men, but most congregants were women. Later, I became an Apostolic (Jesus-only) denomination member. Following Deuteronomy 22:5 (KJV), this passage states that women should not wear clothing that belongs to men (pants were prohibited years ago, but some churches in recent years have changed course on this stance). Skirts had to be below the knees, and blouses and dresses could not show cleavage or be above the elbow. The pastors used to talk about Queen Jezebel, who had a reputation for murder, iniquity, and sexual promiscuity. This causation may be the reasoning behind doctrinal teaching on women. The church may want to consider where they are treading unconsciously with gender bias in this 21st Century. Ephesians 5:23 (KJV) says, "For the husband is the head of the wife, even as Christ is the head of the church: and he is the saviour of the body," and I cannot imagine nor read of Jesus treating women in a degrading manner while on Earth.

"Church leaders have instructed apostolic and Pentecostal women to cover themselves with modesty. Women are encouraged to dress conservatively to not tempt or entice men into sinning or lust. Apostolic and Pentecostals believe women must strictly follow these guidelines to stay pure before God. Since Apostolic, Pentecostal dress codes are particular (i.e., no makeup, no cutting hair, skirts below the knee, etc.), finding a job can be complex. The dress code may get in the way of work tasks, or a company may have its dress standards. It is also important to note that men in these churches are not subject to the same rules as women. Apostolic, Pentecostal men hardly look different from the world, which can be very frustrating for women who feel that they are being held to a higher standard than the men in their church (Wordsmith, 2022)."

In a national sample, the frequency of church attendance was inversely related to domestic violence victimization and perpetration, significantly reducing substantial racial differences in perpetration for men but not victimization for women. I.eEven among those attending services several times a week, Black women were significantly more likely than White women to report abuse (Ellison et al., 2007) (Williams & Jenkins, 2019).

"The two divergent approaches to the question of the role of women which are common among contemporary Evangelical Christians we might call the Traditional View (the majority opinion) and the Egalitarian View (the minority opinion).

> *The Traditional View stresses submission and dependence. A woman's role in relation to home, church and society is to be in submission to her husband (or to male leadership) and dependent upon him/them. She has her own sphere and freedom to exercise her spiritual gifts; but it is ultimately under the leadership of the male, who takes the lead in the home and in the church, that her gifts are expressed (The Role of Women in the Church, in Society and in the Home, n.d.)."*

It was not unusual for faith leaders to encourage women to stay in abusive relationships [I am pleased to report not my pastor], to "submit to their husbands," and to provide biblical misinterpretations that seem to justify the wife's abuse (Clark, 2015; Williams, 2012) (Williams & Jenkins, 2019).

There are several Bible scriptures targeted at women becoming submissive:

- 1 Corinthians 14:33-34 (NASB), "The women are to keep silent in the churches; for they are not permitted to speak, but are to subject themselves, just as the Law also says."
- 1 Timothy 2:11 (KJV), "Let the woman learn in silence with all subjection."

While a member of a Word church in New York in the late 1980s, I married an inspiring minister and experienced intimate partner violence. During my time as a member of this congregation, an elder allegedly received a black eye from her husband, who was also an elder within that ministry. When I was a member of a particular church, the pastor was quite demanding and controlling. While attending a jurisdiction service, members from our congregation were leaving before the end of it. He openly rebuked them, saying they were departing the church service before the benediction (conclusion/final prayer that also provides divine protection). I wonder if it was confusing to gauge after being under this type of pastor who sometimes has aggressive leadership but was also caring. God is love, yet why are church members enduring intimate partner violence?

I recall hearing "some things you need to keep under the Blood [of Jesus]" in Christendom. In these days and times, there comes a point where transparency is the new ministry. Jesus, after the resurrection, visited His disciples behind barred doors for fear of the Jews, according to John 20:19, but Thomas doubted it. John 20:25 (AMP) says, "So the other disciples kept telling him, "We have seen the Lord!" But he said to them, "Unless I see in His hands the marks of the nails, and put my finger into the nail prints, and put my hand into His side, I will never believe." Jesus came on the scene and revealed His scars. John 20:27 (KJV) states, "Then saith he to Thomas, 'Reach hither thy finger, and behold my hands; and reach hither thy hand, and thrust it into my side: and be not faithless, but believing."

"A 2018 Lifeway survey showed that more than 30% of Protestant pastors believe physical and sexual violence don't occur within their churches. Unfortunately, that belief is almost certainly false. Studies have shown that Christian women are abused at roughly the same rate as those outside the Church. The major difference is that Christian women are likely to remain an average of three and a half years longer with an abusive partner, and they are more likely to return to an abuser after leaving (Domestic Abuse: 4 Things Pastors and Churches Need to Know, n.d.)."

As the ecclesia (Church, not the actual edifice but the Body of Christ), we should minister to the whole man (spirit, soul, and body). Churches and Christian groups often instill in young women character traits that, unfortunately, open the gateway to dating violence and domestic abuse (Goertzen-Morrison, 2022). By gendering character traits, the church has increased men's power and women's marginalization. Patriarchal strongholds have further increased the gap between men and women in the home and the church (Goertzen-Morrison, 2022).

The conservative pro-family, pro-church organization *Institute for Family Studies* published a report by researchers DeRose, Johnson, and Wang, who studied intimate partner violence in deeply religious couples in 11 countries, including the U.S. (Gbaskerville, 2022). They found that in the U.S., about one in four couples reported intimate partner violence in their current relationship. Sadly, in the U.S., the finding was the same whether they were highly religious or not (Gbaskerville, 2022). In other countries, religion made a difference, but not in the U.S.; notability the report on page 37 shows that U.S. rates are different from other peer countries (Gbaskerville, 2022).

According to a *Review of Religious Research* article entitled *Couple Religiosity, Male Headship, Intimate Partner Violence, and Infidelity*, the authors acknowledge, "Although women in less/mixed religious couples have a 26% probability of ever having been the victim of violence in their relationship, compared to a 21% probability for women in highly religious couples, and a 23% probability for women in shared secular couples, none of these differences are statistically significant (DeRose et al., 2021)." The article reports predicted probabilities of victimization among women from shared secular couples, less/mixed religious couples, and highly religious couples in the 11-country sample (DeRose et al., 2021).

"[The article] reports predicted probabilities of women's victimization by couple religiosity and belief about male headship (Table 1, Model 2). Popular accounts suggest the idea that wifely submission to husbands provides theological cover for abusive relationships—or at least for men to abuse

women. We see little evidence of this here, though. Women in highly religious couples, be they patriarchal or egalitarian, are not statistically different from any other group of women. The only significant difference is that egalitarian women in shared secular relationships are less likely to be victims of IPV (22%) than patriarchal women in less/mixed religious relationships (30%). Headship beliefs themselves (i.e., not in combination with couple religiosity) are not associated with women's victimization (results not shown). Figure 3 reports predicted probabilities of men being a perpetrator of IPV in the global sample by couple religiosity (Table 1, Model 3). Findings for perpetration of IPV—whether the respondent has abused their current partner—also suggest no influence of couples' religious characteristics. Men are nearly equally likely to report being perpetrators of IPV across the three categories, with predicted probabilities ranging from 21 to 24% (DeRose et al., 2021)."

Stay with God-Faith as a coping mechanism. I must admit that the inspiring, religious Facebook posts and messages from preachers, saints of God, born-again believers, or Christian-oriented groups like *I Know the Bible is Right*, that I viewed after the December 2009 intimate partner violence incident assisted me in recovery. Women who reported higher levels of spirituality reported utilizing more elevated levels of religious coping strategies, and women who reported higher levels of religious involvement reported higher levels of social support (Watlington & Murphy, 2006).

Recommendations to the Community

It's crucial to provide survivors of intimate partner violence with support that is focused on their needs and well-being. They have been through a difficult and traumatic experience and must receive compassionate and empathetic care to help them heal and move forward. An intersectional trauma-informed practice that addresses intimate partner violence's psychological and physical effects is culturally appropriate and empowering for the survivor. In addition, a social network-oriented approach might provide a way to ensure that intimate partner violence interventions are responsive to the needs of the survivor of intimate partner violence (Ogbe et al., 2020).

Conclusion

I ASPIRE FOR my memoir and extensive research on intimate partner violence to be a valuable resource for readers. My ultimate objective is to enlighten and empower the community about this humanitarian crisis. However, my foremost desire is for survivors and victims of this violent crime and traumatic experience to discover healing and retrieve fragments of their souls through my vulnerability in this work and research. Above all, I hope my openness in *Lord, He Hit Me Again: An Insider's Look at Intimate Partner Violence* can help survivors and victims of this traumatic experience find healing and reclaim pieces of themselves. My sincerest wish is that my writing can positively impact those who need it most. The Heavenly Father, in His love letter to you, declares in 3 John 2 (AMP), "Beloved, I pray that in every way you may succeed and prosper and be in good health [physically], just as [I know] your soul prospers [spiritually]."

Appendix

Ungodly Soul Ties

THIS APPENDIX section presents additional insight into ungodly soul ties, previously mentioned in this book. This subject matter is extremely important because its stronghold causes severing relationships, a challenging task or feat. There is a FaithGaint.com article entitled *Understanding Ungodly Soul Ties and How to Break Them* that provides the following revelation on how ungodly soul ties form (FaithGiant, 2022):

We enter the bondage of ungodly soul ties through our wrong choices concerning companionship. Jesus came to liberate us from sin, but the devil can still hold us captive when we form ungodly associations. However, we can resist his tricks when we know his tactics for ensnaring us. 1 Peter 5:8 (NKJV) instructs us, "Be sober, be vigilant; because your adversary the devil walks about like a roaring lion, seeking whom he may devour." Ungodly soul ties can form in a variety of ways, but here are some examples:

- *Sexual Connections*: When we have sex outside of marriage, we can form ungodly soul ties with people who are not our spouse or future spouse. The Bible warns us that sexual immorality and intercourse outside marriage lead only to spiritual death. For example, sexual intercourse with a prostitute might join a person's soul with the prostitute and all her previous clients' souls. Proverbs 5:3-5 (NIV) says, "For the lips of the adulterous woman drip honey, and her speech is smoother than oil; but in the end, she is bitter as gall, sharp as a double-edged sword. Her feet go down to death; her steps lead straight to the grave."

- *Emotional Connections*: We can develop ungodly soul ties with people with strong emotional ties as children, such as our parents and family members (Deuteronomy 13:6). Our souls can become so intertwined with theirs that it feels like we are one person. We end up doing whatever they want. These relationships can be so overpowering that obeying God and loving Him with all our hearts becomes difficult. It can also happen in friendships. For example, consider King Saul's son Jonathan's soul ties with David, the king's attendant. The Bible says Jonathan's soul was knit to David's soul (1 Samuel 18:1). Jonathan risked his own life, even disobeying his father when he tried to save David from King Saul.

Words of Affirmation

"Trauma can impact every area of survivors' lives including their self-perceptions, relationships with others, emotions, thoughts, physical health, and sense of spiritual well-being. One of the biggest challenges for trauma survivors face is reconciling who they were before trauma occurred with who they are as a trauma survivor. Traumatic experiences have a way of shattering previously held assumptions such that the world can feel unsafe, and people are viewed as dangerous or unpredictable. As they attempt to make sense of what happened and why, many trauma survivors struggle with feelings of self-blame and guilt. Stressful thoughts and feelings

can continue for a long time after a trauma, interfering with the survivors' overall happiness and quality of life (Admin, 2019)."

Dr. Robyn L. Gobin, Licensed Clinical Psychologist, author of *The Self-Care Prescription*, and Assistant Professor, has an article on ThinkUp.me wherein she empowers women healing from trauma, which is outstanding as she specializes in women's mental health and interpersonal trauma. Dr. Gobin shared 16 affirmations for trauma that may be beneficial to you:

1. I am capable of transforming negative experiences into something positive.
2. I am worthy of respect and equality.
3. Everything will work out for my highest good.
4. I am opening my heart and learning to trust again.
5. I am rational, balanced, and know my truth.
6. No one can take my truth away from me. I speak my truth, even if my voice shakes.
7. It's okay to not be okay.
8. Every emotion is legitimate. I let myself be happy, sad, frustrated, and hurt. This is my experience, and I am accepting it.
9. Each day, I am creating a more meaningful life.
10. I am changing in positive ways. I am making peace with my past and accepting myself.
11. I make healthy choices and choose to love myself a bit more every day.
12. My life is divinely guided.
13. I am exactly where I need to be on my journey.
14. I am safe at this moment.
15. Today, I chose to focus on the things I can control.

16. My needs and wants are just as important as anyone else's. I trust my instincts and listen to my inner wisdom (Admin, 2019).

Affirmations for Individuals Dealing with PTSD (Kristenson, 2022):

1. I deserve love.
2. I am safe and protected.
3. I am stronger than the trauma that has happened to me.
4. I make good decisions.
5. I surround myself with gentleness.

Faith Affirmations

"A prayer of biblical affirmation: Father, we come to You today because we want You to speak truth into our lives. We recognize that sometimes the things we tell ourselves do not reflect the truth that comes from You. Help us to not only speak good things over our lives but to also believe only those things that line up with Your word. In Jesus' name. Amen (15 Magnificent Biblical Affirmations for Women - Hebrews 12 Endurance, 2021)."

Romans 10:17 (AMPC) says, "So faith comes by hearing [what is told], and what is heard comes by the preaching [of the message that came from the lips] of Christ (the Messiah Himself)." I heard years ago in Christendom that the Bible stands for Basic Instructions Before Leaving Earth. Please know you are a child of the King (Jesus, the King of Glory-Psalm 24 NKJV); a royal priesthood (1 Peter 2:9-10 KJV), and you shall have whatsoever you saith (Mark 11:23 KJV) for death and life are in the power of the tongue (Proverbs 18:21 KJV).

Below are 19 faith affirmations on Kingdom Ambassadors Empowerment Network's website (19 Faith Affirmations, 2014):

1. I am a person of faith, and therefore, I do not focus upon the things that are seen with my natural eyes and which are temporary and subject to change according to the word of God that I speak, but I focus my attention on the things that are unseen in the spirit realm that shall stand forever more. (Scriptural reference 2 Corinthians 4:18)

2. I firmly believe the Word of God that I am a person of faith. I walk by faith and not by sight; I talk by faith; I live by faith, and I therefore have an expectancy to receive that which I pray for by faith. (Scriptural reference 2 Corinthians 5:7)

3. I will not waiver at the promises of God through unbelief, but I will remain strong in my faith as I give glory unto God. (Scriptural reference Romans 4:20)

4. I am fully persuaded in my heart and in my mind that whatever God has promised me according to His word, He is well able to perform and bring it to fruition. (Scriptural reference Romans 4:21)

5. I have a mountain-moving faith that removes all hindrances and spiritual opposition that I face. Therefore, when I command my mountains to be removed, they must move and be cast away and make room for God's promises to take effect into my life, for with my faith in God, nothing is impossible unto me. (Scriptural reference Matthew 17:20)

6. Through Christ, I have strength, power, and the authority He has given to me, and therefore affirm I can do all things through Christ who strengthens me. (Scriptural reference Philippians 4:13)

7. I gird myself up daily with the shield of faith, and it is my faith in God and authority in His word that I am able to quench every fiery dart of Satan, the wicked one. (Scriptural reference Ephesians 6:16)

8. I affirm there is no lack or deficiency in my life because, with my faith in God, I can decree and declare a thing, and according to what I have declared, it shall come to pass. (Scriptural reference Job 22:28)

9. I am grounded, rooted, and settled in my faith in God, and I shall not be moved away from the hope of the gospel which I boldly speak and believe. (Scriptural reference Colossians 1:23)

10. I hold fast to the confession of my faith in God and His word, and I do not doubt, and will not give up because Christ who has made me promises is faithful to deliver as He has promised in His word. (Scriptural reference Hebrews 10:23)

11. My faith produces substance and brings to pass with the evidence of what I speak in faith. (Scriptural reference Hebrews 11:1)

12. I please the Lord with my faith each day, and when I come before the Lord, I believe that He is God, and God alone, and that He is a rewarder of those that come unto Him and diligently seek His face. (Scriptural reference Hebrews 11:6)

13. When I pray and ask the Lord for something, I do not waiver or doubt, but I ask in faith, and I, therefore, receive from the Lord that which I asked Him for. (Scriptural reference James 1:6)

14. I am confident that Jesus Christ is the author and finisher of my faith and, just like Him, my faith will guard, protect, and sustain me so that I can endure my cross, and at the end, I will receive my reward of joy. (Scriptural reference Hebrews 12:2)

15. The word of God does not profit some because they do not mix it with faith, but the word does profit me because I mix God's word with my faith. Therefore, when I release my faith in that which I believe and speak, those things shall profit me and come to pass. (Scriptural reference Hebrews 4:2)

16. When my faith is tried in the fire, my faith shall stand and come through the fire victoriously, just like pure gold. (Scriptural reference 1 Peter 1:7)

17. I am fully persuaded in my heart and in my mind that whatever God has promised me according to His word, He is well able to perform and bring to pass. (Scriptural reference Ephesians 3:20; Romans 4: 21)

18. The righteousness of God is revealed from faith to faith. I am the just, and I live by faith. (Scriptural reference Romans 1:17)

19. My faith comes as a result of me reading, speaking, and hearing the word of God. (Scriptural reference Romans 10:17)

Biblical Affirmations for Self-Esteem

1. According to the Hebrews 12 Endurance website Spiritual Growth section article 15 Magnificent Biblical Affirmations for Women, "The enemy likes to chip away at our self-esteem and replace what God says about us with lies. But we can regain that power when we choose to repeat biblical affirmations to improve our self-esteem (15 Magnificent Biblical Affirmations for Women - Hebrews 12 Endurance, 2021)."

2. I am strong and courageous because the Lord is with me wherever I go (Scriptural reference Joshua 1:9).

3. I am precious in God's eyes (Scriptural reference Isaiah 43:4).

4. I can do all things through Christ who strengthens me (Scriptural reference Philippians 4:13).

5. God loves me with an everlasting love (Scriptural reference Jeremiah 31:3)

"*I will not surrender to my fears (Isaiah 41:10). I claim the biblical freedom to trust that God is powerful enough to work all things for my good. I will not be preoccupied with worst case scenario thinking (Romans 8:28) (11 Affirmations to Build Your Faith, n.d.).*"

References

5 Types Of Friends You Need To Have In Your Life. (n.d.). 5 Types of Friends You Need to have in Your Life.
https://www.tdjakes.com/
posts/5-types-of-friends-you-need-to-have-in-your-life.

7 Tips to Heal after an Abusive Relationship. (8 Sept. 2021). Psych Central,
psychcentral.com/health/how-to-heal-after-an-abusive-relationship#common-thoughts-and-feelings.

10 Signs You're in a Toxic Relationship. (Dec. 3, 2022). Ramsey Solutions,
www.ramseysolutions.com/relationships/
toxic-relationship-signs.

11 Affirmations to build your faith. (n.d). (Nov. 12, 2018). iBelieve.com.
https://www.ibelieve.com/blogs/noelle-kirchner/11-affirmations-to-build-your-faith.html.

15 Magnificent Biblical Affirmations for Women - Hebrews 12 Endurance. (2021, October 7).
https://hebrews12endurance.com/positive/.

19 Faith Affirmations. (2014, February 3). Kingdom Ambassadors Empowerment Network.
https://empowermentmomentsblog.com/
words-of-encouragement/19-faith-affirmations/.

24-HOUR SURVEY of Domestic Violence Shelters and Services Domestic Violence Counts
Report. (2021). https://nnedv.org/wp-content/
uploads/2021/05/15th-Annual-DV-Counts-Report-Full-Re-
port.pdf.

A Holistic Approach to Tackling Intimate Partner Violence among Marginalized Women in Urban Liberia: Guest Post by David Sungho Park. (Dec. 02, 2021).
Blogs.worldbank.org, blogs.worldbank.org/impactevalu-
ations/holistic-approach-tackling-intimate-partner-viole
nce-among-marginalized-women. Accessed 28 Jan. 2023.

A YEAR OF IMPACT. (2020).
https://www.thehotline.org/wp-content/uploads/
media/2021/06/Hotline-EOY-Impact-Report-2020_
FINAL.pdf.

Abrams, A. (Sept. 2, 2018). Does Your Partner Value You? Psychology Today. (n.d.). Retrieved
June 19, 2023, from https://www.psychologyto-
day.com/us/blog/nurturing-self-compassion/201809/
does-your-partner-value-you.

Abuse Hurts. Domestic Violence Awareness at the University of Michigan.
Stopabuse.umich.edu, stopabuse.umich.edu/about/barriers.
html. Accessed 26 Dec. 2022.

Abuse of Older People. (13 June 2022). World Health Organization.
Www.who.int,
www.who.int/news-room/fact-sheets/detail/
abuse-of-older-people.

Ademiluka, S. O. (2019). Reading 1 Corinthians 7:10–11 in the context of intimate partner violence in Nigeria. Verbum Et Ecclesia, 40(1).
https://doi.org/10.4102/ve.v40i1.1926.

Admin. (2019, December 30). Affirmations For Trauma By Dr. Robyn Gobin affirmations for trauma. ThinkUp App.
https://thinkup.me/affirmations-for-trauma/.

Administrator. (Jan. 23, 2016). Unrequited love - IResearchNet. Psychology.
https://psychology.iresearchnet.com/social-psychology/interpersonal-relationships/unrequited-love/.

Affirmations: The Why, What, How, and What If? (2014). Psychology Today.
https://www.psychologytoday.com/us/blog/smart-relationships/201403/affirmations-the-why-what-how-and-what-if.

Allyn, B. (2019, August 7). NPR Choice page. Npr.org,
https://www.npr.org/2019/08/07/749025458/cyntoia-brown-released-after-15-years-in-prison-for-murder.

Anderson, N. E., & Kiehl, K. A. (2014). Psychopathy: developmental perspectives and their implications for treatment. Restorative Neurology and Neuroscience, 32(1), 103–117. National Library of Medicine.
https://doi.org/10.3233/RNN-139001.

Antiracism & Interpersonal Violence. (9 Nov. 2020). School of Social Work,
socialwork.asu.edu/gender-violence/antiracism-interpersonal-violence-10.

APA Dictionary of Psychology. (n.d.). Dictionary.apa.org,
https://dictionary.apa.org/bystander-effect.

APA Dictionary of Psychology. (n.d.)
   Dictionary.apa.org, dictionary.apa.org/defense-mechanism.

APA Dictionary of Psychology. (n.d.)
   Dictionary.apa.org, dictionary.apa.org/gaslight.

APA Dictionary of Psychology. (n.d.). Dictionary.apa.org,
   https://dictionary.apa.org/impostor-syndrome.

APA Dictionary of Psychology. (n.d.)
   Dictionary.apa.org, dictionary.apa.org/psychotherapy.

APA Dictionary of Psychology. (n.d.).
   Dictionary.apa.org, https://dictionary.apa.org/value.

APA PsycNet. (n.d.) Psycnet.apa.org, psycnet.apa.org/doiLand-
   ing?doi=10.1037%2Fvio0000031. Accessed 9 Jan. 2023.

APA PsycNet. Psycnet.apa.org, psycnet.apa.org/record/2017-
   36858-007. Accessed 26 Dec. 2022.

Assault in the second degree. (2021, July 10). NY State Senate.
   https://www.nysenate.gov/legislation/laws/PEN/120.05.

Armstrong, M. (2022, November 24). 45,000 women and girls
killed by family members in 2021. Statista Daily Data.
   https://www.statista.com/chart/28820/
   women-girls-killed-by-partner-family-by-region/.

Ates, D. U. (2021, May 4). Eleven Ways Tech Is Preventing And
Reducing Domestic Violence. Forbes.
   https://www.forbes.com/sites/forbestechcouncil/2021/05/04/
   eleven-ways-tech-is-preventing-and-reducing-domestic-vio-
   lence/?sh=4b1b3bd8ba98.

Bailey, Z., Feldman, J. M., & Bassett, M. T. (2021). How structural racism works — Racist policies as a root cause of U.S. racial
health inequities. The New England Journal of Medicine, 384(8),
768–773.
   https://doi.org/10.1056/nejmms2025396.

Banaji, M. R., Fiske, S. T., & Massey, D. S. (2021). Systemic racism: individuals and interactions, institutions and society. Cognitive Research: Principles and Implications, 6(1).
https://doi.org/10.1186/s41235-021-00349-3.

Bancroft, L. Why Does He Do That? Goodreads.
https://www.goodreads.com/work/quotes/217475-why-does-he-do-that-inside-the-minds-of-angry-and-controlling-men.

Barbara, G., Viero, A., Pellizzone, I., Buggio, L., Facchin, F., Cattaneo, C., D'Amico, M. E., Vercellini, P., & Kustermann, A. (2022). Intimate Partner Violence in the COVID-19 Era: A health, psychological, forensic and legal perspective. International Journal of Environmental Research and Public Health, 19(9), 4973.
https://doi.org/10.3390/ijerph19094973.

Barrios, Veronica R., et al. (Jan. 2020). Future Directions in Intimate Partner Violence Research: An Intersectionality Framework for Analyzing Women's Processes of Leaving Abusive Relationships. Journal of Interpersonal Violence, vol. 36, no. 23-24, p. 088626051990093,
https://doi.org/10.1177/0886260519900939.

Beer-Becker, D. (Mar. 2022). "Psychologist, How to Overcome Emotional Dependency." Blake Psychology,
www.blakepsychology.com/2022/03/how-to-overcome-emotional-dependency.

Ben-Ze'ev, Aaron. (Dec. 9, 2019) Is Self-Fulfillment Essential for Romantic Love? The Self-Other Tension in Romantic Love. Revista de Filosofia Aurora, vol. 31, no. 54, 10.7213/1980-5934.31.054. ds12. Accessed 22 Jan. 2023.

Bishop, B. (2023, April 19). *Report Highlights Sentencing Laws for Criminalized Domestic*
Violence Survivors, Urges Reform. The Sentencing Project. https://www.sentencingproject.org/press-releases/

report-highlights-sentencing-laws-for-criminalized-domes-tic-violence-survivors-urges-reform/

Black Codes (article) | Reconstruction | Khan Academy. (n.d.). Khan Academy. Black Codes
(article) | Reconstruction. (n.d.). Khan Academy. https://www. khanacademy.org/humanities/us-history/civil-war-era/recon-struction/a/black-codes#;~:text=Overview%201%20When%20 slavery%20was%20abolished%20at%20the,racial%20 hierarchy%20within%20the%20southern%20society.%20 More%20items

Blagg, R. D. (2019). Bystander effect. In Encyclopedia Britannica. https://www.britannica.com/topic/bystander-effect

Bonomi, A. E., Altenburger, L. E., & Walton, N. L. (2013). "Double Crap!" Abuse and Harmed Identity in Fifty Shades of Grey. *Journal of Women's Health*, 22(9), 733–744.
https://doi.org/10.1089/jwh.2013.4344

Bolman, L. G., & Deal, T. E. (2021). Reframing organizations: Artistry, choice, and leadership.

Jossey-Bass. Boserup, B., McKenney, M., & Elkbuli, A. (2020). Alarming trends in US domestic violence during the COVID-19 pandemic. American Journal of Emergency Medicine, 38(12), 2753–2755.
https://doi.org/10.1016/j.ajem.2020.04.077.

Both, L. M., Favaretto, T. C., & Freitas, L. H. M. (2019). Cycle of violence in women victims of domestic violence: Qualitative anal-ysis of OPD 2 interview. Brain and Behavior, 9(11).
https://doi.org/10.1002/brb3.1430.

Bottaro, A. (Jan. 4, 2022). How to Recognize and End the Cycle of Abuse. Verywellhealth.
https://www.verywellhealth.com/cycle-of-abuse-5210940.

Brandt, S, and Rudden, M. (Sept. 3, 2020). A Psychoanalytic Perspective on Victims of Domestic Violence and Coercive Control. International Journal of Applied Psychoanalytic Studies, vol. 17, no, pp. 215–231, 10.1002/aps.1671.

Braveman, P., Arkin, E. B., Proctor, D., Kauh, T. J., & Holm, N. (2022). Systemic And Structural Racism: Definitions, Examples, Health Damages, And Approaches To Dismantling. Health Affairs, 41(2), 171–178.
https://doi.org/10.1377/hlthaff.2021.01394.

Breaking Toxic Soul Ties: Healing from Unhealthy and Controlling Relationships. (n.d.). In
www.christianbook.com, www.christianbook.com/break-ing-toxic-healing-unhealthy-controlling-relationships/tom-brown/9781629119540/pd/9119540#CBD-PD-Description. . Accessed 28 Jan. 2023.

Brend, D. M., Krane, J., & Saunders, S. (2020). Exposure to trauma in intimate partner violence human service work: A scoping review. *Traumatology*, 26(1), 127–136.
https://doi.org/10.1037/trm0000199.

Brenner, H., & Letich, L. (2022). Emotional Triggers: Why They're Hard to Spot, and What You Can Do About Them. helenebrenner.com.
https://helenebrenner.com/emotional-triggers-hard-to-spot/.

Bridges, K. M. (2020, June 11). *The many ways institutional racism kills Black people.* Time.
https://time.com/5851864/institutional-racism-america/

Britannica. (2023, February 18). institutional racism | Definition, Meaning, & Examples | Britannica. Www.britannica.com.
https://www.britannica.com/topic/institutional-racism

Brooklyn man accused of fatally stabbing wife, her new lover was acting in self-defense: lawyer. (2014, December 19). New York Daily News.
https://www.nydailynews.com/new-york/nyc-crime/man-accused-killing-wife-lover-acted-self-defense-article-1.2051638.

Brooks, D., Wirtz, A. L., Celentano, D., Beyrer, C., Hailey-Fair, K., & Arrington-Sanders, R. (2020). Gaps in Science and Evidence-Based Interventions to Respond to Intimate Partner Violence Among Black Gay and Bisexual Men in the U.S.: A Call for an Intersectional Social Justice Approach. *Sexuality & Culture.*
https://doi.org/10.1007/s12119-020-09769-7.

Broom, D. (2020, November 25). As the UK publishes its first census of women killed by men, here's a global look at the problem. World Economic Forum.
https://www.weforum.org/agenda/2020/11/violence-against-women-femicide-census/.

Brown, E. (2019, October 4). Five Red Flags of Safety. Hoar Construction.
https://hoar.com/five-red-flags-of-safety/.

Brown, S. (2018). ScholarWorks The Lived Experience of Daughters Who Have Absent Fathers: A Phenomenological Study.
https://scholarworks.waldenu.edu/cgi/viewcontent.cgi?article=5995&context=dissertations.

Bryngeirsdottir, & Halldorsdottir, S. (2022). I'm a Winner, Not a Victim: The Facilitating Factors of Post-traumatic Growth among Women Who Have Suffered Intimate Partner Violence. International Journal of Environmental Research and Public Health, 19(3), 1342.
https://doi.org/10.3390/ijerph19031342.

Burrell, M., White, A., Frerichs, L., Funchess, M., Cerulli, C., DiGiovanni, L., & Lich, K. H. (2021). Depicting "The System": How structural racism and disenfranchisement in the United States can cause dynamics in community violence among males in urban black communities. Social Science & Medicine, 272, 113469. https://doi.org/10.1016/j.socscimed.2020.113469.

Camp, A. R. (Dec. 1, 2023). From experiencing abuse to seeking protection: Examining the shame of intimate partner violence. https://papers.ssrn.com/sol3/papers.cfm?abstract_id=4323805

Caring for Your Mental Health. (2021). National Institute of Mental Health. Www.nimh.nih.gov, www.nimh.nih.gov/health/topics/ caring-for-your-mental-health.

Carr, S. (2022, October 31). Murdered woman, 22, feared social services would "take her baby away." Mail Online. https://www.dailymail.co.uk/news/article-11372901/Mother-22-killed-obsessive-partner-feared-social-services-baby-away.html.

Cartrine Anyango, Goicolea, I., & Fredinah Namatovu. (2023). Women with disabilities' experiences of intimate partner violence: a qualitative study from Sweden. BMC Women's Health, 23(1). https://doi.org/10.1186/s12905-023-02524-8.

Cervantes, M. V., & Sherman, J. (2019). Falling for the Ones That Were Abusive: Cycles of Violence in Low-Income Women's Intimate Relationships. Journal of Interpersonal Violence, 36(13-14), 088626051982977. https://doi.org/10.1177/0886260519829771.

Centers for Disease Control and Prevention. (2023, June 29). Preventing adverse childhood experiences. Www.cdc.gov. https://www.cdc.gov/violenceprevention/aces/fastfact.html.

Chain Gangs | Slavery By Another Name Bento | PBS. (2017). Chain Gangs | Slavery by Another Name Bento | PBS.

> https://www.pbs.org/tpt/slavery-by-another-name/themes/chain-gangs/.

Chalabi, M. (2019, January 12). *Are women punished more harshly for killing an intimate partner?* The Guardian.

> https://www.theguardian.com/news/datablog/2019/jan/12/intimate-partner-violence-gender-gap-cyntoia-brown.

Chapman, G. (n.d.). What are The 5 Love Languages? 5lovelanguages.com.

> https://5lovelanguages.com/learn.

Cherelus, Gina. (Jan. 10, 2022). What Is "Love Bombing"? New York Times,

> www.nytimes.com/2022/01/10/style/love-bombing.html.

Children and Youth Exposure to Domestic Violence. (n.d.). Nccadv.org.

> https://nccadv.org/children-and-youth/.

Christman, Jennifer. (Aug. 1, 2009). Expanding the Theory of Traumatic Bonding as It Relates to Forgiveness, Romantic Attachment, and Intention to Return. Masters Theses,

> trace.tennessee.edu/utk_gradthes/30/.

Cigarette smoking: health risks and how to quit. (April 11, 2023). National Cancer Institute.

> https://www.cancer.gov/about-cancer/causes-prevention/risk/tobacco/quit-smoking-pdq.

Cipriani, G., Vedovello, M., Nuti, A., & di Fiorino, A. (2012). Dangerous passion: Othello syndrome and dementia. Psychiatry and Clinical Neurosciences, 66(6), 467–473.

> https://doi.org/10.1111/j.1440-1819.2012.02386.x

Clements, K., & Schumacher, J. A. (2010). Perceptual biases in social cognition as potential moderators of the relationship between alcohol and intimate partner violence: A review. Aggression and Violent Behavior, 15(5), 357–368.
https://doi.org/10.1016/j.avb.2010.06.004

Clicktivism is Not Enough: What to do About the Bystander Effect. (2021, November 17). Psych Central.
https://psychcentral.com/health/
bystander-effect#bystander-effect-explained.%E2%80%8C

Coates, T.-N. (2015, September 14). 50 Years After the Moynihan Report, Examining the Black Family in the Age of Mass Incarceration. The Atlantic; The Atlantic.
https://www.theatlantic.com/magazine/archive/2015/10/
the-black-family-in-the-age-of-mass-incarceration/403246/

Community-Based Response to Intimate Partner Violence During COVID-19 Pandemic - Bill of Health. (2021, August 10).
Blog.petrieflom.law.harvard.edu. https://blog.petrieflom.law.
harvard.edu/2021/08/10/community-based-response-inti-
mate-partner-violence-covid-pandemic/

Costello, K., & Greenwald, B. D. (2022). Update on Domestic Violence and Traumatic Brain Injury: A Narrative Review. Brain Sciences, 12(1), 122.
https://doi.org/10.3390/brainsci12010122.

Cramer, E. P., & Plummer, S. (2009). People of Color with Disabilities: Intersectionality as a Framework for Analyzing Intimate Partner Violence in Social, Historical, and Political Contexts. *Journal of Aggression, Maltreatment & Trauma, 18(2), 162–181*
https://doi.org/10.1080/10926770802675635.

Cuppy, C. (2022). Fathers Matter: The importance of a father. Focus on the Family.
https://www.focusonthefamily.com/parenting/
fathers-matter-the-importance-of-a-father/.

Cycle of Abuse – Envision.
www.envisioncounsellingcentre.com/innerpage/resources/
partner-abuse/cycle-of-abuse/.

"Cycle of Violence." (2019). Blue Cloud Studio. Shelterforhelpine-
mergency.org,
www.shelterforhelpinemergency.org/get-help/cycle-violence.

Cycle of Violence. (2019).
www.womenscenteryfs.org/index.php/get-info/prevention/
education/14-cycle-of-violence

D'Amore, C., Martin, S., Wood, K., & Brooks, C. (2018). Themes of
Healing and Posttraumatic growth in women survivors' narratives
of intimate partner violence. Journal of Interpersonal Violence,
36(5–6), NP2697–NP2724.
https://doi.org/10.1177/0886260518767909.

Daugherty, J. C., Marañón-Murcia, M., Hidalgo-Ruzzante, N.,
Bueso-Izquierdo, N., Jiménez-González, P., Gómez-Medialdea,
P., & Pérez-García, M. (2018). Severity of neurocognitive impairment in women who have experienced intimate partner violence
in Spain. The Journal of Forensic Psychiatry & Psychology,
30(2), 322–340
https://doi.org/10.1080/14789949.2018.1546886

Davila, J., et al. (Feb. 7, 2017). Romantic Competence, Healthy
Relationship Functioning, and Well-Being in Emerging Adults.
Personal Relationships, vol. 24, no. 1, pp. 162–184,
onlinelibrary.wiley.com/doi/full/10.1111/pere.12175, 10.1111/
pere.12175.

Davis, M., Gilbar, O., & Padilla-Medina, D. (2021). Intimate
partner violence victimization and perpetration among U.S. adults
during the earliest stage of the COVID-19 pandemic. Violence &
Victims, 36(5), 583–603.
https://doi.org/10.1891/vv-d-21-00005.

Davis, M., & Johnson, M. (2020). Exploring Black Clergy Perspectives on Religious/Spiritual Related Domestic Violence: First Steps in Facing those Who Wield the Sword Abusively. Journal of Aggression, Maltreatment & Trauma, 30(7), 950–971.
https://doi.org/10.1080/10926771.2020.1738615.

Decker, M. R., Holliday, C. N., Hameeduddin, Z., Shah, R., Miller, J., Dantzler, J., & Goodmark, L. (2019). "You Do Not Think of Me as a Human Being": Race and Gender Inequities Intersect to Discourage Police Reporting of Violence against Women. *Journal of Urban Health-bulletin of the New York Academy of Medicine, 96(5), 772–783.*
https://doi.org/10.1007/s11524-019-00359-z

Definition of MANIPULATE. (2019). Merriam-Webster.com.
https://www.merriam-webster.com/dictionary/manipulate.

DeRose, L. F., Johnson, B. R., Wang, K., & Salazar-Arango, A. (2021). Couple religiosity, male headship, intimate partner violence, and infidelity. Review of Religious Research, 63(4), 607–627.
https://doi.org/10.1007/s13644-021-00461-2

Domestic abuse: 4 things pastors and churches need to know. (n.d.). Baptist Churches of New England.
https://www.bcne.net/news
domestic-abuse-4-things-pastors-and-churches-need-to-know.

Domestic Violence Basics | NY CourtHelp. (n.d.). Www.nycourts.gov.
https://www.nycourts.gov/CourtHelp/Safety/DVbasics.shtml.

Domestic Violence Dynamics - What Domestic Abuse What It Does to Family. (2011). Domestic Violence Coordinating Council (DVCC) - State of Delaware,
dvcc.delaware.gov/background-purpose/
dynamics-domestic-abuse/.

Domestic Violence Information. (n.d.). Nccadv.org.
https://nccadv.org/domestic-violence-information/.

Domestic Violence: Understanding the Cycle of Violence.
LAPD Online,
www.lapdonline.org/
domestic-violence-understanding-the-cycle-of-violence/.

Ducharme, Jamie. (Jun. 5, 2018) How to Tell If You're in a Toxic
Relationship — and What to Do about It. Time,
time.com/5274206/toxic-relationship-signs-help/.

Dugal, C., Bélanger, C., Brassard, A., & Godbout, N. (2020). A
Dyadic analysis of the associations between cumulative childhood
trauma and psychological intimate partner violence: the mediating
roles of negative urgency and communication patterns. Journal of
Marital and Family Therapy, 46(2), 337–351.
https://doi.org/10.1111/jmft.12414.

Durfee, A. (2011). "I'm Not a Victim, She's an Abuser." Gender &
Society, 25(3), 316–334.
https://doi.org/10.1177/0891243211404889.

DV and IDV Courts | NY CourtHelp. (n.d.). Www.nycourts.gov.
https://www.nycourts.gov/courthelp/Criminal/DV-IDV.shtml.

Dyal, G. (2022). *Community collaborations help protect victims of
intimate partner violence.* Archway Community Services.
https://archway.ca/stories/collaboration-helps-protect-vic-
tims-of-intimate-partner-violence/

Edwards, J. (n.d.). Mutual emotional triggers.
https://www.abcsw.org/index.php?option=com_dailyplanet-
blog&view=entry&year=2021&month=01&day=10&id=9:mu-
tual-emotional-triggers.

Effiong, J. E., et al. (2 June 2022). Traumatic Bonding in Victims of Intimate Partner Violence Is Intensified via Empathy. Journal of Social and Personal Relationships, p. 026540752211062, 10.1177/02654075221106237.

Emezue, C. (2020). Digital or digitally delivered responses to domestic and intimate partner violence during COVID-19. JMIR Public Health and Surveillance, 6(3), e19831.
https://doi.org/10.2196/19831.

Engel, B. (Jun. 7, 2020). Breaking the Cycle of Abuse. Psychology Today.
https://www.psychologytoday.com/us/blog/
the-compassion-chronicles/202006/breaking-the-cycle-abuse.

Facts and figures: Ending violence against women. (n.d.). UN Women – Headquarters.
https://www.unwomen.org/en/what-we-do/
ending-violence-against-women/facts-and-figures.

Fadelici, K. (4 May. 2020). Re-victimization: How Can This Keep Happening? Psychology
Today, www.psychologytoday.com/us/blog/fostering-free-
dom/202005/revictimization-how-can-keep-happening. .

FaithGiant. (2022, June 2024). Understanding ungodly soul ties and how to break them.
FaithGiant. https://faithgiant.com/ungodly-soul-ties/.

Fast Facts: Preventing Intimate Partner Violence - Centers for Disease.
https://www.cdc.gov/violenceprevention/intimatepartnervio-
lence/fastfact.html.

Federal policies can address the impact of structural racism on Black families' access to early care and education. (2021, March 5). Child Trends. ChildTrends.
https://www.childtrends.org/publications/federal-policies-can-address-the-impact-of-structural-racism-on-black-families-access-to-early-care-and-education.

Fielding, S., Torrisi, R., Fielding, S., & Torrisi, R. (2022). 7 signs of a toxic relationship and what to do to fix it, according to couple therapists. Insider.
https://www.insider.com/guides/health/mental-health/toxic-relationship#:~:text=According%20to%20Wood-fin%2C%20subtler%20signs%20of%20hostile%20communica-tion,of%20listening%20to%20hear%20and%20understand%20your%20partner.

Fleming, Paul J., et al. (Mar. 3, 2015). Risk Factors for Men's Lifetime Perpetration of Physical Violence against Intimate Part-ners: Results from the International Men and Gender Equality Survey (IMAGES) in Eight Countries. PLOS ONE, vol. 10, no. 3, p. e0118639, 10.1371/journal.pone.0118639. Accessed 21 Jan. 2023.

Fla. woman Marissa Alexander gets 20 years for "warning shot": Did she stand her ground?
(n.d.). Www.cbsnews.com. https://www.cbsnews.com/news/fla-woman-marissa-alexander-gets-20-years-for-warning-shot-did-she-stand-her-ground/. Accessed 23 Jan. 2023.

Foldy, B. (2018). *A Date Went Terribly Wrong. Was it Murder—Or Self-Defense?* - Bklyner.
https://bklyner.com/he-killed-the-man-who-seduced-him-was-it-murder-or-self-defense/.

Fontes, L. A. "8 Common Post-Separation Domestic Abuse Tactics." DomesticShelters.org,
www.domesticshelters.org/articles/legal/8-common-post-separation-domestic-abuse-tactics.

Foroudi, P. (Jan. 2019). Influence of Brand Signature, Brand Awareness, Brand Attitude, Brand Reputation on Hotel Industry's Brand Performance. International Journal of Hospitality Management, vol. 76, no. A, pp. 271–85,
https://doi.org/10.1016/j.ijhm.2018.05.016.

Forth, A., Sezlik, S., Lee, S., Ritchie, M., Logan, J., & Ellingwood, H. (2021). Toxic Relationships: The Experiences and Effects of Psychopathy in Romantic Relationships. International Journal of Offender Therapy and Comparative Criminology, 66(15), 0306624X2110491.
https://doi.org/10.1177/0306624x211049187.

Fraley R. Chris. A brief overview of adult attachment Theory and research.
http://labs.psychology.illinois.edu/~rcfraley/attachment.htm.

FREE MARISSA NOW. (n.d.). FREE MARISSA NOW.
https://www.freemarissanow.org/.

Fuentes, A. (9 May. 2012). On Marriage and Pair Bonds: Humans bond, love, and marry heterosexually and homosexually. (n.d.). Psychology Today.
https://www.psychologytoday.com/us/blog/busting-myths-about-human-nature/201205/marriage-and-pair-bonds.

Gajanan, M. (2020, March 20). What does 'Shelter in Place' mean? Here's what life is like under the mandate. Time.
https://time.com/5806477/what-is-shelter-in-place/.

Galla, S. (n.d.). Masculinity: The Essential Guide to Manhood and Manliness. MensGroup.com.
https://mensgroup.com/masculinity/.

Gardner, T. (Feb. 17, 2021). A thoroughly horrible incident: Violent jealous boyfriend kept his partner prisoner in his home in Armley and punched out her front teeth. Yorkshire Evening Post. https://www.yorkshireeveningpost.co.uk/news/ crime/a-thoroughly-horrible-incident-violent-jealous- boyfriend-kept-his-partner-prisoner-in-his-home-in-armley- and-punched-out-her-front-teeth-3138261.

"Get the Facts on Elder Abuse." (2021, Feb 23). National Council on Aging. Www.ncoa.org. www.ncoa.org/article/get-the-facts-on-elder-abuse.

Gbaskerville. (2022). 1-in-4 highly religious U.S. marriages have abuse. Life-Saving Divorce. https://lifesavingdivorce.com/1in4/.

Ghidei, W., Montesanti, S., Tomkow, K., Silverstone, P. H., Wells, L., & Campbell, S. (2022). Examining the effectiveness, acceptabil- ity, and feasibility of virtually Delivered Trauma-Focused Domes- tic Violence and Sexual Violence interventions: a Rapid Evidence assessment. Trauma, Violence, & Abuse, 24(3), 1427–1442. https://doi.org/10.1177/15248380211069059.

Goertzen-Morrison, G. (2022, October 12). How the church becomes a grooming place for domestic violence. Baptist News Global. https://baptistnews.com/article/how-the-church-becomes-a- grooming-place-for-domestic-violence/.

Goodmark, L. (Jul. 24, 2019). Stop treating domestic violence differently from other crimes. The New York Times. https://www.nytimes.com/2019/07/23/opinion/domestic-vio- lence-criminal-justice-reform-too.html.

Gordon, K.C., Baucom, D.H., & Snyder, D.K. (2005). Treating couples recovering from infidelity: An integrative approach. Journal of Clinical Psychology. 61(11), 876-893.

Governor Cuomo Signs the Domestic Violence Survivors Justice Act, Longtime Bill Sponsored by Senator Persaud. (n.d.). NYSenate.gov. Retrieved October 29, 2023, from
https://www.nysenate.gov/newsroom/
press-releases/2019/roxanne-j-persaud/
governor-cuomo-signs-domestic-violence-survivors.

Gracia, E. (2014). Intimate Partner Violence against Women and victim-blaming Attitudes among Europeans. Bulletin of the World Health Organization, 92(5), 380–381.
https://doi.org/10.2471/blt.13.131391.

Grady, G., Hinshaw-Fuselier, S., & Friar, N. (2019). Expanding perspectives: A social inequities lens on intimate partner violence, reproductive justice, and infant mental health. *Infant Mental Health Journal, 40(5), 624–639.*
https://doi.org/10.1002/imhj.21809.

Grigsby, N., & Hartman, B. R. (1997). The Barriers Model: An integrated strategy for intervention with battered women. Psychotherapy: Theory, Research, Practice, Training, 34(4), 485–497.
https://doi.org/10.1037/h0087721.

Guide to Affirmations and How to Use Them | Psychology Today. (n.d.).
Www.psychologytoday.com. https://www.psychologytoday.com/us/blog/click-here-happiness/202105/
guide-affirmations-and-how-use-them.

Guy-Evans, O. (2023, September 14). Bronfenbrenner's ecological systems theory. *Simply Psychology*.
https://www.simplypsychology.org/Bronfenbrenner.html.

Hadeed, L. (2021). Why Women Stay: Understanding the Trauma Bond Between Victim and Abuser Case Studies Were Written. In Springer eBooks (pp. 195–207).
https://doi.org/10.1007/978-3-030-73472-5_12.

Hampton, R. L., LaTaillade, J. J., Dacey, A., & Marghi, J. R. (2008). Evaluating Domestic Violence Interventions for Black Women. *Journal of Aggression, Maltreatment & Trauma, 16(3), 330–353.*
https://doi.org/10.1080/10926770801925759.

Harris, B., & Woodlock, D. (2018). Digital Coercive Control: Insights from two landmark domestic violence studies. British Journal of Criminology, 59(3), 530–550.
https://doi.org/10.1093/bjc/azy052.

Health, VHA Office of Mental. Veterans Affairs. Www.va.gov, www.va.gov/HOMELESS/nchav/resources/trauma/intimate-partner-violence.asp. Accessed 27 Dec. 2022.

HeinOnline. (Mar. 8, 2021). HeinOnline.
https://heinonline.org/HOL/LandingPage?handle=hein.journals/calr109&div=7&id=&page=.

Hillstrom, C. (2022, March 1). The hidden epidemic of brain injuries from domestic violence.
The New York Times. https://www.nytimes.com/2022/03/01/magazine/brain-trauma-domestic-violence.html.

Holliday, C. N., Kahn, G., Thorpe, R. J., Shah, R., Hameeduddin, Z., & Decker, M. R. (2019). Racial/Ethnic disparities in police Reporting for partner Violence in the National Crime Victimization Survey and Survivor-Led Interpretation. *Journal of Racial and Ethnic Health Disparities, 7(3), 468–480.*
https://doi.org/10.1007/s40615-019-00675-9.

How Attachment Styles Influence Romantic Relationships. (Feb. 9, 2022). Columbia University
Department of Psychiatry, www.columbiapsychiatry.org/news/how-attachment-styles-influence-romantic-relationships.

How domestic violence leads to murder. (2018, December 9). Washington Post.
https://www.washingtonpost.com/graphics/2018/investigations/domestic-violence-murders/.

How Domestic Violence Perpetrators Manipulate Systems Why Systems & Professionals Are So Vulnerable & 5 Steps to Perpetrator-Proof Your System. (n.d.). Retrieved August 14, 2023, from
https://sfv.org.au/wp-content/uploads/2022/02/How-DV-Perpetrators-Manipulate-Systems.pdf.

How experiences shape who we are. (2020, July 21). Riss.wolfert.nl.
https://riss.wolfert.nl/extra-curricular/rissue/rissue-posts/~board/winter-2020/post/how-shape-who-we-are#:~:text=Mindsets%20are%20a%20culmination%20of.

How Good Is Your "Romantic Competence? Psychology Today. Www.psychologytoday.com,
www.psychologytoday.com/us/blog/talking-apes/202101/how-good-is-your-romantic-competence. Accessed 23 Jan. 2023.

How Important Is An Emotional Connection In A Relationship? (Mar. 22, 2017). Marriage Advice - Expert Marriage Tips & Advice.
https://www.marriage.com/advice/emotional-intimacy/how-important-is-an-emotional-connection-in-a-relationship/.

How to fly in a holding pattern. (2022). Pilot Institute.
https://pilotinstitute.com/holding-patterns/.

How to Overcome Guilt after Leaving a Narcissistic Abuser. Jay Reid Psychotherapy,
jreidtherapy.com/how-to-overcome-guilt/. Accessed 28 Jan. 2023.

Howard, V. (May. 29, 2019) Recognising Narcissistic Abuse and the Implications for Mental Health Nursing Practice. Issues in Mental Health Nursing, vol. 40, no. 8, pp. 1–11, 10.1080/01612840.2019.1590485.

Howell, Kathryn H., Barnes, Sarah E., Miller, Laura E., Graham-Bermann, Sandra A. (2016) "Developmental variations in the impact of intimate partner violence exposure during childhood." Journal of injury & violence research vol. 8,1: 43-57. doi:10.5249/jivr.v8i1.663
https://www.browardbar.org/wp-content/uploads/orientation-%20seminar/domestic-violence-cha rt-dominique.pdf.

https://www.researchgate.net/publication/313406102_Romantic_competence_healthy_relationsh p_functioning_and_well-being_in_emerging_adults_Romantic_competence.

https://www.researchgate.net/publication/320348312_Intimate_Partner_Violence_Victimization_and_Cognitive_Function_in_a_Mixed-Sex_Epidemiological_Sample_of_Urban_Adults.

Hu, R., Xue, J., Lin, K., Sun, I. Y., & Wang, X. (2019). Bidirectional Intimate Partner Violence among Chinese Women: Patterns and Risk Factors. Journal of Interpersonal Violence, 36(21–22), NP12252–NP12278.
https://doi.org/10.1177/0886260519888523.

Huecker, M. R., Shreffler, J., McKeny, P. T., & Davis, D. (2022). Imposter Phenomenon. PubMed; StatPearls Publishing.
https://www.ncbi.nlm.nih.gov/books/NBK585058/.

Huecker, M., & Smock, W. (2023, April 9). Domestic Violence. Nih.gov; StatPearls Publishing.
    https://www.ncbi.nlm.nih.gov/books/NBK499891/.

Hulley, J., Bailey, L., Kirkman, G., Gibbs, G. R., Gomersall, T., Latif, A., & Jones, A. (2022). Intimate Partner Violence and Barriers to Help-Seeking among Black, Asian, Minority ethnic and Immigrant Women: A Qualitative Metasynthesis of Global research. *Trauma, Violence, & Abuse, 24(2), 1001–1015.*
    https://doi.org/10.1177/15248380211050590.

Isen, R. (2022). The contribution of social media toward racial trauma and post-traumatic stress disorder in Black Americans: a forensic perspective. The Journal of Forensic Psychiatry & Psychology, 1–16.
    https://doi.org/10.1080/14789949.2022.2105250.

Ivert, A.-K., Merlo, J., & Gracia, E. (2017). Country of residence, gender equality and victim blaming attitudes about partner violence: a multilevel analysis in EU. European Journal of Public Health, 28(3), 559–564.
    https://doi.org/10.1093/eurpub/ckx138.

Jackson, S. (12 Feb. 2021). What Is Emotional Attachment & When Does It Become Unhealthy? Choosing Therapy,
    www.choosingtherapy.com/emotional-attachment/.

James, A. G., Coard, S. I., Fine, M. A., & Rudy, D. (2018). The Central Roles of Race and Racism in Reframing Family Systems Theory: A consideration of choice and time. *Journal of Family Theory and Review*, 10(2), 419–433.
    https://doi.org/10.1111/jftr.12262.

Jantz, G. L. (Nov. 16, 2021). Break Free from the Trap of Toxic People. Psychology Today.
    Www.psychologytoday.com, www.psychology-today.com/us/blog/hope-relationships/202111/break-free-the-trap-toxic-people.

Jhoydapsych. (2023, April 5). My partner triggers my trauma: Tips and coping strategies. Veritas Psychotherapy and Counselling. https://veritaspsychotherapy.ca/blog/ my-partner-triggers-my-trauma/.

Jock, Brittany W. I., Dana-Sacco G, Arscott J, Bagwell-Gray ME, Loerzel E, Brockie T, Packard G, O'Keefe VM, McKinley CE, Campbell J. We've Already Endured the Trauma, Who is Going to Either End that Cycle or Continue to Feed It?: The Influence of Family and Legal Systems on Native American Women's Intimate Partner Violence Experiences. Journal of interpersonal violence vol. 37,21-22 (2022): NP20602-NP20629. doi:10.1177/08862605211063200

Joseph-Edwards, A., & Wallace, W. C. (2020). Suffering in Silence, Shame, Seclusion, and Invisibility: Men as Victims of Female Perpetrated Domestic Violence in Trinidad and Tobago. Journal of Family Issues, 42(8), 0192513X2095704. https://doi.org/10.1177/0192513x20957047.

Kearney, M. S., & O'Brien, K. M. (2018). Is it love or is it control? Assessing warning signs of dating violence. Journal of Interpersonal Violence, 36(11–12), 5446–5470. https://doi.org/10.1177/0886260518805105.

Kelly, L., Spencer, C., Stith, S. M., & Beliard, C. A. (2020). "I'm Black, I'm strong, and I need help": Toxic Black femininity and intimate partner violence. *Journal of Family Theory & Review, 12(1), 54–63.* https://doi.org/10.1111/jftr.12358.

Kennedy, A. C., & Prock, K. A. (2018). I Still Feel Like I Am Not Normal: A Review of the Role of Stigma and Stigmatization Among Female Survivors of Child Sexual Abuse, Sexual Assault, and Intimate Partner Violence. Trauma, Violence, & Abuse, 19(5), 512–527. https://doi.org/10.1177/1524838016673601.

King, J. (2018). Too Good to Go Too Bad to Stay: 5 Steps to Finding Freedom from a Toxic Relationship. Morgan James Publishing. ProQuest Ebook Central,
http://ebookcentral.proquest.com/lib/bmcc/detail.action?docID=6448502. Created from bmcc on 2023-01-22 05:48:13.

Kippert, A. (2020, Aug 10). The ways racism fuels the fire of domestic violence. DomesticShelters.org.
https://www.domesticshelters.org/articles/race-gender-religion-immigration/the-ways-racism-fuels-the-fire-of-domestic-violence.

Kippert, A. (2020, June 22). Women Serve Longer Prison Sentences After Killing Abusers.
DomesticShelters.org. https://www.domesticshelters.org/articles/in-the-news/women-serve-longer-prison-sentences-after-killing-abusers.

Kluger, J. (3 Feb. 2021). Domestic violence is a pandemic within the COVID-19 pandemic.
Time. https://time.com/5928539/domestic-violence-covid-19/.

Knaul, F. M., Bustero, F., & Horton, R. (Jan. 2020). Countering the Pandemic of Gender-Based Violence and Maltreatment of Young People: The Lancet Commission. The Lancet, vol. 395, no. 10218, pp. 98–99, 10.1016/s0140-6736(19)33136-8.

Kristenson, S. (2022, August 25). 101 Affirmations for People Dealing with PTSD. Happier
Human. https://www.happierhuman.com/affirmations-ptsd/.

Kulkarni, S. (2018). Intersectional Trauma-Informed Intimate Partner Violence (IPV) Services: Narrowing the Gap between IPV Service Delivery and Survivor Needs. *Journal of Family Violence*, 34(1), 55–64.
https://doi.org/10.1007/s10896-018-0001-5.

Kupferman & Golden Family Law – The Role of Isolation in Domestic Violence. (n.d.).
https://www.kgfamilylaw.com/
the-role-of-isolation-in-domestic-violence/.

'Amie, L. (29 Mar. 2019). Are You Being Love Bombed? Cosmopolitan.
www.cosmopolitan.com/sex-love/a26988344/
love-bombing-signs-definition/.

Lahav, Y., Renshaw, K. D., & Solomon, Z. (2018). Domestic Abuse and Forgiveness among Military Spouses. Journal of Aggression, Maltreatment & Trauma, 28(2), 243–260.
https://doi.org/10.1080/10926771.2018.1531335.

Lahav, Y. (Dec. 2021). Painful Bonds: Identification with the Aggressor and Distress among IPV Survivors. Journal of Psychiatric Research, vol. 144, pp. 26–31, 10.1016/j.jpsychires.2021.09.046. Accessed 18 Jan. 2023.

Lambert, C. A. (2016). Women with Controlling Partners: Taking Back Your Life from a Manipulative Or Abusive Partner.

Lane, R., Gribble, R., Alves-Costa, F., Taylor, A., Howard, L. M., Fear, N. T., & MacManus, D. G. (2022). Intimate Partner Violence and Abuse: A qualitative exploration of UK military personnel and civilian partner experiences. Journal of Family Violence.
https://doi.org/10.1007/s10896-022-00446-x.

Langhinrichsen-Rohling, J., Schneider, M., Selwyn, C., Lathan, E., Sayegh, L., & Hamberger, L. K. (2020). Addressing Intimate Partner Violence Within the Healthcare System. *Handbook of Interpersonal Violence and Abuse across the Lifespan, 1–29.*
https://doi.org/10.1007/978-3-319-62122-7_153-1.

Lansford, J. (2021, June 15). The Importance of Fathers for Child Development. Psychology
Today. Www.psychologytoday.com. https://www.psychol-ogytoday.com/us/blog/parenting-and-culture/202106/the-importance-fathers-child-development.

Lausi, G., Pizzo, A., Cricenti, C., Baldi, M., Desiderio, R., Giannini, A. M., & Mari, E. (2021). Intimate Partner Violence during the COVID-19 Pandemic: A Review of the Phenomenon from Victims' and Help Professionals' Perspectives. International Journal of Environmental Research and Public Health, 18(12), 6204.
https://doi.org/10.3390/ijerph18126204.

Lazaridou, F., & Fernando, S. (2022). Deconstructing institutional racism and the social construction of whiteness: A strategy for professional competence training in culture and migration mental health. *Transcultural Psychiatry*, 59(2), 175–187.
https://doi.org/10.1177/13634615221087101.

LGBTQ: Sexual Assault, Partner Violence, and Stalking. Inside.nku.edu,
inside.nku.edu/studentaffairs/departments/nvp/about-us/resources/lgbtq.html. Accessed 13 Nov. 2022.

Lippy, C., Jumarali, S. N., Nnawulezi, N., Williams, E., & Burk, C. (2019). The Impact of Mandatory Reporting Laws on Survivors of Intimate Partner Violence: Intersectionality, Help-Seeking and the need for change. *Journal of Family Violence, 35(3), 255–267.*
https://doi.org/10.1007/s10896-019-00103-w.

Lmhc, C. H. M. (2017, November 17). 7 Steps of Healing from Domestic Violence. Psych Central.
https://psychcentral.com/pro/exhausted-woman/2017/11/7-steps-of-healing-from-domestic-violence#1.

Lpc/Mhsp, J. C. M. (2023). UNREQUITED LOVE—What to do When Love is One-Sided. Verywell Mind.
https://www.verywellmind.com/unrequited-love-4175362.

Lynn, N. (n.d.). Understanding Intimate Partner Violence in the Church: A Call for Church Leaders to Engage in Dialogue. Retrieved August 31, 2023, from
https://bpb-us-w2.wpmucdn.com/wordpress.lehigh.edu/dist/5/694/files/2020/01/IPV-the-Church-White-Paper.pdf.

Maftei, A., & Dănilă, O. (2021). Give me your password! What are you hiding? Associated factors of intimate partner violence through technological abuse. Current Psychology, 42(11), 8781–8797.
https://doi.org/10.1007/s12144-021-02197-2digit.

Mahapatro, M., & Prasad, M. M. (2021). Role of popular media and breaking the cycle of domestic violence. Journal of Public Affairs.
https://doi.org/10.1002/pa.2618.

, A. I., Cunradi, C. B., & Nápoles, A. M. (2020). Racial/Ethnic Discrimination and Intimate Partner Violence Perpetration in Latino Men: The Mediating Effects of Mental Health. *International Journal of Environmental Research and Public Health, 17(21), 8148.*
https://doi.org/10.3390/ijerph17218148.

Martin, B. A., Cui, M., Ueno, K., & Fincham, F. D. (2013). Intimate Partner Violence in Interracial and Monoracial Couples. Family Relations, 62(1), 202–211.
https://doi.org/10.1111/j.1741-3729.2012.00747.x.

Mating. Psychology Today. (n.d.). Www.psychologytoday.com.
https://www.psychologytoday.com/us/basics/mating.

Matthew, D. C. (2022). Against "institutional racism." *Philosophy & Social Criticism*, 019145372211149.
https://doi.org/10.1177/01914537221114910.

McDermott, N. (2023, March 31). Trauma Bonding: What You Need To Know—And How To Get Help. Forbes Health.
https://www.forbes.com/health/mind/what-is-trauma-bonding/.

McLeod, D. A., Pharris, A., Boyles, E., Winkles, R., & Stafford, W. (2021). The Model of Systemic Relational Violence: Conceptualizing IPV as a Method of Continual and Enforced Domination. Trauma Care, 1(2), 87–98.
https://doi.org/10.3390/traumacare1020009.

Michaels, Samantha. New York Just Passed a Bill to Prevent Domestic Violence Survivors from Being Evicted for Calling 911. Mother Jones.
www.motherjones.com/crime-justice/2019/05/new-york-just-passed-a-bill-to-prevent-domestic-violence-survivors-from-being-evicted-for-calling-911/. Accessed 27 Dec. 2022.

Miller, E., & McCaw, B. (2019). Intimate partner violence. *The New England Journal of Medicine, 380(9), 850–857.*
https://doi.org/10.1056/nejmra1807166.

Mirshahzadeh, D. (Apr. 1, 2015). The Power of Symbols to Transform Your Business. Forbes.
www.forbes.com/sites/theyec/2015/04/01/pink-unicorns-and-the-power-of-symbols-to-transform-your-business/?sh=295b2a00113e. Accessed 25 Mar. 2023.

Moffitt, P., Aujla, W., Giesbrecht, C. J., Grant, I., & Straatman, A.-L. (2020). Intimate Partner Violence and COVID-19 in Rural, Remote, and Northern Canada: Relationship, Vulnerability and Risk. Journal of Family Violence.
https://doi.org/10.1007/s10896-020-00212-x.

Monahan, K. (2019). Intimate Partner Violence (IPV) and Neurological Outcomes: A Review for Practitioners. Journal of Aggression, Maltreatment & Trauma, 28(7), 807–825.
https://doi.org/10.1080/10926771.2019.1628154.

Morrison, P. K. & Wentling, R. (October 23, 2023). COVID-19 and its impact on intimate partner violence. SSRI COVID-19 Resources.
    https://covid19.ssri.psu.edu/articles/covid-19-and-its-impact-intimate-partner-violence.

Murray, C., Crowe, A., & Overstreet, N. (2015). Sources and components of stigma experienced by survivors of intimate partner violence. Journal of Interpersonal Violence, 33(3), 515–536.
    https://doi.org/10.1177/0886260515609565.

National Center for Injury Prevention and Control, Division of Violence Prevention. Preventing Intimate Partner Violence. (2 Nov. 2021). Centers for Disease Control and Prevention,
    www.cdc.gov/violenceprevention/intimatepartnerviolence/fastfact.html.

National Coalition Against Domestic Violence. (n.d.). NCADV. Ncadv.org. Retrieved August 16, 2023, from
    https://ncadv.org/blog/posts/after-the-laughter.

National Domestic Violence Hotline. "Power and Control." The Hotline,
    www.thehotline.org/identify-abuse/power-and-control/.

Navigating Racial Trauma in the Aftermath of Police Killings | The Takeaway. (2021, March 16).
    WNYC Studios. https://www.wnycstudios.org/podcasts/takeaway/segments/racial-trauma-police-killings. Accessed 23 Jan. 2023.

New Approaches to Policing High-Risk Intimate Partner Victims and Those Committing the Crimes. (n.d.). National Institute of Justice.
    https://nij.ojp.gov/topics/articles/new-approaches-policing-high-risk-intimate-partner-victims-and-those-committing#Model%20Focused%20on%20Persons%20Committing%20The%20Offense.

Niemeyer, K. (2022, August 14). Killing of Black, Gay Ole Miss Student has School's LGBTQ community "terrified," his former roommate says. Insider.
https://www.insider.com/killing-of-black-gay-ole-miss-student-has-lgbtq-community-terrified-2022-8.

Nyc.gov. (2022).
comptroller.nyc.gov/reports/housing-survivors/?utm_source=Media-All&utm_campaign=6277f0addf-EMAIL_CAMPAIGN_2017_05_31_COPY. Accessed 24 Dec. 2022.

Obituary for Ellen Louise Pence. (2012, January 11). Star Tribune. Retrieved October 28, 2023,
from https://www.startribune.com/obituaries/detail/13335325/.

Obsessive love disorder: Symptoms and treatment. (2019, November 22).
Www.medicalnewstoday.com. https://www.medicalnewstoday.com/articles/327098.

Ogbe, E., Harmon, S., Van den Bergh, R., & Degomme, O. (2020). A systematic review of intimate partner violence interventions focused on improving social support and/ mental health outcomes of survivors. PLOS ONE, 15(6), e0235177.
https://doi.org/10.1371/journal.pone.0235177.

Pace, R., Pace, R., & Pace, R. (2022). 10 Benefits of the 80/20 rule in relationships. Marriage Advice - Expert Marriage Tips & Advice.
https://www.marriage.com/advice/relationship/rule-in-relationships/.

Pache, Stéphanie. "A History of Interpersonal Violence: Raising Public Concern." Handbook of Interpersonal Violence and Abuse across the Lifespan, 2020, pp. 1–22, 10.1007/978-3-319-62122-7_284-1. Accessed 23 Jan. 2023.

Padgett, D. (2022, June 25). *Police Say Man Killed Gay Lover, Burned Corpse to Hide Relationship.* Advocate.com.
https://www.advocate.com/crime/2022/6/25/police-say-man-killed-gay-lover-burned-corpse-hide-relationship.

Park, Y., Sullivan, K., Riviere, L. A., Merrill, J. C., & Clarke-Walper, K. (2021). Intimate Partner Violence Perpetration among Military Spouses. Journal of Interpersonal Violence, 37(15–16), NP13497–NP13517.
https://doi.org/10.1177/08862605211004139.

Perspective: The Difference Maker in Memories & Experiences. (2017). Psychology Today.
https://www.psychologytoday.com/us/blog/trauma-and-hope/201704/perspective-the-difference-maker-in-memories-experiences.

Petersson, J., and Thunberg, S. (18 Oct. 2021). Vulnerability Factors among Women Victimized by Intimate Partner Violence and the Presence of Children. Journal of Family Violence, 10.1007/s10896-021-00328-8.

Pocock, M., Jackson, D., & Bradbury-Jones, C. (2019). Intimate Partner Violence and the Power of Love: A qualitative systematic review. Health Care for Women International, 41(6), 621–646.
https://doi.org/10.1080/07399332.2019.1621318.

Pokharel, B., Hegadoren, K., & Papathanassoglou, E. (2020). Factors influencing silencing of women who experience intimate partner violence: An integrative review. *Aggression and Violent Behavior*, 52, 101422.
https://doi.org/10.1016/j.avb.2020.101422.

Porter, S. (2023). Cycle of Abuse: What it is & How to heal. Choosing Therapy. Choosing Therapy.
  https://www.choosingtherapy.com/cycle-of-abuse/.

Power and Control Wheel. Michigan State University. (n.d.). Michigan State University.
  https://safeplace.msu.edu/info-resources/
  relationship-violence/power-control-wheel.

Practice Profile: Interventions for Domestic Violence Offenders: Duluth Model. (n.d.). CrimeSolutions, National Institute of Justice.
  https://crimesolutions.ojp.gov/ratedpractices/17#pd.

Preventing violence before it occurs A framework and background paper to guide the primary prevention of violence against women in Victoria. (n.d.). Retrieved August 31, 2023, from
  https://prevention-collaborative.org/wp-content/
  uploads/2021/08/VicHealth_2007_Primary-Prevention-Framework-in-Victoria.pdf.

Prevention Institute. (n.d.). Www.preventioninstitute.org.
  https://www.preventioninstitute.org/publications/
  what-why-how-answers-faqs-about-acer-framework.

Products, C. F. T. (2023). Cigarettes. U.S. Food And Drug Administration.
  https://www.fda.gov/tobacco-products/
  products-ingredients-components/cigarettes.

PSAs Highlight Domestic Violence Awareness Among Native Americans. (2022, January 17).
  Www.acf.hhs.gov. https://www.acf.hhs.gov/media/press/2022/
  psas-highlight-domestic-violence-awareness-among-native-americans.

"Psychoanalytic Theory & Approaches" (2009). American Psychoanalytic Association.
  Apsa.org. apsa.org/content/psychoanalytic-theory-approaches.

Puri, L. (21 Sept. 2016). The Economic Costs of Violence against Women. UN Women.
www.unwomen.org/en/news/stories/2016/9/speech-by-laksh-mi-puri-on-economic-costs-of-violence-against-women.

Racial justice. (n.d.). Institutional Diversity, Equity, and Inclusion.
https://diversity.williams.edu/racial-justice/.

Rafferty, B. (2019). Repetition Compulsion and Choice of Love Object. Esource.dbs.ie, esource.dbs.ie/handle/10788/3974. Accessed 19 Jan. 2023.

Ragavan, M. I., & Miller, E. (2022). Healing-Centered care for intimate partner violence survivors and their children. Pediatrics, 149(6).
https://doi.org/10.1542/peds.2022-056980.

Rakovec-Felser, Z. (2014). Domestic violence and abuse in inti-mate relationship from public health perspective. Health Psychol-ogy Research, 2(3), 62–67.
https://doi.org/10.4081/hpr.2014.1821.

Reid, J., Haskell, R., Dillahunt-Aspillaga, C., & Thor, J. (1 Jan. 2013). Trauma Bonding and Interpersonal Violence. Psychology of Trauma.
digitalcommons.usf.edu/fac_publications/198/.

Re-Traumatizing Domestic Violence Victims | Psychology Today. (n.d.).
Www.psychologytoday.com. Retrieved August 16, 2023, from https://www.psychologytoday.com/us/blog/intersecting-law-and-mental-health/202204/re-traumatizing-domestic-violence-victims.

Rice, J., West, C. M., Cottman, K., & Gardner, G. (2020). The Inter-sectionality of Intimate Partner Violence in the Black Community. *Handbook of Interpersonal Violence across the Lifespan, 1–29.*
https://doi.org/10.1007/978-3-319-62122-7_240-1.

Robbins, T. 13 Proven Ways to Maintain a Healthy Relationship with Tony. Tonyrobbins.com,
www.tonyrobbins.com/ultimate-relationship-guide/healthy-relationship-you-deserve/.

Romero, J. (25 Nov. 2014). Father Figure Wanted: The Effect of Absence of a Father in a Woman's Love Relationships. The Composition of Happiness.
https://openlab.citytech.cuny.edu/the-composition-of-happiness-f2014/2014/11/25/father-figure-wanted-the-effect-of-absence-of-a-father-in-a-womans-love-relationships/#:~:text=Research%20shows%20that%20women%20are%20specifically%20damaged%20in,the%20emotional%20absence%20of%20a%20father%20throughout%20childhood.

Romero-Martínez, Á., Lila, M., Gracia, E., Rodriguez, C. M., & Moya-Albiol, L. (2019). Acceptability of Intimate Partner Violence among Male Offenders: The Role of Set-Shifting and Emotion Decoding Dysfunctions as Cognitive Risk Factors. International Journal of Environmental Research and Public Health, 16(9), 1537.
https://doi.org/10.3390/ijerph16091537.

Ryzik, M, and Benner, K. (18 Mar. 2021). Biden's Aid Package Funnels Millions to Victims of Domestic Abuse. The New York Times,
www.nytimes.com/2021/03/18/us/politics/biden-domestic-violence.html.

Sabri, B., Tharmarajah, S., Njie-Carr, V. P. S., Messing, J. T., Loerzel, E., Arscott, J., & Campbell, J. C. (2021). Safety Planning With Marginalized Survivors of Intimate Partner Violence: Challenges of Conducting Safety Planning Intervention Research With Marginalized Women. Trauma, Violence, & Abuse, 23(5), 152483802110131.
https://doi.org/10.1177/15248380211013136.

Sahdan, Z., Pain, R., & McEwan, C. (2021). Demonic possession: Narratives of domestic abuse and trauma in Malaysia. Transactions of the Institute of British Geographers, 47(2), 286–301.
https://doi.org/10.1111/tran.12485.

Sangeetha, J., Mohan, S., & Hariharasudan, A. (1 June 2022). Strategic Analysis of Intimate Partner Violence (IPV) and Cycle of Violence in the Autobiographical Text –When I Hit You. Heliyon, vol. 8, no. 6, p. e09734,
www.sciencedirect.com/science/article/pii/
S2405844022010222#bbib35, 10.1016/j.heliyon.2022.e09734.

Santa Clara University. (2022). *Theoretical Framework*. Www. scu.edu.
https://www.scu.edu/oml/about-us/theoretical-framework/.

Sexual Assault. (3 Jan. 2019). The United States Department of Justice. Justice.gov,
www.justice.gov/ovw/sexual-assault.

Saunders, D. G. (2020). Barriers to Leaving an Abusive Relationship. Handbook of Interpersonal Violence and Abuse across the Lifespan, pp. 1–23, 10.1007/978-3-319-62122-7_186-1.

Selva, Joaquin. (5 Jan. 2018). How to Set Healthy Boundaries: 10 Examples + PDF Worksheets.
PositivePsychology.com, positivepsychology.com/
great-self-care-setting-healthy-boundaries/.

Sexual Violence and Intimate Partner Violence Among People with Disabilities |Violence Prevention|Injury Center|CDC. (2021, February 23).
Www.cdc.gov. https://www.cdc.gov/violenceprevention/sexu-
alviolence/svandipv.html.

Shorey, R. C., Tirone, V., & Stuart, G. L. (2014). Coordinated community response components for victims of intimate partner violence: A review of the literature. *Aggression and Violent Behavior, 19(4)*, 363–371.
https://doi.org/10.1016/j.avb.2014.06.001.

Sikweyiya, Y., Nduna, M., Khuzwayo, N., Mthombeni, A., & Mashamba-Thompson, T. P. (2016). Gender-based violence and absent fathers: a scoping review protocol. BMJ Open.
https://doi.org/10.1136/bmjopen-2015-010154.

Shapper, A. (25 Jul. 2022). 7 Stages of Trauma Bonding | Banyan Boca. Banyan Treatment Center.
www.banyantreatmentcenter.com/2022/07/25/7-stages-of-trauma-bonding-boca/. Accessed 22 Jan. 2023.

SITNFlash. (19 Jun. 2020). Love, Actually: The science behind lust, attraction, and companionship - Science in the News. Science in the News.
https://sitn.hms.harvard.edu/flash/2017/love-actually-science-behind-lust-attraction-companionship/.

Sokoloff, N. J., & Dupont, I. (2005). Domestic violence at the intersections of race, class, and gender. Violence Against Women, 11(1), 38–64.
https://doi.org/10.1177/1077801204271476.

Sosnoski, K., Ph.D. (5 Feb. 2022). Differences Between Love and Attachment. Psych Central,
psychcentral.com/health/attachment-vs-love#love.

Specialty Institute June 2022: Addressing the Spectrum of Housing for Victim/Survivors for DV, Sexual Violence and Trafficking in Tribal Communities | NIWRC. (2023, October 25).
https://www.niwrc.org/resources/traininginstitute/specialty-institute-june-2022-addressing-spectrum-housing.

Sprang, G. (17 Dec. 2020). Attachment Styles, and Vicarious Trauma. Handbook of Interpersonal Violence and Abuse across the Lifespan, pp. 1–17, 10.1007/978-3-319-62122-7_285-2. Accessed 23 Jan. 2023.

Staff report, Knoxville News Sentinel. (2019, January 7). Read Cyntoia Brown's full statement on her clemency. The Tennessean. https://www.knoxnews.com/story/news/2019/01/07/cyntoia-brown-clemency-read-her-full-statement-gov-bill-haslam-decision/2502303002/.

Statement of U.S. Attorney's Office for the District of Columbia before D.C. Council Regarding Measures to Strengthen Protections for Victims-Survivors of Domestic Violence. (13 May 2021). Www.justice.gov, www.justice.gov/usao-dc/pr/statement-us-attorneys-office-district-columbia-dc-council-regarding-measures-strengthen. Accessed 9 Jan. 2023.

Stith, Sandra M., and Chelsea M. Spencer. (2019). Couples Counseling to End Intimate Partner Violence. Handbook of Interpersonal Violence across the Lifespan, pp. 1–19, 10.1007/978-3-319-62122-7_146-1. Accessed 23 Jan. 2023.

Strucke, M., & Hajjar, K. (2009). Battered Woman Syndrome. Cornell.edu. https://courses2.cit.cornell.edu/sociallaw/student_projects/BatteredWomanSyndrome.htm

Sultana, R., Ozen-Dursun, B., Femi-Ajao, O., Husain, N., Varese, F., & Taylor, P. (2022). A Systematic Review and Meta-Synthesis of Barriers and Facilitators of Help-Seeking Behaviors in South Asian Women Living in High-Income Countries Who Have Experienced Domestic Violence: Perception of Domestic Violence Survivors and Service Providers. Trauma, Violence, & Abuse, 152483802211261. https://doi.org/10.1177/15248380221126189.

Team, F. (2022, October 15). Why are fathers overprotective of their daughters? - FatherResource. FatherResource.
https://fatherresource.org/overprotective-fathers-and-daughters/.

Teen Dating Violence. National Institute of Justice,
nij.ojp.gov/topics/crimes/teen-dating-violence.

The 3 Core Skills That Every Person Needs for Healthy Romantic Relationships. (18 Nov. 2019).
Ideas.ted.com, ideas.ted.com/the-3-core-skills-that-every-person-needs-for-healthy-romantic-relationships/.

The 7 Stages of Trauma Bonding. Choosing Therapy,
www.choosingtherapy.com/stages-of-trauma-bonding/.

The 4 Stages of the Cycle of Abuse: From Tension to Calm and Back. (2022, July 15). Psych Central.
https://psychcentral.com/health/cycle-of-abuse#recap.

The 80/20 Rule: Dating Using The Pareto Principle Rule | ReGain. (n.d.).
https://www.regain.us/advice/dating/the-80-20-rule-dating-using-the-pareto-principle/.

The Correlation of Domestic Violence & Systemic Oppression. (2020, October 1). The Women's Center.
https://twcwaukesha.org/the-correlation-of-domestic-violence-and-systemic-oppression/.

The Cycle of Violence. Mpdc.
Mpdc.dc.gov, mpdc.dc.gov/page/cycle-violence.

THE HRSA STRATEGY TO ADDRESS INTIMATE PARTNER VIOLENCE. (2017).
https://www.hrsa.gov/sites/default/files/hrsa/owh/hrsa-strategy-intimate-partner-violence.pdf.

The National Intimate Partner and Sexual Violence Survey Report on Sexual Violence. (2016).
https://www.cdc.gov/violenceprevention/pdf/nisvs/nisvsReportonSexualViolence.pdf.

The Role of Women in the Church, in Society and in the Home. (n.d.). CBE International. Retrieved August 29, 2023, from https://www.cbeinternational.org/resource/role-women-church-society-and-home/#:~:text=A%20woman%E2%80%99s%20role%20in%20relation%20to%20home%2C%20church.

Torrisi, R. Fielding, S. (2021). 7 Tell-Tale Signs of a Toxic Relationship and How to Fix It, according to Couple Therapists. Insider, www.insider.com/guides/health/mental-health/toxic-relationship.

Training Curriculum for Intimate Partner Abuse Prevention and Intervention among American Evangelical Keralite Women - ProQuest. (n.d.).
Www.proquest.com. https://www.proquest.com/openview/39f49bb23f1f3bf42d52dc962d67f48a/1?pq-origsite=g-scholar&cbl=18750&diss=y.

Trauma Bonding: What You Need to Know—and How to Get Help. (23 Sept. 2022). Forbes Health.
www.forbes.com/health/mind/what-is-trauma-bonding/.

Tullio, V., Zerbo, S., Lanzarone, A., Spagnolo, E. V., Malta, G., & Argo, A. (2019). The violence of men against women: Medico-legal and psychological issues. Medico-legal Journal, 88(1), 37–40.
https://doi.org/10.1177/0025817219882169.

Tullio, V, Lanzarone, A., & Zerbo, S. (Jan. 2021). Violence against Women in Heterosexual Couples: A Review of Psychological and Medico-Legal Considerations. Medicine, Science, and the Law, vol. 61, no. 1_suppl, pp. 113–124, 10.1177/0025802420936081. Accessed 19 Jan. 2023.

Tyler Perry - 80/20 clip. (n.d.). [Video]. @Amazon. https://www.amazon.com/live/video/4aae5c226f5843449556dc1554926ec3?ref_=asvh_vdp

Understanding and addressing violence against women BOX 1. FORMS OF INTIMATE PARTNER VIOLENCE (2). (n.d.). https://iris.who.int/bitstream/handle/10665/77432/WHO_RHR_12.36_eng.pdf

Understanding Emotional Triggers and Building Healthy Relationships. (n.d.). Sunshine City Counseling. Retrieved August 16, 2023, https://www.sunshinecitycounseling.com/blog/emotional-triggers-and-relationship-issues-in-therapy.

Understanding Florida's Stand Your Ground Defense. (n.d.). Valiente, Carollo and McElligott PLLC. https://valientelaw.com/understanding-floridas-stand-your-ground-defense/#:~:text=The%20statute%20states%20that%20a.

Understand Relationship Abuse. National Domestic Violence Hotline. The Hotline, www.thehotline.org/identify-abuse/understand-relationship-abuse/.

United Nations Office on Drugs and Crime. (2021). Killings of Women and Girls by Their Intimate Partner or Other Family Members.

United Nations. Transforming Our World: The 2030 Agenda for Sustainable Development |

Department of Economic and Social Affairs. (2015). United Nations,
  sdgs.un.org/2030agenda.

Unrequited Love. (n.d.). Psychology Today.
  https://www.psychologytoday.com/us/blog/
  in-it-together/202003/unrequited-love

Valera, E. M., Cao, A., Pasternak, O., Shenton, M. E., Kubicki, M., Makris, N., & Adra, N. (2019). White Matter Correlates of Mild Traumatic Brain Injuries in Women Subjected to Intimate-Partner Violence: A Preliminary Study. Journal of Neurotrauma, 36(5), 661–668.
  https://doi.org/10.1089/neu.2018.5734.

Varina, R. (2023, January 3). What's Unrequited Love? Experts Explain Why It Can Be So Painful and What to Do About It. Cosmopolitan.
  https://www.cosmopolitan.com/sex-love/a42305495/
  unrequited-love.

Victims of Crime Act (VOCA). (n.d.). The Hotline.
  https://www.thehotline.org/resources/victims-of-crime-act-
  voca/. Accessed 9 Jan. 2023.

Violence against women prevalence estimates. (2018). WHO.
  https://www.who.int/
  publications-detail-redirect/9789240026681.

Voith, L. A., Topitzes, J., & Berg, K. A. (2020). The transmission of violence and trauma across development and environmental contexts: Intimate partner violence from the perspective of men with histories of perpetration. *Child Abuse & Neglect*, 99, 104267.
  https://doi.org/10.1016/j.chiabu.2019.104267.

Walker, L. E. A. (2006). Battered woman syndrome: Empirical findings. In F. L. Denmark, H. H. Krauss, E. Halpern, & J. A. Sechzer (Eds.), Violence and exploitation against women and girls (pp. 142–157). Blackwell Publishing.

Waller, B., Harris, J., & Quinn, C. R. (2021). Caught in the Crossroad: An intersectional examination of African American women intimate partner violence survivors' help seeking. *Trauma, Violence, & Abuse*, 23(4), 1235–1248.
https://doi.org/10.1177/1524838021991303.

Waller, B., Joyce, P. A., Quinn, C. R., Shaari, A. a. H., & Boyd, D. T. (2022). "I am the one that needs help": The Theory of Help-Seeking Behavior for Survivors of Intimate Partner Violence. *Journal of Interpersonal Violence, 38(1–2), 288–310.*
https://doi.org/10.1177/08862605221084340.

Watch Deon Cole: Cole Hearted | Netflix Official site. (n.d.).
https://www.netflix.com/title/80995737.

Wathen, C. N., & Macmillan, H. L. (2013). Children's exposure to intimate partner violence: Impacts and interventions. Paediatrics & Child Health, 18(8), 419–422.
https://www.ncbi.nlm.nih.gov/pmc/articles/PMC3887080/.

Watlington, C. G., & Murphy, C. M. (2006). The roles of religion and spirituality among African American survivors of domestic violence. Journal of Clinical Psychology, 62(7), 837–857.
https://doi.org/10.1002/jclp.20268.

WBA Referee Manual. (2009, February 26). World Boxing Association.
https://www.wbaboxing.com/officialarticles/wba-referee-manual.

Weiss, A. (2020, December 9). Helping Survivors Can Be as Simple as Changing the Way We Speak - Partners for Peace.
https://www.partnersforpeaceme.org/helping-survivors-can-be-as-simple-as-changing-the-way-we-speak/.

Westenberg, L. (2017). 'When She Calls For Help'—Domestic violence in Christian families. Social Sciences, 6(3), 71.
https://doi.org/10.3390/socsci6030071.

White, D. G., Bay, M., & Martin, W. E., Jr. (2016). Freedom on my mind: A History of African Americans, with Documents. Macmillan Higher Education.

Whitfield, D. L., Coulter, R. W., Langenderfer-Magruder, L., & López, D. J. (2018). Experience of intimate partner violence among lesbian, gay, bisexual, and transgender college students: the intersection of gender, race, and sexual orientation. *Journal of Interpersonal Violence, 36(11–12)*, NP6040–NP6064.
https://doi.org/10.1177/0886260518812071.

Why Do I Keep Attracting Toxic Partners? Psychology Today." www.psychologytoday.com,
www.psychologytoday.com/us/blog/women-autism-spectrum-disorder/202011/why-do-i-keep-attracting-toxic-partners. Accessed 28 Jan. 2023.

Why Gaslighters Accuse You of Gaslighting | Psychology Today. (n.d.).
Www.psychologytoday.com. Retrieved August 29, 2023, from https://www.psychologytoday.com/us/blog/here-there-and-everywhere/201702/why-gaslighters-accuse-you-of-gaslighting#:~:text=Gaslighters%20often%20accuse%20others%20of%20harmful%20actions%20even.

Why is it important to bring a racial justice framework to our efforts to end domestic violence? (2018). VAWnet.org.
https://vawnet.org/news/why-it-important-bring-racial-justice-framework-our-efforts-end-domestic-violence.

Wikipedia Contributors. (2019, March 9). Duluth model. Wikipedia; Wikimedia Foundation.
https://en.wikipedia.org/wiki/Duluth_model.

Williams, O. J., & Jenkins, E. J. (2019). A survey of Black churches' responses to domestic violence. Social Work and Christianity, 46(4), 21–38.
https://doi.org/10.34043/swc.v46i4.110.

Williams, M. R., Murphy, C. M., Dore, G. A., Evans, M. K., & Zonderman, A. B. (2017). Intimate Partner Violence Victimization and Cognitive Function in a Mixed-Sex Epidemiological Sample of Urban Adults. Violence and Victims, 32(6), 1133–1148.
https://doi.org/10.1891/0886-6708.vv-d-16-00118.

Women of Color Network. (n.d.). Retrieved August 25, 2023, from
https://womenofcolornetwork.org/docs/factsheets/fs_domestic-violence.pdf.

Women of Intimate Partner Abuse: Traumatic Bonding Phenomenon. ProQuest.
Www.proquest.com, www.proquest.com/openview/464ba-033849288b9e402569e9b02af48/1?pq-origsite=gscholar&cbl=18750.

Wong, J. Y.-H., Fong, D. Y.-T., Lai, V., & Tiwari, A. (2013). Bridging Intimate Partner Violence and the Human Brain. Trauma, Violence, & Abuse, 15(1), 22–33.
https://doi.org/10.1177/1524838013496333.

Woodlock, D., McKenzie, M., Western, D., & Harris, B. (2019). Technology as a weapon in domestic violence: Responding to digital coercive control. Australian Social Work, 73(3), 368–380.
https://doi.org/10.1080/0312407x.2019.1607510.

Wordsmith, N. (2022, March 3). Apostolic Pentecostal Women: Looking different. The Real Church Hurt. https://doi.org/10.1037/ccp0000722tps://blog.therealchurch-hurt.com/2021/12/apostolic-pentecostal-women-looking.html.

Zarling, A., & Russell, D. W. (2022). A randomized clinical trial of acceptance and commitment therapy and the Duluth Model classes for men court-mandated to a domestic violence program. *Journal of Consulting and Clinical Psychology*, 90(4), 326–338. https://doi.org/10.1037/ccp0000722.

Zurick, M. (2023, July 23). *Florida man kills pregnant trans partner in murder-suicide: sheriff.* Newsweek. https://www.newsweek.com/florida-man-kills-preg-nant-trans-partner-murder-suicide-sheriff-1814763.

Crime trends in U.S. Cities: Mid-Year 2023 Update - Council on Criminal Justice. (2023, July 20). Council on Criminal Justice. https://counciloncj.org/mid-year-2023-crime-trends/

Domestic Violence Services Network, Inc. (DVSN). (2023, October 30). Infographics - Domestic Violence Services Network, Inc. (DVSN). Domestic Violence Services Network, Inc. (DVSN) - a Coordinated Community Response to Domestic Violence. https://www.dvsn.org/infographics/

https://www.whitehouse.gov/wp-content/uploads/2023/05/National-Plan-to-End-GBV.pdf

About the Author

Smiley Grace is a New York City resident pursuing an associate degree in Public and Non-profit Administration at the Borough of Manhattan Community College (BMCC) with a Myers–Briggs Type Indicator (MBTI) defender personality trait. Grace is honored to be a member of BMCC Phi Theta Kappa Alpha Kappa Chapter and BMCC National Society of Leadership for Success Sigma Alpha Pi.

As a survivor of intimate partner violence, Grace escaped traumatic occurrences, and her abuser was imprisoned and pleaded guilty to third-degree assault. *Lord, He Hit Me Again: An Insider's Look at Intimate Partner Violence* shares her story and empowers others. Birthed after two presentations on the subject matter of intimate partner violence, it is her first autobiography. For over two years, Grace was classified as chronically homeless within the New York City Department of Homeless Services (DHS) system. But God took her from the pit to the palace, transforming this survivor from victim to victor. When not penning their latest novel, Smiley Grace binge-watches streaming diverse cultural drama series, court shows, The Lead Attorney, Pam Esq.-The Law Intellect, "Border Patrol," "Border Security," or "To Catch A Smuggler" or Marital Arts YouTube videos. Grace designed *Lord, He Hit Me Again: An Insider's Look at Intimate Partner Violence* to be informative and conceptualize intimate partner violence.

"CONGRATULATIONS!!!!! I look forward to reading and sharing your book out. What an important contribution you are making to our world. Thank you for sharing the exciting news with me. Proud of you, my friend. " – *Professor Rajni S., FL*

Wow, this is a very heartbreaking story. I want this book. I almost cried, because it was a similar issue for me as well. Love you sis. Yes, I will appreciate it; it is a must read. This should be published to help others who witnessed this ordeal. I thank you for sharing this book. Love you very much. – *Korita R., Irvington*

This book covers all areas of domestic violence-mental, physical and emotional abuse and how to get through it and out of a deadly situation. – *Ireama R., NYC*

I truly appreciate you sharing this with me. I can't imagine what you've been through, but I can clearly see how strong you are. This seems like such an important piece of work, and I admire you very much for having the courage to write about these experiences. Sending strength to you as you write this important book. – *James N., NYC*

Also, read the abstract in your upcoming publication – writing this must have been a real challenge – you are a strong person to have taken on telling this story, empowering, lifesaving.... Sending you all good thoughts! – *Professor Peter H., NYC*

The work is really great. I loved how it pictures the symbolic aspect of organization, discussed in our book, Reframing organizations. This is a very good work. I would love to read more. I will gladly read and enjoy it! – *Nana K., NYC*

Wow, that was amazing, and you are very intelligent. Lots of research too, wow, amen – *Arlene G., Brooklyn*

Congratulations! I look forward to looking at this and reading the book once it is published. No doubt it will impact many lives. – *Professor Sara K., NYC*

Made in United States
North Haven, CT
17 March 2024

49939420R00153